If You're an Egalitarian, How Come You're So Rich?

If You're an Egalitarian, How Come You're So Rich?

G. A. COHEN

HARVARD UNIVERSITY PRESS

Cambridge, Massachusetts

London, England

Third printing, 2001

First Harvard University Press paperback edition, 2001

Library of Congress Cataloging-in-Publication Data

Cohen, G. A. (Gerald Allan), 1941–
    If you're an egalitarian, how come you're so rich? / G. A. Cohen.
        p.   cm.
    Includes bibliographical references and index.
    ISBN 0-674-00218-0 (cloth)
    ISBN 0-674-00693-3 (pbk.)
    1. Equality. 2. Distributive justice. 3. Social justice. 4. Communism.
5. Liberalism. 6. Religion and social problems. I. Title.

HM821.C64 2000
303.3'72—dc21   99-086974

With gratitude to my beloved brother Michael

CONTENTS

PREFACE

These are the Gifford Lectures of 1996. Before I had the opportunity to
spend the month in Edinburgh during which I delivered them, I had
heard and read a great deal about the architectural splendor of that city,
but, having only glimpsed it for a day or two on a couple of hectic occasions, I had not experienced the truth of the praise it receives. Edinburgh is glorious, partly because of its grand buildings and its monu-
ments, its parks and its hills, but also—and, for me, more so—because of
the brilliantly conceived and faithfully maintained straight and curved
terraces of the eighteenth-century New Town that lies to the north of
Prince's Street. On the second evening of my lecturing engagement, full
of good red wine from the cellar of the Roxburgh Hotel in Charlotte
Square, where I was fortunate enough to be lodged, I treated myself to an
after-dinner walk through the New Town's stately terraces, and at no
other time in my life—not even in Oxford or Cambridge—have I been
so enthralled by the eloquence of stone.

There is a certain incongruity between the sumptuous circumstances
of the delivery of these lectures—the hotel, the wine, the lush sojourn in
a handsome, wealthy (in the latitudes of it where I had occasion to
move) city—and their egalitarian content. I am greatly preoccupied with
that incongruity. It is a large part of what this book is about, and it helps
to explain the book's title.

I focus here on Marxism and on Rawlsian liberalism, and I draw a
connection between each of those thought-systems and the choices that
shape the course of a person's life. In the case of Marxism, the relevant
life is my own. For, as I have occasion to recount in Lecture 2, I was
raised as a Marxist (and Stalinist communist) the way other people are
raised Roman Catholic or Muslim. A strong socialist egalitarian doctrine
was the ideological milk of my childhood, and my intellectual work has
been an attempt to reckon with that inheritance, to throw out what

should not be kept and to keep what must not be lost. The impact of belief in socialism and equality on my own life is given some prominence in what follows.

In the case of Rawlsian doctrine, the relevant life is not mine in particular, but people's lives as such. For I argue, at some length, that egalitarian justice is not only, as Rawlsian liberalism teaches, a matter of the rules that define the structure of society, but also a matter of personal attitude and choice; personal attitude and choice are, moreover, the stuff of which social structure itself is made. These truths have not informed political philosophy as much as they should inform it, and I try to bring them to the fore in Lectures 8–10.

When Rosa Luxemburg wrote that "history . . . has the fine habit of always producing along with any real social need the means to its satisfaction, along with the task simultaneously the solution," she was expressing a thought, descended from Hegel, that had lodged itself deeply in Marxist theory and practice. The proposition that, as Karl Marx himself put it, "mankind sets itself only such tasks as it can solve," comforted and inspired Marxist thinkers and activists, but it was, I argue in Lectures 3–6, a disastrous mistake, one that bore a large responsibility for Marxism's failure in the twentieth century.

Because I shall labor to expose that failure, I consider it important to emphasize, at the outset of this book, two things—one personal and one political. The personal thing is that I remain unambivalently grateful to the people who ensured that my upbringing was Marxist, and I have in no measure abandoned the values of socialism and equality that are central to Marxist belief. The political thing is that the task which Marxism set itself, which is to liberate humanity from the oppression that the capitalist market visits upon it, has not lost its urgency. That goal is not less worth fighting for when we have forsaken the belief that history ensures that it will be accomplished.

Accordingly, while I shall oppose the fundamental Marxist conception that Luxemburg expressed with beguiling pungency, my opposition to it reflects no weakening of my commitment to socialism. Far from urging a reconsideration of socialist equality itself, I am engaged in rejecting Marxist (and Rawlsian) postures that seek to reduce the force of equality as a moral norm.

* * *

The last seven of the lectures presented here concern Marxism and liberalism. These are preceded by an opening lecture in which I provide an examination of the problematic issue of why we adhere to commitments which, like mine, are ones that we know originated in the contingencies of a particular upbringing: in my case, of the upbringing that I describe in Lecture 2.

The lectures appear here in a somewhat different form from the one in which they were delivered. The Prospectus, here presented separately, was originally part of Lecture 1; Lecture 7 (as readers will learn) could not be reproduced in print; and in the reworking of the lectures for publication, some have been substantially expanded—particularly so Lecture 10, which is less polished than the rest, and which remains open-ended.

My greatest Edinburgh debt is to Paul McGuire of the Faculty of Arts, who discharged a considerable organizational burden with diligence and grace. I also thank Marsha Caplan, who prepared handouts for the audience, often at short notice, and Ross Sibbald, who prepared the lecture hall and who ensured that entry into it and exit from it were appropriately uneventful. Finally, I am grateful to those who chaired the lectures: John Richardson, Ronald Hepburn, Carole Hillenbrand, Timothy Sprigge, Duncan Forrester, John O'Neill, Russell Keat, and Sir Stewart Sutherland.

Most of these lectures have reached their present form following superb criticism by many people. I apologize to those commentators whose names I failed to record for future mention, and I am happy to be able to thank Daniel Attas, John Baker, David Bakhurst, Jerry Barnes, Brian Barry, Paul Boghossian, Diemut Bubeck, Paula Casal, Joshua Cohen, Miriam Cohen Christofidis, Ronald Dworkin, Cécile Fabre, Margaret Gilbert, Keith Graham, Betsy Hodges, Susan Hurley, John McMurtry, Andrew Mason, Liam Murphy, Thomas Nagel, Michael Otsuka, Derek Parfit, Guido Pincione, Thomas Pogge, Joseph Raz, John Roemer, Amélie Rorty, Michael Seifert, Horacio Spector, Gopal Sreenivasan, Hillel Steiner, Christine Sypnowich, Larry Temkin, Peter Vallentyne, Frank Vandenbroucke, Robert Van der Veen, Alan Wertheimer, Martin Wilkinson, Andrew Williams, Bernard Williams, Erik Wright, and two anonymous Harvard referees. Apart from those referees, Paul Levy, David Miller, and Derek Parfit were the only people who read the whole thing;

their advice was invaluable. My most indefatigable and productive critic was, as always, Arnold Zuboff, with whom I spent many instructive (for me) hours debating most of the themes of the lectures.

Lindsay Waters has been a dream editor: I do not think anyone could have been more supportive. Maria Ascher improved the prose at many junctures. And those who know her will not be surprised by the size of the gratitude that I feel to my wife Michèle.

If You're an Egalitarian,
How Come You're So Rich?

Prospectus

So we beat on, boats against the current, borne back ceaselessly into the
past.

F. Scott Fitzgerald, *The Great Gatsby*

I read *The Great Gatsby* in 1963, and I found its final sentence, which is
reproduced above, particularly arresting. Over the course of the past
thirty-three years, I have often repeated that sentence to myself, with a
mixture of good and sad feelings.

Scott Fitzgerald's sentence is, of course, about everybody: "we," here,
means all of us. But while each person's past weighs strongly on his or
her present, for some it weighs more heavily than for others, and it certainly weighs very heavily for me. For I was raised in a working-class
communist family in a communist community in the 1940s in Montreal,
on a very strongly egalitarian doctrine, and, with all the history both
public and private that I have since witnessed and undergone, I have remained attached to the normative teachings of my childhood, and, in
particular, to a belief in equality, which I continue to hold and to pro-
pound. I cannot escape from it. A powerful current bears me back to it
ceaselessly, no matter where I might otherwise try to row.

I am deeply grateful for the opportunity these lectures afford me to
reflect on my belief in equality, and on the several ways that other thinkers have conceived both the character of equality and the mode of its advent. Three currents of thought for which social equality, in some form,
is in some sense morally imperative have influenced the content of these
lectures: first, classical Marxism; second, egalitarian liberalism, as it presents itself in the work of John Rawls; and, finally, the egalitarian strain
within Christianity. These three doctrines regard equality, in one or

1

other form, as the answer to the question of distributive justice—the question, that is, about what distribution of benefits and burdens in society is just. But the three understand equality as something to be delivered by very different agencies.

According to classical Marxists, as I shall explain in Lectures 3–6, we come to equality through and as a result of history. Marxists live in the faith that the consummation of centuries of exploitation and class struggle will be a condition of material abundance that confers on each human being full scope for self-realization, in a society in which the free development of each will be the condition of the free development of all. For Rawlsians, delivering equality is a task not of class struggle (crowned by a future abundance) but of constitution-making. Democratic politics must institute principles of an egalitarian kind, or, to be more precise, principles that mandate equality save where inequality benefits those who are worst off in society. For Christians, both the Marxist and the Rawlsian conceptions are misguided, since equality requires not mere history and the abundance to which it leads, or mere politics, but a moral revolution, a revolution in the human soul.[1]

When I was a child, and then an adolescent, I knew about and I believed Marxism, and I knew about and I *dis*believed Christianity. A radical liberalism no doubt existed in some pre-Rawlsian form, but I didn't know about it. My attitude to the Christian attitude to equality—to the attitude, that is, of those Christians who believed in equality—was surprise mixed with mild contempt: I thought that the Christian prescription for equality was utterly naive, and that the transformation of society not by class struggle but by the moral struggle that Christianity demanded was not only impractical but also unnecessary. It was impractical because you could not change society by a sequence of individual self-transformations, and it was unnecessary because history was destined to make equality unavoidable. With all the moral striving in the world, equality would be *impossible to achieve* under the material scarcity that divides society into classes, and equality would be *impossible to avoid* under the material abundance which obliterates class difference and thereby makes a moral struggle for equality pointless. So in neither case—neither under past and present scarcity, nor under future abundance—would moral struggle be called for. And as for egalitarian liberalism, had I encountered it, then I would have said that its faith in constitution-building as a means to equality was also misconceived. I would have said that egalitarian constitution-building presupposes a social unity for which equality is itself a prerequisite. I would have said that we cannot make a constitution *together* unless and until we are already equals, unless we are already the equals that only history can make us become.

As I shall indicate in Lecture 6, I have lost my Marxist belief in the inevitability of equality. As I shall indicate in Lecture 9, I also reject the liberal faith in the sufficiency of political recipes. I now believe that a change in social ethos, a change in the attitudes people sustain toward each other in the thick of daily life, is necessary for producing equality, and that belief brings me closer than I ever expected to be to the Christian view of these matters that I once disparaged. So in one big respect I have outrowed Scott Fitzgerald's stream; in one big respect I have outgrown my past.

I would indeed have been shocked to foresee, when I was, say, in my twenties, that I was to come to the point where I now am. For the three forms of egalitarian doctrine that I have distinguished can in one dimension be so ordered that my present view falls at the opposite end to the Marxist view with which I began. That is so because an emphasis on ethos is at the center of my present view, and the Marxist view has less time for ethos, as an engine of social transformation, than the liberal one does. I have, then, proceeded, within one understanding of the following contrast, from the hardest position to the softest one (without, as it happens, having at any point embraced the middle, liberal, position). Very roughly speaking, I have moved from an economic point of view to a moral one, without ever occupying a political one. (Needless to say, I regard this progression as an improvement, induced by increased appreciation of truth, rather than a piece of backsliding for which I should apologize.)

Three views may be taken about what might be called the *site* of distributive justice—about, that is, the sorts of items to which principles of distributive justice apply. One is my own view, for which there is ample Judeo-Christian precedent, that *both* just rules *and* just personal choice within the framework set by just rules are necessary for distributive justice. A second view, held by some Christians, is that all justice is a matter of morally informed personal decision; on this particular Christian view, the rules set by Caesar can achieve little or nothing in the direction of establishing a just society. And a third possibility, which is hard to envisage in a Christian form, is the Rawlsian view that distributive justice and injustice are features of the rules of the public order alone. What others might see as justice in personal choice (within such rules), Rawls would see as some different virtue, such as charity, or generosity, or self-denial; or, if indeed justice, then not justice in the sense in which it is the central concern of political philosophy.[2] I shall argue in Lectures 8–10 that this Rawlsian and, more generally, liberal view represents an evasion—an evasion of the burden of respecting distributive justice in the choices of everyday life, an evasion which may (or may not: it is very hard to tell) be encouraged by the circumstance that contemporary egalitarian political philosophers are, on average, much wealthier than other people are.

So this is my aim: to explore the theme of egalitarian justice and history, and of justice in state-imposed structure and in personal choice, in a fashion that brings together topics in Marxism, issues in recent political philosophy, and standing preoccupations of Judeo-Christian thought.

I *believe* that my topic is a suitable one for the Gifford Lectures. There is some basis for anxiety about that, since, in the testament in which he established these lectures, Lord Gifford directed that they be devoted to "Promoting, Advancing, Teaching, and Diffusing . . . the knowledge of God, the Infinite, the All, the First and Only Cause, the One and Sole Substance, the Sole Being, the Sole Reality, and the Sole Existence,"[3] and so forth, and I cannot say that this will be my topic, in a very strict sense. But in the 110 years that have passed since Lord Gifford endowed this chair, its "patrons"[4] have wisely failed to insist on a strict construal of the condition that I have just quoted.

The "patrons" have interpreted Lord Gifford's directive very broadly, in two respects. First, one is not required to discuss God in the severely metaphysical terms, just illustrated, in which He is portrayed in Lord Gifford's will. A focus on religion itself, rather than on the supreme object of religious devotion in its most abstract specification, will do. Thus, for example, an existential treatment of religion, an examination of religious belief as it is lived by the believer, or a study of the social or historical emplacement of religion: these, too, are allowed to pass muster. And the second respect in which Lord Gifford's directive has been subjected to a relaxed interpretation is that the lecturer is not required to devote all of his or her attention to religious themes, however broadly the idea of a religious theme may be construed. Only a portion of the lectures need be concentrated in that direction.

Now, I happen to hold old-fashioned views about the terms of bequests. To accept a bequest is to make a promise, and promises should, normally, be kept. Accordingly, I felt able to accept the invitation to deliver these lectures only after correspondence and reflection which satisfied me that I could offer something at least as close to the spirit of the bequest as what the invitation had specified. You may come to think that I shall not go very far toward satisfying Lord Gifford's wishes, but you should not reach that conclusion without taking into account a perhaps surprising liberality in the terms of his bequest which is expressed at a different point in his will from the one at which there appears the phrase that I quoted a moment ago. I have in mind Lord Gifford's willingness to allow that the lecturers

> may be of any denomination whatever or of no denomination at all (and many earnest and high-minded men prefer to belong to no ecclesiastical denomination); they may be of any religion or way of thinking, or, as is sometimes said, they may be of no religion, or they may be so-called sceptics or agnostics or free-thinkers, provided only that the "patrons" will use diligence to secure that they be able reverent men, true thinkers, sincere lovers of and earnest inquirers after truth.[5]

So we have, on the one hand, a requirement that the lectures be devoted to promoting the knowledge of God, and, on the other hand, a considerable liberality, or openness, with respect to who may deliver these lectures. Now, either those two parts of Lord Gifford's will are consistent with each other, or they are not. If the two parts are indeed *incon*sistent, if the liberality as to *who* is inconsistent with the stringency as to *what,* then Lord Gifford contradicted himself, and it's hard for me to know what I'm supposed to try to do. But if, as we may more charitably suppose, his will was consistent, then Lord Gifford envisaged promotion of the knowledge of God being effected in a great variety of ways. If an agnostic—for that, not an atheist, is what *I* am—if an agnostic can advance the knowledge of God, then perhaps I shall do so here.

In addressing my chosen theme, I hope to bring together two interests of mine that I have not otherwise had the opportunity to connect. The first interest is pursued in my recent research work in political philosophy, which is devoted to a critique, from the left, of John Rawls's theory of justice. The second is a long-standing interest in scripture that I have not pursued academically. Let me explain.

My critique of Rawls reflects and supports a view that justice in personal choice is necessary for a society to qualify as just. This view shines forth in parts of the Bible that have occupied me nonacademically for a long time. Following a severely antireligious upbringing, which I shall permit myself to describe in Lecture 2, I began to rebel in the direction of tolerance for religion; I became, so to speak, anti-antireligious, in my late teens, and I progressed from tolerance to deep interest and sympathy as a result of seeing, on television, in 1969, a film by the late Pier Paolo Pasolini called *The Gospel According to Saint Matthew.* I was so taken with the figure and the teaching of Jesus as they were presented in that film that I was moved to read the Gospels for the first time, and I was deeply impressed. Since then I have been a Bible reader, in both Testaments, but I have never publicly commented on scriptural material. Well then, my first such comment will be this one: that Jesus would have spurned the liberal idea that the state can take care of justice for us, provided only that we obey the rules it lays down, and regardless of what we choose to do *within* those rules. And I believe that Jesus would have been right to spurn that idea.

So much by way of introduction. I shall now raise some questions that have puzzled me and troubled me about our relationship to the central religious and political and moral convictions that help to give value to our lives. I am not sure what the correct answers to these questions are, but I raise them as a cautionary preface to the exploration of my own convictions that you have given me an opportunity to conduct.

1

Paradoxes of Conviction

We have all of us considerable regard for our past self, and are not fond
of casting reflections on that respected individual by a total negation of
his opinions.

George Eliot, *Scenes of Clerical Life*

1

I did not have a religious upbringing, but I did have a strongly political
upbringing, and strongly political upbringings, of the sort that I had, re-
semble religious ones in several important respects. In each case, intense
belief is induced in propositions that other people regard as false; indeed, very often, *most* people regard the propositions in question as *obviously* false. And, both in religion and in high-temperature politics, there
is a powerful feeling of unity with other believers. They—we—feel embattled together, or triumphant together, according to circumstance. In
both cases, there are texts and hymns that rally conviction and cement
community. The melodies of some of the hymns that we sang in the
North American communist movement in which I was raised were taken
from Christian gospel songs. Some relevant verses from our communist
hymns will appear in later lectures.

So I was brought up in a culture of conviction, and therefore in some
ways my upbringing was like that of those raised in religious belief. I
shall set out the early stages of my political and religious, and irreligious,
beliefs in Lecture 2. But before I describe the development of my convictions, I should like to explore some aspects of the development of conviction in general, aspects that I came to find puzzling as I reflected on
my own development. In the case of what are properly called convictions, but even, as we shall see, in the case of beliefs which might be con-

sidered too cool in temperature to be called "convictions," there is a problem about how we manage to go on believing what we were *raised* to believe, in the face of our knowledge that we believe it *because* (in a certain sense, which I shall specify at p. 10 below) we were raised to believe it. F. Scott Fitzgerald's point about the power of the past (see p. 1 above) is comparatively easy to accept with respect to our feelings and emotions. But, for many of us, his point also has force with respect to our beliefs, and that is more unsettling, since it raises questions about the rationality of those beliefs—questions that are more unsettling than parallel ones that might be raised about our feelings and emotions.

Suppose that identical twins are separated at birth. Twenty years later, they meet. One was raised as, and remains, a devout Presbyterian. The other was raised as, and remains, a devout Roman Catholic. They argue against each other's views, but they've heard those arguments before, they've learned how to reply to them, and their opposed convictions consequently remain firm.

Then each of them realizes that, had she been brought up where her sister was, and vice versa, then it is overwhelmingly likely that (as one of them expresses the realization) *she* would now be Roman Catholic and her sister would now be Presbyterian. That realization might, and, I think, should, make it more difficult for the sisters to sustain their opposed religious convictions. Or, to come closer to home—or, at any rate, to where I am—suppose I were to discover that I have an identical twin, who was raised not in a communist home but in a politically middle-of-the-road home, and that my twin has the easy tolerance toward limited inequality which I learned to lack. That, I confess, would disturb my confidence in my own uncompromising egalitarianism, and not because my twin could supply me with an argument against egalitarianism of which I was previously unaware.

To be sure, the surprise which the twin sisters undergo need not make it hard for them to remain Christians; and the revelation which my twin brother and I experience need not make it hard for us to remain anti-Tory. But such further difficulty will supervene if the sisters turn out to be not twins but triplets, and they now meet their long-lost and now Jewish third sister. Which, so far as it goes, will no doubt leave their belief in (a) *God* secure, until they meet their long-lost and now atheist quadruplet, whose confidence in her atheism may be shaken when *she* confronts *them*. And a similar extension of the story about me and my brother can, of course, also be rolled out.

Now, most of us are solo-birth children; most of us were, that is, born twinless, tripletless, and so forth. But it would be crazy to infer that the story about the twins has no bearing on *our* convictions. That I am *in fact* twinless should not reduce the challenge to my inherited convictions which is posed by the story I've told. An entirely plausible story could be told about a *hypothetical* disagreeing twin, and it would, or should, be just as challenging as a true story, to those of us who believe what we were brought up to believe.

That is not, of course, all of us. But it is very many of us. And although it does not follow from the fact that we believe what we were brought up to believe that we believe it in any sense *because* we were brought up to believe it, it is very widely true that people *do* believe what they do in some sense[1] because they were brought up to believe it: the statistics of parent-to-child belief replication prove that. And I think these stories about twins and so forth should give pause to those of us who are steadfastly devoted to the beliefs of our upbringing, while being aware that people of different upbringing are steadfastly devoted to beliefs contrary to our own. It should give us pause that we would not have beliefs that are central to our lives—beliefs, for example, about important matters of politics and religion—if we had not been brought up as we in fact were. It is an accident of birth and upbringing that we have *them,* rather than beliefs sharply rival to them, and (here's the rub) we shall frequently[2] have to admit, if we are reflective and honest, that *we consequently do not believe as we do because our grounds for our beliefs are superior to those which others have for their rival beliefs.*

The problem I am posing does not require a narrow view of the sorts of grounds that one can have for a belief. Consider, for example, the person who says that she believes in God because she underwent a profound experience that she cannot fully describe, an experience that induced faith in God within her. I am not skeptical about that claim as such. I do not find appeal to a special religious experience intrinsically unacceptable. The skepticism in focus here arises, rather, when we *compare* A's grounds for believing that *p* with B's grounds for believing that *q,* and we notice that, however good or bad those grounds may *otherwise* be, they do not relevantly differ in quality; so that, so it seems, it *should* be difficult for each to maintain his convictions, when he confronts the other. For neither can reasonably believe that he believes what he does, rather than what the other does, because he has better grounds for his belief than the other does for his, as opposed to: because he was brought up differently.

So I do not say: because faith-inducing experiences are not pieces of scientific reasoning, they cannot credentialize belief. What I do say is that if, for example, profoundly Catholic religious experiences tend to take place in Catholic homes and profoundly Protestant ones in Protestant homes, then it looks as though both Catholics and Protestants should be wary about the messages apparently conveyed by their religious experiences.

Let me say something about what I mean by "because" here, in such sentences as "she believes it because she was brought up to believe it." When I say such a thing here, I do not mean that her belief is groundless. Nor do I mean to deny that she has reflected on and assessed the grounds she has for holding it, and continues to hold it only because her belief survived that reflection. I have in view, throughout, nurtured beliefs which have indeed passed the test of reflection for the believer. But even so, even though the beliefs I am targeting are not (any longer) held for no reason, they are there in a crucial sense *because* of the believer's upbringing. The reflective nurtured Catholic and the reflective nurtured Presbyterian *may,* for all that I am concerned to contend, believe what their beliefs *have in common* entirely because they have drawn the right conclusions from the evidence available to them. But the whole explanation of the *difference* between their beliefs, the explanation for why one believes *p* as opposed to *q,* and the other believes *q* as opposed to *p,* lies, typically, in their upbringing,[3] *rather than in the quality of the data that were presented to them or in the quality of their reflection upon that data.*

I emphasize that contrast because what disturbs me in the cases under inspection here is not, just in itself, that the person believes differently because of a different upbringing, but that she cannot honestly identify a relevant further difference. These cases differ from that, for example, where one person was brought up to believe that the earth is round and another that the earth is flat. When the round-earther reflects that, had he been brought up flat-earthly, he would now believe the earth to be flat, that need not give him pause, for he can reasonably say that his grounds for believing it to be round are overwhelming. Round-earthers (justifiably) think they can prove their position. But Catholics—or, at any rate, enough Catholics to make my point interesting—would acknowledge that they are in the same epistemic boat as Presbyterians are, that the Presbyterians' grounds are no worse than theirs are. Since, in the relevant cases, you can't find anything except nurture that makes the difference, since you can't say, on independent grounds, that their nurture was defective, you can't say that you have better grounds for believing that *p* than they have for believing that not-*p*. And this flies in the face of what seems to me an undeniable principle about reasons for belief— namely, that *you lack good reason to believe p rather than a rival proposition q when you cannot justifiably believe that your grounds for believing p are better than another's are for believing q* (call that principle "the Principle").[4] For you have to believe that your grounds make it more likely than not that *p* is true, and they don't do that if they make *p* no more likely than his grounds make *q* likely.

Now, paradox looms here, not because there *exist* the truths about nurtured beliefs that I have labored, but because we, the believers, or anyway those of us who are reflective, are (at least implicitly) aware of these truths. Thus, for example, no intelligent and reflective Scots Presbyterian can *herself* suppose it irrelevant to the explanation for why she is a Christian and not a Jewess that she did not wind up in the wrong hospital cot at birth, and her reflection may tell her that she would not then have received a less good case for Judaism than the one she actually got for Christianity. And while you may think it unsurprising, at first glance, that I hold the egalitarian views that were instilled in me, you should perhaps find it a little surprising that I do, when you realize that I stick to them even though I *know* that I hold them *because* they were instilled in me, and that less radical views with no less good epistemic credentials might have been instilled in me if, for example, I had been brought up in the upper-middle-class Jewish part of Montreal instead of in the working-class Jewish part of Montreal.

To believe that *p rationally*[5] is to believe that one has a good reason to believe that *p*, that one has grounds for believing that *p* which constitute a good reason for believing it;[6] and, in particular, that the grounds for holding the beliefs one does must be such that they give one good reason to hold *those* beliefs, *as opposed* to the competing beliefs that others hold. To be sure, one need not believe, on pain of irrationality, that one could state the grounds for one's belief, forthwith, or even that one could, with sufficient time, recover them. One can believe that one has forgotten, irrecoverably, what one's good grounds are. Or one can believe that they are there, in one's mind, but not yet capable of being articulated. One can say that one *senses* that one has good grounds for believing that p which have not yet surfaced into consciousness. But, so soon as one confesses that one's belief lacks appropriate grounding, one condemns oneself as irrational.[7]

Those qualifications constitute a partial explication of the claim that to believe, non-irrationally, that p is to believe that one has good grounds for believing that p (grounds, that is, which constitute a good reason for believing that p). But the qualifications do not erase the paradox toward which I am moving. For, even when we review the qualifications, it will remain evident, in leading cases of nurtured disagreement, that what distinguishes me from her is not that I possess special grounds of a kind that she lacks, or that I have a hunch of a kind that she cannot claim to have, but *just* my upbringing. And then I appear to be in difficulty. For the fact that I was brought up to believe it is no reason for believing it, and I know that.[8]

We have to believe about our beliefs that we have good reasons for holding them. Yet even when we become apprised of these facts about the genesis of our convictions and these norms internal to the holding of conviction, we, or many of us, still don't give up our beliefs; we feel that we needn't, in the face of all that, give them up. So it seems we can prove what we think we know is false: that we should give up our (controversial) inherited beliefs. An exceedingly familiar fact that belongs to what can be called the elementary sociology of conviction, one that we all know about from our ordinary experience, thereby appears to generate a paradox.

The argument implicit in the foregoing discussion, the argument which is the locus of paradox, has three premises. The premises look hard to fault and the conclusion seems to follow; yet the conclusion looks hard to accept, because at least many people's considered convictions contradict it and their behavior appears to conflict with it:

(1) It is not rational to believe p rather than q when you know that you lack good reason to believe p rather than q.

(2) You lack good reason to believe p rather than a rival proposition

q when you cannot justifiably believe that your grounds for believing *p* are better than another's grounds for believing *q*. (The Principle.)[9]

(3) In a wide range of cases of nurtured belief, people *who continue to believe p* (can readily be brought to) realize that they believe *p* rather than *q* not because they have grounds for believing *p* that are better than the grounds for believing *q* that others have, but because they were induced to believe *p* without being supplied with such differentiating grounds.

∴ (4) The beliefs described in (3) are irrational (and the people who believe them are *pro tanto* irrational).[10]

Call that argument "the Argument." Note that its conclusion flatly contradicts what we (or, anyway, many of us) are confident is true, for we do not usually think that nurtured beliefs of the sort under contemplation here are irrational. That is the interest of the argument; that is what gives it its air of paradox, whether or not it is sound.

And I am, indeed, not sure that the argument is sound. If the Argument is unsound, and (4) has therefore *not* been shown to be true, then that would be good news, but we would then have the intellectual difficulty that it isn't so easy to see what's wrong with the Argument. But if the Argument is indeed sound, then our intellectual difficulty is not, of course, to show what's wrong with it, but to determine how (some of us) manage to sustain our strong impression that the beliefs here in view are *not* irrational. If the Argument is sound, then people are starkly irrational in contexts where we do not normally account them irrational. It is not, of course, news that people can be irrational, nor is it news that it can be puzzling to see how they manage to be so. What's puzzling here, if the Argument is sound, is not that people can be irrational (that puzzle isn't *especially* strongly raised in *this* sort of case) but just that we do not normally consider beliefs of the sort that I have identified as instances of our (perhaps even commonplace) irrationality.

Now, there are many significant challenges to the Argument, and examining all of them would take us too far afield.[11] But I shall now address three of them, the first two of which, so it seems to me, are defeated by the self-same compelling counterexample, which is presented in section 3.

2

The first challenge may be called the *depth solution*. It says that the case for competing convictions can be put more or less deeply, and that the case for *p* is put more deeply—with, that is, greater sophistication and circumspection—within a community sustaining *p* than in a community sustaining rival *q*, where, in turn, the case for *q* is put more deeply. That is how proponents of an inherited view are able rightly to dismiss so much of the attack on their view as superficial, as I have often done and can still do with respect to Marxism and socialism, and as some of you have often done and can still do with respect to Roman Catholicism. And so premise (3) of the Argument is an overstatement—those nurtured within a *p*-affirming community typically *do* have particularly good grounds for believing *p*, and need not, therefore, so readily admit their (comparative) cognitive nakedness as premise (3) suggests.

The depth solution works well enough for an easier question than ours—the question, namely, which asks: How can equally intelligent and open-minded people have utterly opposed beliefs? But that is not our question, because it formulates a purely third-person problem. The depth solution collapses just where we need it—at the reflexive level, where the relevant questions are posed in the first person. For how can *I* stick to *p* even when I can truly say that I see a deeper case for it than I do for *q*, when I have no reason to think that the *q*-believer sees a case for *q* that is less deep than the case *I* see for *p*? The strength of that question is confirmed by the example laid out in section 3 below.

The second challenge is not to the soundness of the argument but to the interest of its conclusion. It runs as follows: "It is no accident that the beliefs which come from nurture, and, more generally, beliefs which display an irreducible element of (comparative) groundlessness, are characteristically religious or heavily political in subject matter. The strength with which such beliefs are held, the emotion that characteristically attaches to them—all that makes them suspect *anyway;* and it is therefore not surprising that their genesis, too, is suspect. Rational people should abandon them. They partake, more or less, of fanaticism." Call that the *credal cleansing* proposal.

There are two objections to the credal cleansing proposal. I am more sure of the soundness of the second one, but I enter the first one too because it would be extremely interesting if it is sound, and I am not sure that it is not.

The first objection is that, if we *were* to abandon all religious and heavily political views, then most of us would be stripped of the convictions which structure our personality and behavior. Life would be bland, lacking in élan and direction. Everybody would be *l'homme moyen sensuel*. Maybe irrationality is preferable to a dull existence.[12]

And the second objection to the credal cleansing proposal is that it is, to an important extent, false that beliefs which have a significant trace of nurture are all of a religious, heavily political, or similarly high-temperature sort. As I shall show in the next, and closing, section of this lecture, quite reconditely theoretical beliefs also display substantial traces of nurture. It accordingly begins to look as though the credal cleansing policy is more drastic than it presents itself as being. If their suspect genesis shows that religious and political beliefs have to go, then much more has to go with them.

The credal cleansing proposal is also very drastic because it would cut away a great mass of nontheoretical quotidian beliefs. For a belief's being due to upbringing is neither necessary nor sufficient for it to be at variance with rationality; I have focused on upbringing because it is, nevertheless, an especially potent source of beliefs that have the power to resist rationality. Plenty of other widespread belief differences are not more rationally based than inherited belief differences are, but reference to nurture immediately generates a host of compelling examples, which are especially relevant here, because of my focus on my own beliefs in the next lecture.

Realizing that the Argument would also impugn casual beliefs of ordinary life, one critic of the Argument (Brian Barry) adduced the following example, which is the third challenge to the Argument that I shall consider. You and I go to the same play, and we disagree about how good it is. There must be something about *us* that accounts for the disagreement, something about personality or history or whatever, since we are responding to the same thing. We may agree about the good-making and bad-making characteristics of the play, yet simply be differently impressed by their relative importance. Does this make it irrational to hold the views we do? Why should it? We both have reasons for our views, and we admit they're not conclusive. If, though, our disagreement is not irrational, then the standards that I have laid down for rationality are pitched too high.

There is, in Barry's example, something unapparent that explains the difference between our judgments about the play. Barry says that we are not being irrational, but I think that whether or not we are being irrational here depends on our view, speculative though it perforce is, about what the unapparent explanation of our difference of judgment is. Each of us might think that his faculty of judgment and/or sensibility is, in general, superior to the other's, and that this explains why we do not agree. If so, we can indeed comfortably persist in our disagreement, but the case is then not parallel to one where we assign our difference to mere differences of nurture. On this interpretation of Barry's example, it does not represent a counterexample to my position.

If, however, we avow that the reason we're differently impressed by the play is not different quality of judgment and/or sensibility but *simply* different background etc., *then* our disagreement, on my view, becomes peculiar—not that it breaks out, but that we persist in it at that point. It is *at that point* that we become placed as nurtured believers are; but then the suspicion of irrationality persists, and the example is, once again, no special threat to my claims.

I do not, accordingly, regard Barry's example, taken in whichever of the two ways it may be interpreted, as an embarrassment for my view that persistence in a belief which one assigns to one's upbringing appears to be irrational.

3

The problem that I have canvassed arises not only in the region of heavy-duty matters of religious and of moral and political conviction, and in the region of casual ordinary belief, but also with respect to quite abstractly theoretical tenets. This fact defeats the tough-minded types who featured in the second challenge in section 2 and who say: "Well, all those ideological and religious beliefs are garbage anyway; their sensitivity to upbringing only confirms that. If we stick to scientific and technical matters, we shall unsaddle ourselves of beliefs for which we lack impressive grounds." Here is a counterexample to that policy of selective credal disburdenment.

In 1961 I was on the eve of doing graduate work in philosophy, and I was able to choose between going to Harvard and going to Oxford. Against the advice of some of my McGill University teachers (and of one in particular, who said, I recall, that Harvard's Willard Van Orman Quine "could put [Oxford's] A. J. Ayer in his pocket"), I chose Oxford, not because, despite the stated advice, I was more drawn to Ayer than to Quine—I was agnostic about their comparative merits—but because it seemed much more exciting to leave Montreal for Europe than to leave Montreal for Massachussetts.

I was pretty ignorant of Oxford-style philosophy before I arrived in Oxford, and I spent my first year there absorbing what I could. One thing I learned to do was to ask questions about the *status* of truths, and of supposed truths. If someone said "*p*," you'd then pounce, as follows: Is that analytic (that is, true by virtue merely of the meanings of the words in which it is expressed), or is it synthetic (that is, true for some more substantial reason)? An example would be the contrast between "All bachelors are unmarried," which is analytic, if anything is, and "All bachelors are tetchy and demanding," which may be just as true as that they are all unmarried, but whose truth depends on more than just that they are rightly *called* "bachelors."

"Is that analytic or synthetic?" was a terrifically important question in the Oxford of 1961. If, as sometimes happened, someone, perhaps from Germany or Italy, said something rather grand and general, such as that memory falsifies experience, or that God is everywhere, or that reason is tripartite, or that man is distant from being, or from the isness of being, then he or she would be subjected to the cited interrogative pounce, and if the response was "Um . . . er . . . ," as it often was, then that would be that as far as *they* were concerned.[13]

By the end of my first year at Oxford, I was reasonably agile at distinguishing (apparently) analytic points from synthetic ones, and I enjoyed doing it. Then, in the autumn of my second Oxford year, I read a famous article by Quine, called "Two Dogmas of Empiricism." Quine there said, among other things, that it was a false dogma that truths could be sorted into analytic and synthetic ones, for there was no such thing as analytic truth: all truths depended for their truth on the way the world is.

I did not want to believe that Quine was right, but I also did not want to believe or disbelieve anything just because I wanted to believe or disbelieve it. So I worked hard at Quine's arguments, and, in the event, I decided that they were not good arguments. In reaching that conclusion I was helped by my reading of various anti-Quine articles—by, in particular, H. P. Grice and P. F. Strawson and Jonathan Bennett, and also by a pro-Quine-ish (or pro-ish-Quine) article or two by Hilary Putnam. I still think Quine was wrong, but I don't care about the issue as much as I did then.

Now people of my generation who studied philosophy at Harvard rather than at Oxford for the most part *reject* the analytic/synthetic distinction. And I can't believe that this is an accident. That is, I can't believe that Harvard just *happened* to be a place where both its leading thinker rejected that distinction and its graduate students, for independent reasons—merely, for example, in the independent light of reason itself—also came to reject it. And vice versa, of course, for Oxford. I believe, rather, that in each case students were especially impressed by the reasons respectively for and against believing in the distinction, because in each case the reasons came with all the added persuasiveness of personal presentation, personal relationship, and so forth.[14]

So, in some sense of "because," and in some sense of "Oxford," I think I can say that I believe in the analytic/synthetic distinction because I studied at Oxford. And that is disturbing. For the fact that I studied at Oxford is no reason for thinking that the distinction is sound. Accordingly, if I believe it sound because I studied at Oxford, if that *explains* why I believe in it whereas, say, Gilbert Harman does not, then my belief in the distinction is ill-grounded. But I can't comfortably believe that a belief of mine is ill-grounded. So I can't comfortably believe that the only reason I believe the distinction to be sound is that I went to Oxford. I can readily believe that this is how I came to believe it in the first place, but I have to believe that my present reason for sticking to it is that I have good reasons to do so. But what in the world are they? Might they include the reason that Oxford is a better belief-producer than Harvard is, because, for example, it has better architecture? (And one thing that I must believe, of course, if I stick to my belief in the analytic/synthetic distinction, is that I am *lucky*, with respect to the view I have of this matter, that I went to Oxford, rather than to Harvard. Maybe I am lucky that I did *anyway*.)

Consider, in the light of the analytic/synthetic distinction example, the depth solution, which I floated, and sank, in section 2. Perhaps a deeper case for the distinction was available at Oxford than at Harvard. But that doesn't make it right for me to believe the Oxford doctrine now,

since I can be pretty sure that a commensurately deeper case for rejecting the distinction was available at Harvard. You see the deeper case at
home, but that doesn't help, since you know that the other guy sees the
deeper case against it where he is.[15]

Well, enough of these morose meanderings. In the next lecture I shall
lay before you some of the history of my own formation of conviction,
under the title "Politics and Religion in a Montreal Communist Jewish
Childhood."

Politics and Religion in a Montreal Communist Jewish Childhood

Nit zuch mich vu die mirten grinen,
Gefinst mich dortn nit, mein shatz;
Vu lebens velkn bei mashinen,
Dortn is mein ruhe platz.

(Don't look for me where myrtles blossom,
You will not find me there, my love;
Where lives are withered by machines,
That is my place of rest.)

Morris Rosenfeld, "Mein Ruhe Platz," in
Let's Sing the Songs of the People

I consider myself very Jewish, but I do not believe in the God of the Old Testament. Some people, more especially some gentiles, find that strange. One purpose of what follows is to demonstrate how one might be very Jewish, yet cut off from the Jewish religion.

1

I was brought up to be both Jewish and antireligious, and I remain very Jewish, and pretty godless, though not as godless as my parents intended and expected me to be—not as godless, indeed, as they took for granted that I would be. My mother influenced my outlook and my development more than my father did, and I'll begin by saying something about her.[1]

She was born, in Kharkov, in the Ukraine, in 1912, to areligious Jewish parents of ample means: her father was a successful timber merchant. When my mother was exactly five years old, the Bolshevik Revo-

20

lution occurred. My grandfather's business continued to provide well for the family during the 1920s in the period of the New Economic Policy,[2] which was a form of compromise between socialist aspiration and capitalist reality. My mother was consequently quite well-heeled, with plenty to lose, but she nevertheless developed, across the course of the 1920s, in schools and in youth organizations, a full-hearted commitment to the Bolshevik cause. She took this commitment with her to Canada in 1930, by which time the New Economic Policy had given way to a regime that was less amenable to bourgeois existence, and my mother's parents had therefore decided to emigrate. As a result, my mother left the Soviet Union and settled in Montreal, not because she wanted to, certainly not because she had any objection to the Soviet Union, but because she did not want to be separated from her emigrating parents and sister.

In Montreal, my mother, who spoke no English and, at eighteen, lacked an advanced education, tumbled down the class ladder to a proletarian position. She took employment as a sewing-machine operator in a garment factory. Before long, she met my father, a dress cutter, who, like my mother, had no use for the Jewish religion, but who, unlike her, had an impeccably proletarian pedigree (his father was a poor tailor from Lithuania) and no secondary education.

My parents' courtship unrolled in the context of long hours of factory work, struggles, often in the face of police violence, to build unionism in the garment trade, and summer weekends at the country camp some forty miles from town that was set up by and for left-wing Jewish workers. My parents married in 1936, and I, their first-born, appeared in 1941.

My mother was proud to be—to have become—working class, and through the Thirties and Forties, and until 1958, she was an active member of the Canadian Communist Party. My father belonged to the United Jewish People's Order, most of whose members were antireligious, anti-Zionist, and strongly pro-Soviet. He did not join the Communist Party itself, not because he had ideological reservations, but because his personality was not conducive to party membership. Members of the Communist Party were expected to express themselves with confidence and with regularity at branch meetings, and my father was an unusually reticent man with little disposition to self-expression.

Because of my parents' convictions, I was raised in a militantly antireligious home (not just areligious, or nonreligious, but *anti*religious). As far as I know, my father never underwent the *bar-mitzvah,* or confirmation, that, in his day, was de rigueur even in the majority of *atheist* Jewish households, and my mother's background was certainly free of belief. And my upbringing was as intensely political as it was antireligious. My first school, which was run by the United Jewish People's Order, and which I entered in 1945, was named after Morris Winchewsky, a Jewish proletarian poet. At Morris Winchewsky we learned standard primary-school things in the mornings, from noncommunist gentile women teachers;[3] but in the afternoons the language of instruction was Yiddish, and we were taught Jewish (and other) history, and Yiddish language and literature, by left-wing Jews and Jewesses whose first and main language was Yiddish. The education we got from them, even when they narrated Old Testament stories, was suffused with vernacular Marxist seasoning—nothing heavy or pedantic, just good Yiddish revolutionary common sense. Our report cards were folded down the middle, with English subjects on the left side and Yiddish on the right, because of the different directions in which the two languages are written. One of the Yiddish subjects was *"Geschichte fun Klassen Kamf"* (History of Class Struggle), at which, I am pleased to note, I scored a straight *aleph* in 1949.

At Morris Winchewsky, and in our homes, we had secular versions of the principal Jewish holidays: our own kind of *Chánnukah,*[4] our own kind of *Púrim,* our own kind of Passover. The stories attaching to those holidays were generalized without strain into a grand message of resistance to all oppression, so that our Passover was as much about the 1943 Warsaw Ghetto uprising as it was about liberation from Egypt. Our parents and grandparents attended special evenings at which politically scarlet Yiddish themes were celebrated by their *kinder* and *ainiklach* in songs and narrations and plays. We felt proud as we performed, we knew we were the apples of our elders' eyes; and they *shepped nachas,* they glowed with satisfaction, as they watched us.

2

I entered Morris Winchewsky School in April 1945, as the Second World War was coming to a close. It was the sunset after a long day of harmony between Western capitalist democracy and Soviet communism. If you want to know how strong that harmony was, at the popular level—as opposed to at the level at which statesmen operate—try to get hold of a copy of the special edition of the American magazine *Life* which appeared sometime in 1943, and which was the best advertisement for the Soviet Union that anyone has ever produced. Shining young faces in well-equipped classrooms, heroic feats of industrialization, prodigious works of art and music, and so on. *Life* magazine did it better than homemade Soviet propaganda ever could.

In the Morris Winchewsky School we believed profoundly both in democracy and in communism, and we did not separate the two—for we knew that communism would be tyranny unless the people controlled how the state steered society, and we thought that democracy would be only formal without the full citizen enfranchisement that required communist equality.

As Jewish children growing up in the shadow of the Holocaust, the Nazi destruction filled us with fury and sorrow. Nazism was a great fierce black cloud in our minds, and we thought of anti-Nazism as implying democracy and therefore communism, and we therefore thought of Jewish people as natural communists; the many left-wing Yiddish songs we were taught to sing confirmed those ideological linkages. Nor was it eccentric of us, in that particular time and place, to put *Yiddishkeit* and leftism together. To illustrate that, let me point out that the area of Montreal in which I lived, at whose geographic center the Morris Winchewsky School stood, elected a Communist Party member, the Polish-Canadian Jew Fred Rose, to the Parliament of Canada in Ottawa in 1943.

So in our childhood consciousness, being Jewish, being anti-Nazi, being democratic, and being communist all went together. All tyranny was the same, whether it was the tyranny of Pharaoh or of Antiochus Epiphanes or of Nebuchadnezzar or of Hitler or of J. Edgar Hoover.[5] And if the Winchewsky School training had not sufficed to keep that ideological package well wrapped up, there was also in July and August Camp Kinderland,[6] forty miles from Montreal, where *Yiddishkeit* and leftism flourished together among the fir trees and the mosquitoes.

This ideologically enclosed existence was brought to an end one Friday in the early summer of 1952. It was, I remember, a day of glorious sunshine. On that sunny day, the Anti-Subversive (or, as it was commonly known, the Red) Squad of the Province of Quebec Provincial Police raided the Morris Winchewsky School and turned it inside out, in a search for incriminating left-wing literature. We were in the school when the raiders came, but, whatever happened in other classes, the raid was not frightening for those of us who were then in *Lérerin* Asher's charge, because, having left the room for a moment in response to the knock on the door, Mrs. Asher soon returned, clapped her hands with simulated exuberance, and announced, in English: "Children, the Board of Health is inspecting the school and you can all go home early." So we gaily scurried down the stairs, and lurking at the entrance were four men, each of them tall and very fat, all of them eyes down, and looking sheepish.

In the event, no compromising materials were found, since the school had been careful to keep itself clean, but a parallel raid on the premises of the school's sponsoring organization, the United Jewish People's Order, did expose pamphlets and the like. These UJPO premises were consequently padlocked by the police and the organization was denied access to the building, within the terms of a Quebec law, known as the Padlock Law, which was later struck down by the Supreme Court of Canada.[7] And although Morris Winchewsky itself was permitted to remain open, the raids caused enough parents to withdraw their children from the school to make its further full-time operation impractical.

Accordingly, we were cast forth, as far as our formal schooling was concerned, into the big wide noncommunist world. But some of us—and I, now eleven, was one of them—departed with a rock-firm attachment to the principles it had been a major purpose of Morris Winchewsky to instill in us, and with full and joyous confidence that the Soviet Union was implementing those principles.

3

The first blow to that confidence fell in June 1956, when the U.S. State Department published the text of a speech discrediting Stalin that Nikita Khrushchev had delivered, four months earlier, at a closed session of the Twentieth Congress of the Communist Party of the Soviet Union. The party in Quebec was stunned by (what were called) the "Khrushchev revelations," and its top six leaders resigned their memberships in September 1956. The six Quebec party leaders were dismayed by what Khrushchev had said, because it implied that they had conducted their political lives (and, therefore, their lives) under a massive illusion. But the Quebec leaders also felt dismayed for the further reason that national (that is, Toronto) Communist Party leaders who were fraternal delegates at the Twentieth Congress had concealed Khrushchev's secret de-Staliniization speech when reporting back to the Canadian party.[8] The six Montreal-based Quebec leaders felt betrayed by the national leadership, and, once they had left, the membership of the party in Montreal felt not only, like its erstwhile local leadership, betrayed, by Moscow and by Toronto, but also abandoned, by six admired and much-loved comrades whose departure was accompanied by no explanatory statement, who called no meeting to share their burden with the membership, who just went without saying good-bye.

In an atmosphere of confusion and distress, high-tension meetings of an unstructured kind and open to all party members were held in the remaining months of 1956, at the premises of the Beaver Outing Club,[9] which was a recreational society sponsored by the party. As leader of the younger teenage portion of the Quebec Division of the Communist Party youth organization (which was called the NFLY, the letters standing for "National Federation of Labour Youth"),[10] I sat agog at those meetings, a silent witness of a little piece of history in the making. I watched the Quebec party split into two groups: hardliners and softliners. While willing (just) to repudiate Stalin, the hardliners were for minimal change in the party's mode of work, while the softliners had an appetite for reconstruction and renovation.[11] The hardliners called themselves "Marxists" and their opponents "revisionists," and the latter called themselves "the New" and the others "the Old" (or, sometimes, the "dogmatists"). My mother was enthusiastically New, as were the other members of the party branch she chaired: the line of fracture in the party was running between rather than within branches.

After eighteen more months of factional dispute, a convention was called to elect a new executive for the still leaderless Quebec Communist Party. Two high functionaries came from Toronto, where the party was far less wracked, to supervise accreditation of delegates to a Quebec electoral convention. The sympathy of the men from Toronto was with the hardliners, and they ensured that duly selected representatives of "New" party branches were denied their right to vote, on spurious technical grounds. I believe—but here my recollection is somewhat hazy—that this was the trick the Toronto supervisors pulled: they delayed dispatching to New branches the forms on which delegates' names were to be inscribed, so that, when those forms were filled in and returned, they could be declared invalid for having arrived too late. Through that or some comparable form of manipulation, the convention was made to produce a uniformly Old executive, and, in the aftermath, those of the New persuasion, my mother included, gradually fell away from the party: they had, in effect, been disenfranchised. Six or seven years later, when my mother taxed one of the Toronto emissaries, a personal friend, with the role he had played in the misconstruction of the 1958 convention, I heard him say: "Bella, in politics you sometimes have to do things that are not pleasant."

A year or so before the 1958 convention, the leader of the Quebec division of the National Federation of Labour Youth resigned in disillusionment (to become an academic anthropologist), and the Quebec NFLY just collapsed—so fast that I would not have been able to leave it had I wanted to. Nor would I have wanted to leave it then: my mother, after all, was at the time still a committed party member. I felt, morosely, that the NFLY was leaving me.

In September 1957, with the NFLY gone and me too young for a party that was anyway growing too Old for me, I entered McGill University, a convinced Marxist with no suitable organization to belong to, and I joined (and soon became the president of) the thoroughly tame Socialist Society, which was all that McGill then had to offer.

4

Through the rest of the Fifties, and into the early Sixties, I was what some would have called a "fellow traveler." The party rapidly became too rigid for me to consider submitting myself anew to its authority, but I remained basically pro-Soviet. Seeds of doubt had been sown, and I knew that there was much over there that deserved to be criticized, yet I still believed that the Soviet Union was a socialist country, struggling toward community and equality, and amply meriting every leftist's allegiance. (Thorough disillusion with the Soviet Union came only later, when I was in my twenties, as a result of personal travels—to Hungary in 1962, and to Czechoslovakia in 1964—and public events; see note 11 above. By the time I first visited the Soviet Union itself, in 1972, I expected, and found, little that was inspiring.)

5

I have thus far said quite a bit about politics in my childhood, but very little about religion. In order to redress that imbalance, I want to go back to 1952, which was the year my friends and I were forced to leave the Morris Winchewsky School.

I did not proclaim my communist beliefs in the state primary school, called Alfred Joyce, in which, at the age of eleven, I came to be installed, or in Strathcona Academy, the secondary school to which I progressed a year later. I did not publicly expose my red connections, because those years were the apex of the Cold War McCarthy period, and I did not have the guts to lay bare my leftism, and my persisting allegiance to communism and to the Soviet Union and, now, to China, an allegiance which was practiced within various Komsomol-type organizations. When I was twelve, I made a speech before an audience of a couple of thousand at the Canadian Peace Congress in Toronto; it was duly reported, with a photograph of me at the podium, in various low-circulation journals, and I was proud of all that, but I would not have known how to cope if my classmates had learned about it. Later, as teenagers, my comrades and I did quite scary things, like secretly carrying newspapers and leaflets in our bicycle baskets, for delivery at sympathetic destinations. When doing so, we were always wary when we saw policemen, who would not have approved of our activity, and who knew how to rough people up without leaving a mark. (McCarthyism was less insidious and more brutal in its Quebec manifestation than it was in the United States. Fewer people lost their jobs, but more people were beaten in police stations.) I think I might have preferred to be beaten up, just a little bit, than to face classmates who knew what I was doing.

For geographic reasons, 90 percent of those classmates were Jewish; we had only three gentiles in a class of twenty-six. This was so even though Montreal was only 6 percent Jewish at the time, and even though Jews were not a majority where I lived. Let me explain why my schools were predominantly Jewish as far as pupil intake was concerned, while being 100 percent lily-white *goy* on the teaching side.

Alfred Joyce and Strathcona Academy were run under the authority of the Protestant School Board of Greater Montreal. Until 1998, all state schools in Montreal were run either by the Protestant School Board of Greater Montreal or by the Catholic School Board of Greater Montreal, and none were run by both. (The phrase "*Greater* Montreal," by the way, does not mean "greater than some other city"—such as, maybe, Toronto; it means "greater than Montreal in a merely narrow sense of 'Montreal.'")

Now, in the catchment area of these schools, where I lived, there were very few Protestants. Almost everybody was either a believing or a non-believing Jew, or a French Canadian Roman Catholic. The French Canadian Roman Catholic children, who formed the majority in the area, went to French Catholic schools run by the Catholic School Board of Greater Montreal, and the majority of Jewish children—those, that is, who did not go to privately funded Jewish schools—went to English Protestant schools.

It was for several reasons that we Jews did not go to the French Catholic Schools. A major reason is that we would have hated to go to them. First of all, we would then have been educated in French, and English was for most of us our mother tongue, and for all of us the language to be favored as between French and English, because English, being more North American, was more modern, and because the French were, many of them, pretty openly anti-Semitic. Plenty of English Protestants were also anti-Semitic, but, because they were more genteel and better groomed, their anti-Semitism was less open, and anyway they mostly lived in a faraway, and cleaner, part of town. (Let me give you an example of genteel anti-Semitism. Many English-speaking hotels and clubs bore discreet signs near their entrances which said "Restricted Clientele." Nonwhites and Jews were to take note of that. But we were never kicked out of such places (which would have been *un*genteel) because, in that era, none of us would have tried to get in.)

So one reason why we did not go to the French Catholic schools is that we did not want to be educated in a language that we dispreferred and whose speakers were hostile to us. And a second reason was that we disliked the Catholic religion more than we disliked the Protestant one. Once again, it was more associated with anti-Semitism in our minds: we all knew about the Spanish Inquisition and about the pope's inaction on the holocaust. But, also, Catholicism seemed more freaky than Protestantism and more oppressive in its rules and rituals and liturgy. We thought of Protestantism as rather bland and empty and unthreatening, and anyway with less blood on its hands and on its altars. Finally, a third reason why we did not go to the French Catholic schools was that we weren't *allowed* to. Unless you were Catholic, you couldn't enroll in those schools. The Protestants, by contrast, let non-Protestants in, as long as they were not Catholics. Or maybe the Catholics didn't *let* the Protestants let Catholics in. But whichever way it went, Catholics weren't allowed to go to Protestant Schools, only Catholics could go to Catholic schools, and all non-Catholics went to Protestant Schools. So we Jews went to Protestant Schools.

The fact that my classmates were mostly Jewish—mostly, indeed, Jewish boys (for the schools were mixed-sex but individual classes were not)—meant that it was not only my communism that I had to conceal. I also had to conceal, or, anyway, I thought I had to conceal, and I did conceal, the fact that I was not preparing for a *bar-mitzvah*. I would have been mortified to admit, then, that I was out of step on that one. It was relatively easy to hide this shaming fact in the first of my post-Winchewsky school years, because I was six months to a year younger than my classmates, since I had entered school early, because Morris Winchewsky, being private, was able to admit children ahead of the normally required age. But everyone knew, after April 1954, that I had passed my thirteenth birthday, and now I could not avoid the *bar-mitzvah* issue.

So I lied. I said that I *had* had a *bar-mitzvah*. That always caused the boys to ask *where* I'd had my *bar-mitzvah*, which *shul*. Since "which *shul*" was a matter of keen interest, and a false answer to it could and would be exposed within five minutes, I lied that the rabbi had come to our apartment. I can't remember whether I got challenged to name the rabbi, but I seemed to get away with my lie. It provoked more puzzlement than disbelief.

There was a grain of truth in the lie that a rabbi had conducted a *bar-mitzvah* for me in our apartment. The grain of truth was that a kind of *bar-mitzvah* did occur in our apartment on or around my thirteenth birthday. It was attended by dozens of my parents' communist Jewish friends, and, instead of *dávening*, I recited a Yiddish short story by Sholem Aleichem, called "Berel Isaac." How could I have explained such unusual goings-on to my conventionally Jewish classmates? How could I have *justified* substituting such goings-on for the standard procedure?

Two years later, when I was fifteen, and still active in communist organizations, the truth about me emerged, because it was disclosed to someone by an incautious or disloyal friend. The news raced through the school: "Cohen's a Commie! Cohen's a Commie!" (Those were the words that were used.) For a few days I felt embattled, up against it, and I do not recall how I coped, initially, with the "revelation." But after those few days I came to realize that, far from being condemning, my schoolmates were, for the most part, intrigued and impressed, and, after that incident, I wore my ideological colors on my sleeve, with no sense of heroism, since I was conscious of how sheepishly I had hidden those colors before I learned that there was promotional mileage to be got from flourishing them.

6

So I belonged to two Jewish worlds, one forthrightly antireligious and anti-Zionist, save for the brief interlude when Israel had Stalin's blessing, and the other—the mainstream Jewish world, to which I belonged (or, better, in which, *faute de mieux,* I was present and I functioned)—mildly religious, more or less reflectively Zionist, and heartily anti-Soviet. My ideologically significant life was pursued within the first world, and I managed a different existence, with a substantial measure of self-concealment from the age of eleven to the age of fifteen, within the margins of the second.

In my teens, my summers were spent at the children's camp—Kinderland—to which I have already referred. That camp underwent two metamorphoses in the 1950s. In 1953, it passed out of the control of the United Jewish People's Order, and it came to be run by the Communist Party's Beaver Outing Club. The camp's name was therefore changed, from "Kinderland" to "Beaver Camp." And now, instead of being 95 percent Jewish, it was only about 60 percent so, with much of the remaining 40 percent being composed of Ukrainian kids, whose parents belonged to the Association of United Ukrainian Canadians, a pro-Soviet organization which played for left-wing Ukrainians the role that the UJPO played for us Jews. There were also some pure-white Anglo-Saxon kids, and a few French-Canadians. The first lines of the Beaver Camp song made out that the camp's ethnic mix was more balanced than it actually was. They ran as follows:

> French and English,
> Slav and Jewish,
> Junior Beavers All. . .

When, in 1956, in the wake of Nikita Khrushchev's exposure of Stalin's crimes, the Communist Party of Quebec collapsed, Beaver Camp collapsed with it. The land on which the camp was sited reverted to the United Jewish People's Order, and Camp Kinderland was revived, but now it was a very pale pink, by the standards of its crimson past. I worked at Kinderland as a counselor in the summers of 1958 and 1959, but I had conflicts with the camp director, which meant that I didn't return in 1960. One reason he and I quarreled was that he'd been to the Soviet Union and knew it was a disaster, whereas I still thought otherwise and taught the kids otherwise. But we also couldn't get along because he was self-loving and dictatorial and I was too headstrong and too self-important to subordinate myself to such a person. So the summer of 1960 found me, for the first time, at a mainstream Jewish noncommunist children's camp, which was called Wooden Acres, and which was run by the B'nai Brith (a Jewish charity organization similar to the Rotary Club). This was to be my first full-scale engagement within the authority of a noncommunist Jewish organization, and it led to my closest encounter ever with the Jewish religion.

At this point I was nineteen, I'd never laid eyes on *tefillen,* I'd hardly ever been in a synagogue—perhaps twice with my father's father at Simchas Torah, and on two further occasions when each of my two male Montreal cousins, who were brothers, celebrated their *bar-mitzvahs.* These cousins came from an unbelieving family, and they too had attended Morris Winchewsky, but although their mother had been in the Communist Party, their Dad was now becoming a *mácher* in the B'nai Brith, so *bar-mitzvahs* were de rigueur. I remember sitting in the synagogue and contemning the hypocrisy of undergoing a *bar-mitzvah* when you don't believe in God. I wouldn't call that hypocrisy now. Now I'm older, and I believe in preserving tradition.

Anyway, off I went at nineteen to the B'nai Brith charity camp, to take charge of six recently *bar-mitzvah*'ed fourteen-year-old boys. Also at the camp was a young orthodox rabbi from New York, called Josh Tarsis. Josh decided to run a morning *minyan,* which is to say a prayer group of ten or more men, ten men being the quorum required for heavy-duty praying in orthodox Judaism. My six boys formed its core; Josh was the seventh; the camp *meshkiách,* or food inspector, or dietary warden, was the eighth; I forget who was the ninth—and there they stuck, one under par, until my boys succeeded, without much difficulty, because I had a lot of affection for them, in nagging me into joining them as the magic

Number Ten. So I got up early and, ignorantly and awkwardly, I wrapped the *tefillen* around my arm and my head and I tried my best to read the Hebrew prayers, which were alien to me, cast in a language that felt somewhat *goyish* because it was not Yiddish. (Very little Hebrew had been taught at Morris Winchewsky; and because it was the language of religion, I didn't like it much and therefore didn't study it conscientiously.)

Participating in the *minyan,* and also (for I did this too) carrying a prayer book around with me and reading it that summer in isolated moments of privacy—all that was a kind of quiet rebellion against my parents' excessive antireligiousness. For it occurred to me then that so much of humanity, high and low, had believed in religion that it could not be *just* the pile of garbage that my parents thought it was. One had to take seriously the fact that people whom one had to take seriously had taken and took religion seriously. That by no means showed that religion was right-headed, if only because plenty of other people whom one also had to take seriously rejected it. I still thought, as I still indeed think, that the onus is on religious belief to vindicate itself, since it appears to claim for itself a form of knowledge which is different from what everyone—that is, religious and irreligious people alike—thinks of as forms of knowledge, but I did become (and I have remained) more respectful of religion as such, and I was intrigued by and somewhat attracted to religious Judaism in particular, although I was also shocked by the content of some of the *bróches* in the prayer book. But getting up very early in the morning was a drag, and my command over the Hebrew prayers wasn't progressing, so, after a couple of weeks, I quit the *minyan.* This dismayed my six kids, since my departure destroyed the *minyan,* but I was unmoved by their disapproval, because I had told them at the outset that it would be a limited-term engagement, and also because the camp had a good twenty-five *bar-mitzvah*'ed men, many of whom professed belief and any of whom could have served as the tenth that they needed. I felt contemptuous that a camp teeming with *bar-mitzvah*'ed men relied on *me,* who was probably not *minyan*-eligible anyway (since I had not been *bar-mitzvah*'ed) to complete a *minyan.*

My attitude to that mainstream noncommunist Jewish world was profoundly ambivalent. I was drawn toward it and repelled by it at the same time. On the one hand, its citizens and I were of one substance, from one history, connected, together, with one still-recent rending tragedy. On the other hand, they rejected my beliefs, and their beliefs, for me, were unheroic and conformist, lacking in courage and adventure.

At Beaver Camp our song had been full of all that internationalist inspirational "French and English, Slav and Jewish" stuff, and we sang with conviction that "children of our mighty country hate the thought of war." By contrast, the Wooden Acres camp song was ideologically bland: "Round the campfire, brightly blazing," and so on. But every evening before dinner we would gather, all 250 or 300 of us, outside the dining hall, to sing "Hatikvah," which is the Israeli national anthem, with music by Bedřich Smetana. That beautiful hymn, whose words were translated for me, rocked me hard, and the solemnity and feeling with which it was sung made me somewhat anti-anti-Zionist, just as, that same summer, I was becoming anti-antireligious. Then, having completed "Hatikvah," we would file into the dining hall, to stand at our places and wait to say the *bróche,* first in Hebrew and then in English, with hand on head; and I was enchanted by the idea of the Lord bringing forth bread from the earth. I must have been a very impressionable young man, because a few words in a song or a prayer could stir me a lot and unsettle my deeply fixed convictions.

It's amazing how what goes on in your head can differ from what goes on in your heart, without your head knowing about it. Despite the appealing strains of "Hatikvah," I remained if not anti- then at least non-Zionist by conviction. But when the June 1967 (or "Six-Day") war broke out and it looked at first, or was made to look at first, as though Israel might be destroyed, everything in my being strained toward Jerusalem, and there was in me a powerful urge to go there and do whatever I could to help—an urge I did not pursue, if only because our first-born child was then just seven months old.

I am still not a Zionist, but a Jew does not have to be a Zionist to feel strongly implicated in Israel's fate. I have no use for the Israeli state, *as such,*[12] just as I have no use for any other state, but I care disproportionately about the fate of the Jewish people there. I do not have the indifference to the Jews of Israel which is felt or faked by many Jewish leftists. I feel a strong identification not so much with Israel as such but certainly with its Jewish population, and I care about their safety, and about their deeds. When Americans kill Vietnamese, when Indonesians kill East Timorese, when Soviets mow down Czechs, when Serbs murder Bosnians, I am angry, frustrated, and sad. But when Israelis, under whatever provocation, blow up houses and kill men, women, and children in the occupied territories, there is blood on my *own* hands and I weep with shame.

7

Why do I *feel* so Jewish?

A large part of the answer to that question is implied by what I have already said: so much of Jewish tradition, albeit of only one stream in Jewish tradition, was pumped into my soul in childhood. But another thing that has certainly helped me to feel Jewish is anti-Semitism. Jean-Paul Sartre exaggerated when he said in his essay on the Jewish question that it is the anti-Semite who *creates* the Jew. But who could deny that the anti-Semite *reinforces* the Jew's sense that he is Jewish?

Kids like me experienced anti-Semitism in two forms. On the one hand in a coarse form, and on the other hand in a form that was not exactly subtle but, let us say, more clean-shaven. The coarse kind of anti-Semitism came from some of the French-Canadian working-class people with whom we lived cheek by jowl. I don't know how many of them harbored it in their hearts, but it certainly sometimes came out of some of their mouths, such as those of certain rough French-Canadian kids who, at least once or twice, called me "maudit Juif" as I made my way to school along the sidewalk. When I heard "maudit Juif" ("damn Jew"), I walked swiftly on, eyes averted from the name-caller, and probably most of those at whom such epithets were hurled did the same. But there did exist a more or less organized West-Side-Story-type Jewish gang, called "the Lords," which, so I believe, conducted gladiatorial contests against French-Canadian gangs and, although I do not know how much of what we heard about the Jewish gang's exploits was myth, and I never saw them in action, I was glad that such a gang was in business. In any case, the "maudit Juif" name-calling didn't happen very often—not, anyway, in my immediate experience; but it doesn't have to happen a lot for it to be a preoccupation as you walk along the streets where it sometimes happens.

The well-bred variety of anti-Semitism was projected at us by some of the schoolteachers in our high school, Strathcona Academy. Strathcona was named after the Baron Strathcona and Mount Royal, a one-time High Commissioner of Canada to Great Britain and, at an earlier stage in his life, the man who had built the Canadian Pacific Railway. He had not built it single-handedly, but when the line being laid from the east met the line being laid from the west, he had driven in the final spike, which was made of gold.

As I've already said, the great majority of the pupils at Strathcona Academy were Jewish. Something on the order of 90 percent were Jewish, the residual 10 percent being formed out of Greeks, Syrians, a French Huguenot or two, and a very few Protestants whose native language was English. The teachers, by contrast, every last man-Jack and woman-Jill of them, from the principal down to the raw recruits, were pure-white Protestants of British extraction. Elsewhere in the city, there were Jewish teachers teaching Jewish kids, under the auspices of the Protestant School Board, but it was a principle or anyway a policy at Strathcona Academy that no Jews were to be hired. I suppose Jews were so overrepresented among the pupil intake that they thought it would needlessly tilt things even further away from Protestantness if they took in Jewish *teachers* as well.

The fact that 90 percent of us were Jewish and almost none of us were Protestant did not prevent the school from laying little bits of Protestant religious observance on us. We said the Lord's Prayer every morning; I sometimes very quietly recited a Yiddish parody version of it invented by Irving Zucker (who is now a distinguished professor at Berkeley specializing in reproductive physiology). And every Christmastime we assembled to sing carols and to listen to some *nárishkeit* intoned by a local clergyman. The extraordinary thing—and this tells you much about the North American 1950s—is that, in my secure recollection and that of my friends, not a single one of us ever voiced even a mild squeak of protest against this incongruous imposition. We were only too glad not to be subjected to the weirder stuff that would surely have been thrust upon us if we'd been at a *Catholic* school.

Few teachers ever adverted to this curious ethnic divide between teachers and taught. But one of them, Mr. Herbert Jordan, was uninhibited about it. Jordan taught us two subjects: "Guidance" (which is called "Careers" in Britain) and English literature. In his capacity as teacher of Guidance, Mr. Jordan from time to time warned us with relish that, since we were Jewish—he blankly ignored the three non-Jews in our thirty-strong class when making such warnings—we would gain admission to McGill University only if we scored rather better in our examinations than the minimum required for non-Jews: that was McGill's policy.

Now, to go to McGill was a widespread hope and expectation in our class. (I was once traveling on a bus on Sherbrooke Street, and as it passed the Roddick Gates, where McGill University begins, a little Jewish boy asked his mother, "What's that?" "That's McGill, that's where you're gonna be a doctor," she replied, in a European accent.) Anyway, we did want to go to McGill, and one could imagine someone telling us about the special threshold at McGill for Jews matter-of-factly, or even in a tone of compassion and anger; but Jordan would rehearse this piece of information with a certain satisfaction, in a spirit of: Don't get too big for your boots; you may be clever, but you are *Jewish,* after all. And once again, we never protested against this display.

I should say as a footnote at this point that McGill's delicate discrimination policy (don't *prohibit* Jews, but make sure that only the smarter ones come) had, I think, come to an end *before* Herbert Jordan was still ignorantly admonishing us in the aforementioned terms. A massively wealthy Montreal Jewish family, the Samuel Bronfman family (which owned, among other things, Seagrams Distilleries), had by then, so I believe, poured a lot of money into McGill's coffers on the understanding that McGill would reciprocate by lifting its *numerus clausus,* and it duly did.

I say that we did not protest against Jordan, yet we did have contempt for him. But if you think that *all* we had for him was contempt, then you do not understand what sort of contempt we had and you do not understand what it is to be on the receiving end of ethnic discrimination. We did have contempt, but we also had respect, because men like Jordan were on top; they were the official people who ran things and who made things go like they were supposed to go. *They* didn't get called "maudit Juif" as they walked home from school. *They* didn't—even their parents didn't—speak with more or less strong European accents. They were the bright, clean, white people, not underhanded-clever and street-smart and sly, like we were, but full of a spotless surface virtue.[13]

When I look back, I find it remarkable that my respect for Jordan was so robust, despite my contempt for him and despite the many opportunities he created for me to withdraw my respect. Thus, for example, in his manifestation not as Guidance teacher but as teacher of English literature, Jordan many times told us that there were only seven kinds of plot in all works of fiction, and, he added, with Christian pride, that all seven plots were to be found in the Bible. I found this claim both fascinating and incredible, and there was also inside me when I heard it a proto-philosophical stirring about what exactly the criteria of identity would be for plot types, what the criteria were for saying this story has the same plot as that different one, and so forth.

Now, whenever Jordan made this claim, he'd illustrate it by saying that there is, for example, the plot based on the return of the prodigal son. But that was the only example he ever gave. So, because I found Jordan's claim baffling, I one day gathered my courage and I went to him after class and I asked him—because I really wanted to know the answer, I wasn't just trying to trip him up—what the other six plots were. I suppose it was my intention to then see if I could find a counterexample, a truly different eighth type of plot. What was my surprise and disappointment when a *somewhat* embarrassed Jordan (I have to say that his embarrassment wasn't as great as it should have been) replied with little hesitation that he couldn't quite remember any of the other six plots. He'd look up the point in a book he had at home and get back to me on this.

Now, that *should* have undermined my respect for Jordan, but it didn't, even though he never came back with a single one of the six missing plots, and I, of course, never reminded him of his undischarged obligation. This shows how a member of a despised minority can continue to have a kind of deference toward the man in charge even when the man has proved himself to be an empty windbag. And because you have a kind of deference to him, and therefore to his views, you have a kind of deference to his view that Jews are not quite human, or that they have all too many of the less agreeable human characteristics, and that doesn't help you to respect yourself. Which shows that Sartre was onto something in his essay "On the Jewish Question," even if he exaggerated the point with characteristic Gallic excess.

8

When I left high school and entered McGill, I found myself for the first time among classmates who were mostly not Jewish, but the Jewish minority at McGill was sufficiently large for most of my immediate associates to be Jewish, since it was to Jews that I gravitated. Four years later, I passed on to Oxford for graduate study, and there things were different: I was, finally, in a non-Jewish world. There were, of course, plenty of Jews both at Oxford and in Britain more generally, but it was months, if not a couple of years, before I could identify them, when they did not bear names like Birnbaum or Goldstein, because these British Jews looked and behaved differently from the Montreal Jews that I knew inside-out. It took me a while to get the gestalt into which these alien Jews fitted.

It seemed to me that British Jews were, on the whole, both more as-similated *and* more religious than the recently postimmigrant Jews of Canada. The British Jews belonged to an older community, dating back to Victorian times. Because they had settled generations ago, and be-cause they were less Slav and more Germanic, I did not feel immediately drawn to them; their life experience was very different from mine, along the dimensions that mattered to me. There was little heritage of left-wing Jewishness or *Yiddishkeit* within their ranks, not much of the Rus-sian Bund in their backgrounds, and they carried themselves with a con-fidence which betrayed lack of anxiety about anti-Semitism. The present chief rabbi, Jonathan Sacks, said on the radio in January 1994 that he could not recall a single experience of anti-Semitism in Britain when he was a child (whereas, he added, there are plenty of manifestations of anti-Semitism in Britain now). Perhaps their lack of anxiety about anti-Semitism helped to make British Jews both more assimilated *and* more religious: lack of anti-Semitism means you do not have to give up your religion to be part of the wider society.

I was confused about British Jews. I could not find my feet with them. Years later, around 1980, I was recruited, somewhat accidentally, to the National Yad Vashem[14] Committee of the United Kingdom, which oper-ates under the auspices of the Board of Deputies of British Jews. There I sat, with businessmen and rabbis, sharing with them a desire to perpetu-ate the memory of the Holocaust, but so divided from them in outlook and attitude that this (for me uncustomary) engagement with mainline British Jewry was to last just a couple of years. And I have not had the energy to liaise with the small Jewish socialist organization that exists in Britain. For me, now, my Jewishness is a private thing. It no longer has much connection with my leftism, which remains public, on a modest scale.

9

So much on the particular ways that I *feel* Jewish. But feelings (more or less) aside, in what sense *am* I Jewish?

A person who practices the Jewish religion is clearly a Jew: practicing the religion is a sufficient condition of being Jewish. But it is not also a necessary condition. I am Jewish not because I practice the religion, but because I descend from the people who practiced that religion (and still do). That is clearly a way of being Jewish. But it is being Jewish in a derived or secondary way, even if it is consistent with *feeling* no less Jewish, no less connected with the historical people, than an orthodox Jew does.

We learned a lot of true things at Morris Winchewsky, but a lot of false ones too. Setting aside all the false things we learned about Soviet communism, the biggest falsehood was the idea that religion was not central to being Jewish. They made us think that just as some Frenchmen or Italians were religious and some not, so some Jews were religious and some not.

But that, I now know, is not true. Individual Jews, like me, can be irreligious, yet we are Jewish only by virtue of connection with a people defined not by place or race but by religion. The areligious cultural periphery cannot become the core, or even *a* core, of something new, and when I meet third- and fourth-generation secular American Jews whom I teach at Oxford, I observe, with regret, that the sense of connection to the Jewish past is decaying and that the special sensibility is disappearing. (To forestall misunderstanding, let me add that, when I say that the cultural periphery cannot become a core, I do not think that is true by virtue of the very definition of "culture," "religion," "Jewish," or anything else, nor do I put it forth as any sort of general truth. It is an empirical claim about this particular people.)

So, while I need not tell you that being Jewish means an enormous amount to me—much more, for example, than being Canadian—I no longer have the illusion which Morris Winchewsky nourished, that Jews could go on and on without a religion to carry our identity.

Israel is a different matter. The religion is powerful there, but even if it declines, the people will remain an entity. Yet, if the religion goes, then, in time, those people will no longer be a Jewish entity, any more than the Italian citizens of Rome are a Roman entity in the classical sense. Judaism would have contributed centrally to their formation, but they will not be Jews (as I understand what Jews are).

Whatever happens to Israel, and to Judaism as a religion, the secular *Yiddishkeit* in my identity will not last, except as an object of academic attention—albeit, perhaps, of *affectionate* academic attention. *This* way of being Jewish depended on the shtetl, on the prohibition on speaking *lóshen kóydish,* the holy language, in daily life, and on an environing exclusion from gentile society and institutions. As that context goes, so *Yíddishkeit* as a lived thing will also go, outside Hassidic and similar communities.

I find that very sad. It is sad to contemplate the disappearance of one's own identity, and it is awkward to acknowledge that *Yíddishkeit* will persist in some lived form only as long as beliefs and practices from which I remain cut off are perpetuated. But that's how it is. History doesn't always go the way you want it to go.

I sometimes imagine myself, as my death creeps up on me, reciting the "Sh'má Yísroel," which is the prayer to be said when dying, and which runs: "Hear, O Israel! The Lord is our God, the Lord is one." I don't know whether that is just an idle fantasy on my part, or something deeper. If it is deeper, then the desire it expresses is not to pay final homage to the God of the Old Testament, whom I find unattractive,[15] but to solidarize with my forebears, from Canaan to Kishinev, from Belsen to Brooklyn.

Glossary
(Prepared with the help of Dovid Katz)

aínikl, aíniklach = grandchild, grandchildren
bar-mítzvah = male confirmation ceremony at age thirteen
bróche = blessing
Chánnukah = holiday celebrating the victorious revolt of the Maccabees
    against the king of Syria, Antiochus Epiphanes
dávenen = to pray
goy = gentile
kínder = children
lérerin = teacheress
lóshn kóydish = traditional Hebrew (literally, "the holy language")
mácher = wheeler-dealer, mover and shaker (literally, "maker")
meshkiách = kitchen functionary whose task is to ensure that all the food is
    kósher and all *káshrus* rules (of preparation of food, kitchen cleaning, etc.)
    are observed
mínyan = quorum of ten men, required for full communal prayer services
nárishkeit = foolishness, nonsense

Púrim = holiday celebrating events in the Book of Esther

shépn náchas = to derive prideful pleasure from (typically, a younger relative)

Sh'má Yísroel = first words of prayer to be said when dying: "Shmá Yísroel! Adóynoy eloyhéynu, Adóynoy ékhod" ("Hear, O Israel! The Lord is our God, the Lord is one")

shul = synagogue

tefillen = phylacteries—i.e., small leather boxes containing sacred passages from the Pentateuch, held in place by leather straps, one on the forehead and the other on the nondominant arm; worn by men during weekday morning prayers

Yíddishkeit = Yiddishness

3

The Development of Socialism from Utopia to Science

Solemnly our young voices
Take the vow to be true to the cause,
We are proud of our choices,
We are serving humanity's laws.

L. Oshanin, "World Youth Song," in
Silber, ed., *Lift Every Voice!*

1

Because I was born into, and grew up in, a working-class family that belonged to a Communist Party community, I heard a great deal of vernacular Marxism being talked around me, from a very early age. I listened eagerly, and I avidly absorbed Marxist ideas about capitalism, socialism, and revolution, including the idea that the revolution transforming capitalism into socialism would come at a more or less predictable time, since the advent of that revolution was assured by the laws of history.

When I was about twelve years old, I met a man called Tim Buck, who was then general secretary of the Canadian Communist Party.[1] I was dazzled when I met him, not because he had a brilliant personality, but because I believed that his expert grasp of the laws of history meant that he knew *when* socialism would come to Canada. How amazing it must be (so I thought, in my dazzlement) to know a thing like *that!* It puzzles me, in retrospect, that I did not ask Tim Buck to tell *me* when socialism would come. Perhaps I thought that it was the special privilege of the leader to know when the revolution would happen. Or maybe I thought that twelve-year-olds were too young to be told, or that they did not have the right to ask.

But, while thinking that Tim Buck knew when socialism would come, I did not also think that he would simply watch it come—that he would arrange not to be too busy in the month in question, so that he could have a ringside seat at the revolutionary action. Of course I did not think that. I thought that he would be, and that he thought he would be, in the thick of the struggle himself.

Yet what role might there be for him, and indeed for human will in general and for political action in particular, if the advent of socialism was foredoomed? Well, think about pregnancy. The expectant mother may believe that she will have a baby in a particular week or month, but she need not therefore believe that there will be no role for a midwife when she comes to term. So, too, capitalism is pregnant with socialism, but good politics is needed to ensure its safe delivery. Classical Marxism was dominated by an *obstetric* conception of political practice; Lectures 3 and 4 are devoted to exposing that conception.

In prosecution of that aim, I shall begin by addressing the Marxian distinction between utopian and scientific socialism. After nodding, briefly, in the direction of Friedrich Engels' book on that subject, I shall offer a short exposition of Marxism, taking as my text Lenin's pamphlet "The Three Sources and Component Parts of Marxism"—these sources and components being, so he rightly said, German philosophy, French socialism, and British political economy. I shall strive, in my reconstruction of Lenin, to convey how powerful Marxism was, in its own conception of itself, and how strong and prideful a contrast Marx and Engels and their followers felt able to draw between themselves and the socialists whom they stigmatized as utopian. I shall describe what made the utopians count as such, in the view of Marx and Engels, and then what, in their own view, ensured that they themselves counted as scientific. And in Lecture 4 I shall investigate the obstetric motif itself, after expounding a view about mathematics which was propounded by Hegel and which was undoubtedly one source of Marxism's obstetric conception. You won't have to be a mathematician to follow that. To understand Hegel's view, you will only have to know, in the broadest terms, what mathematics *is*.

In later lectures, I shall confront the problem that the big factual claims which were to ensure delivery of the ideal are no longer believable. This means that socialists must abandon the obstetric conception,[2] and that they must, in some measure, be utopian designers, which does not mean that they must be utopian in every respect in which those called utopian by Marx and Engels were utopian. And then I shall ask whether structural design is indeed enough—whether we can settle for changing the world and not *also* the soul.

2

I begin, then, with the Marxian distinction between utopian and scientific socialism, "scientific socialism" being the name that Engels gave to what came to be called "Marxism."[3] The most extended presentation of the distinction between scientific and utopian socialism, by a Marxist, is the one that Engels provided in 1878 in his book *Anti-Dühring*, but the relevant chapters of *Anti-Dühring*[4] were published separately from it, in 1880, in French, under the title *Socialisme utopique et socialisme scientifique* (Utopian Socialism and Scientific Socialism). The chapters then reappeared, again as a separate book, in German, in 1882, under the instructively different title *Die Entwicklung des Sozialismus von der Utopie zur Wissenschaft* (The Development of Socialism from Utopia to Science). The conventional English title of the work, *Socialism: Utopian and Scientific,* displays a significant loss of information, relative to the German title, since it fails to convey what the German title implies: that socialism was utopian *before* it was scientific. It is, as we shall see, a major thesis of scientific socialism that socialism could not but have been first utopian and only later scientific.[5] Note, further, the extraordinary suggestion in the German title of Engels' book that socialism became not merely scientific, but *a science*. That is a stronger claim than the claim that it became scientific. One might say of a body of doctrine which is centrally a political philosophy that it has in certain respects a scientific character and is therefore not only philosophical but also scientific. But to call socialism *a science* suggests that scientificity is the centrally correct classification of the socialism Engels commends, and that is a stronger, and more puzzling, claim.

3

When Engels contrasted utopian and scientific socialism, he had a conception of Marxism in mind. The best brief classical exposition of that conception, an exposition which underlines its self-interpretation as scientific, is Lenin's "Three Sources and Component Parts of Marxism," which was published in 1913. I shall here indicate, following Lenin, what the three components were. But I shall strive to do a bit better than Lenin (in this particular respect!) by displaying more clearly than Lenin did how the three parts of Marxism that he identified were so combined by Marx as to make each part far more consequential than it was in the isolated condition in which Marx had first encountered it.

I shall expound this material without a word of criticism, as though I believed it all, which I do not. This I do in fulfillment of my announced intention to make vivid how powerful Marxism was in the conception of Marxism that the classical Marxists entertained.

The three sources of Marxism came from three European countries, in each of which a single one of them was most highly developed.[6] And each source was a field of thought which presented itself without relationship to the other two, so that it was an act of supreme ingenuity on Marx's part to bring the three together. In the order in which Marx appropriated the three elements, they were: first, the dialectical mode of analysis, which he drew from the philosophy he had studied as an adolescent and as a young man in his native Germany; second, French socialist ideas that flourished among intellectuals critical of capitalism in the France of Marx's day, the France which was the country of his first exile; and, finally, the classical political economy, or economics, which Marx mastered in his final exile, in Great Britain.

4

I start where Marx started, with philosophy, and more particularly with the rich philosophical notion that I shall call the "dialectical idea."[7]

Now, the words "dialectic," "dialectical," "dialectically," and especially "*un*dialectical," which is the most popular of these words, because it is the most aggressive—these words have been used with undisciplined abandon across the Marxist tradition, but I shall mean one reasonably precise thing by the word "dialectical" here. The dialectical idea that I have in mind appears in embryonic form in various episodes in the history of thought, but its most powerful exponent was the German philosopher Hegel, who died in 1831, less than ten years before Marx became a student of law and philosophy in a German academic world that was then still under Hegel's shadow.

This dialectical idea is that every living thing, every functioning thing, every live thing, including not only the literally living things studied by biology but also live systems of ideas or trends in art or smoothly functioning societies or vigorous families—every such thing develops by unfolding its inner nature in outward forms and, when it has fully elaborated that nature, it dies, disappears, is transformed into a successor form precisely because it has succeeded in elaborating itself fully. So the dialectical idea is the idea of self-destruction through self-fulfillment, of self-fulfillment in a self-destruction which generates a new creation.

Examples: The flower runs to seed, and new flowers come. The family brings the children to maturity and thereby dissolves itself and enables the creation of new families. The genre of painting flourishes when it has not yet been entirely explored, and becomes stale and dead when it has been; a new genre then emerges. Every developing thing is a victim of its own success.

Now, the broadest canvas on which Hegel sketched the dialectical idea was world history, which, so he thought, was the story of the *Weltgeist,* the world spirit, which is God in His manifestation on earth in human consciousness. God knows Himself only in human beings, so that His self-knowledge is their self-knowledge, and their knowledge of Him is also their knowledge of themselves.[8]

What happens in history is that the world spirit undergoes growth in self-awareness, and the vehicle of that growth at any given time is a (geographically located) culture, a culture which stimulates the growth of God's self-awareness, and therefore of human self-awareness, and which perishes when it has stimulated more growth than it can contain. Cultures, the spirits of distinct societies, are the units of historical development to which the dialectical principle is applied. Thus, for example, the civilization of medieval Europe perfects itself in its visual arts, in its conception of nature, in its religion, in its literature, and so forth and is then fully self-aware; nothing is hidden, and, as a result, what was medieval Europe is ripe for transformation into Renaissance protomodern Europe.

A one-sentence summary of the Hegelian philosophy of history:

History is the history of *the world spirit and, derivatively, of human consciousness,* which undergoes growth in *self-knowledge,* the stimulus to and vehicle of which is a *culture,* which perishes when it has stimulated more growth than it can contain.

In that summary, the dialectical idea of self-destruction through self-fulfillment plays a key role: the culture destroys itself by perfecting itself, just as the acorn does in the course of transforming itself into an oak.[9] Later (see the end of section 6 below), I shall indicate how Marx preserved the dialectical idea, and, therefore, the structure of Hegel's account of history, while transforming its content (the italicized part of the foregoing summarizing sentence) from a spiritual one into a materialist one.

5

Marx encountered the second source and component part of Marxism[10] during his French exile.[11] This was the socialist project, as propounded by such authors as Etienne Cabet, Henri de Saint-Simon, and Charles Fourier—a vision of a better society, one lacking the manifest injustice and misery of capitalism; one, too, that was rational in its workings because planned, rather than market-driven and therefore anarchic and irrational, as was capitalism. This French socialism was, however, utopian, which means a number of things, but one thing it means is that French socialism was undialectical, in the sense of "dialectical" that I have expounded. French socialism was undialectical because it offered no account of capitalism which showed how capitalism would transform itself and generate socialism as its own proper successor.

The problem with the utopians was *not* that they were too optimistic in what they thought could be accomplished. Marx and Engels were not less optimistic than they were, and therefore could not (and in fact did not) accuse the utopians of being utopian in the vulgar sense of being too optimistic. Rather, the socialists were utopian in the sense that they lacked a realistic conception of how socialism would come to be: they did not see that it was to be produced by social reality itself.

A dialectical approach to the problem of overcoming capitalism demands an account of how capitalism itself produces socialism, as a consequence of its own self-transformation. The French socialists provided a deep critique of capitalism, but it was a moralizing rather than a dialectical critique, showing the evils and irrationalities of capitalism without pointing out how capitalism would induce socialism as its own supersession. And the associated utopian conception of practice simulated the engineering model of alteration from without: it is utopian and undialectical so to construe the relationship between political ideals and political practice that the socialist project gets represented as one of clearing away capitalism to produce an empty plane on which socialism is constructed, like the project of an engineer who demolishes a rotten building in order to raise one of her own design in its place. Dialectically inspired political practice is, by contrast, a matter of working with the forces within capitalism itself which are destined to transform it. Hence, the socialist transformation for Marx is not, as it is for the French socialists, merely *for* the proletariat, to relieve their misery, but *by* the proletariat—the proletariat being the force within capitalist reality that subverts it, the creation of capitalism that overturns its creator.

6

But this application of the dialectical idea to capitalism so as to generate socialism, this synthesis of German philosophy and French socialism, remained schematic without provision of a third component: an analysis of the economic dynamic of capitalism. And that was the major intellectual appropriation of Marx's final exile, in Britain, where he studied the classical political economists more thoroughly than perhaps anyone else has ever done.[12]

Bourgeois political economy was undialectical. In its debased postclassical (that is, post-Adam-Smith-and-David-Ricardo) form, it depicted capitalism as a smoothly self-reproducing system, destined for lasting success. In its more tragic and truly classical form it indeed depicted a development for capitalism, but one culminating not in a higher form of economy but in the "stationary state," at which development stops. Marx refashioned the classical analysis so as to show how capitalist competition abolishes itself by creating enterprises of implicitly social character in which the capitalist becomes obsolete, so that little but his removal is needed to establish socialism. It is not a great exaggeration to say that, in the view of Marx and Engels, socialism is what capitalism has made of itself, minus the capitalist class.[13]

Capitalism was thereby placed within the dialectical frame that Hegel had used to describe cultures, as an entity governed by a principle of self-development that was also a principle of self-destruction and self-transcendence into a higher form. But Marx generalized that account of capitalist self-transformation to the universal plane of history as a whole and thereby generated the theory of historical materialism, which, as I said earlier, preserves the structure of the Hegelian philosophy of history but alters its content. The content is now materialist, since history is now the history of human industry, and not, as it was for Hegel, the history of the world-spirit manifesting itself in human consciousness. Correspondingly, the central growth is not, now, in the historical subject's self-awareness but in its productive power, in its sovereignty over nature rather than over self; and the unit of development is not, now, a culture, but an economic structure. So the following sentence both conveys the theory of historical materialism and displays how it alters the content of Hegel's theory while preserving its structure, the common structure of the two theories being given by the nonitalicized parts of the sentence:

> History is the history of *human industry,* which undergoes growth in *productive power,* the stimulus to and vehicle of which is *an economic structure,* which perishes when it has stimulated more growth than it can contain.

7

The human problem now lies in humanity's relationship to the world, not to itself. The problem is to turn the world into a home for humanity, by overcoming the scarcity in the relationship between humanity and nature which induces social division. Scarcity induces social division because it imposes repugnant labor and a consequent class antagonism between those whose lives must be given over to that labor and those whose lighter task it is to see to it that others carry out the repugnant labor that scarcity imposes. With the massive productive power generated by capitalism, repugnant labor is no longer required, and class division therefore loses its progressive function.

So, with the transition from Hegel to Marx, self-awareness is no longer at center stage. Deficiencies in human self-awareness are no longer due to the immaturity of the development of consciousness as such, but are rooted in defective social structures which produce ideological illusions that conceal and/or defend their inequities.[14]

8

We can now understand how Lenin was able to boast that Marx's teachings "arose as a direct and immediate *continuation* of the teachings of the greatest representatives of philosophy, political economy, and socialism," and that Marxism "is the legitimate successor of the best that was created by humanity in the nineteenth century in the shape of German philosophy, English political economy, and French socialism."[15] We can appreciate the grandeur, or at least the grand ambition, of Marx's theoretical structure by contrasting its plenitude with the restricted character of each of the three components that he brought together, as that component presented itself in its original, isolated form.

The Hegelian philosophy was profound and fertile. But it was also a fantasy, one that could have been produced only in a country bewitched by its romance with philosophy—so bewitched, indeed, by its romance with philosophy that German idealism could represent history as, in essence, a succession of states of consciousness. Thus, by implication, German idealism depreciated the material roots of human existence. Its upward spin into abstracted other-worldliness is corrected by the this-worldly focus of French socialism and British political economy, which Marx united with the revolutionary dialectical idea that he took from German philosophy.

The French provided the necessary vision of a better social reality, but with the French it was nothing *but* a vision, because the French lacked, on the one hand, the dialectical idea, and, on the other, British political economy, which could be used to produce a realistic application of the dialectical idea to capitalism. Socialism then emerges not as a mere vision but as a realistic projection of the future of capitalism itself.

Finally, British political economy was without a conception of a better future and condemned humanity to capitalism, precisely because it lacked the German dialectical principle which counseled search for self-transcendence in self-destructive self-development, and also because it lacked the socialist ideal which it fell to France to provide.

9

I now want to explore the Marxist self-conception further, by looking more closely at the distinction that Marxism drew between itself and utopian socialism.

As we have seen, utopian socialism counts as utopian because of its unrealistic conception of the practice that leads to socialism. It models that practice on the activity of an engineer, and engineers proceed undialectically. They prescribe a new form *to* reality. Contrast midwives, who deliver the form that develops *within* reality.

But that utopian unrealism about political practice followed, according to Marx and Engels, from the utopians' illuded conception of the causes and grounds of their own thought and aspiration. The heart of their utopianism was their idea that their proposals were warranted by, and caused by their perception of, universally valid principles of freedom and justice, rather than warranted and caused by the needs of the time, by what was now historically possible and necessary. The utopians' primary lack of realism was about what they were: it was a lack of self-understanding. Considerable social criticism does not spring, otherwise uncaused, from reflection by hard-thinking people of good will; considerable social criticism is the necessary consequence of the tensions and demands of social reality itself. The utopian movement was indeed such a consequence, but the utopians did not think of it in that way. The dialectic of social reality rising to consciousness of itself was instanced in their own case, but they were unaware of that dialectic. They thought they could direct a historical process which was, in fact, directing them.

10

If the heart of the utopians' unrealism was their unrealistic self-perception, as masters, not servants, of the historical process, then to ask what *caused* them to be utopian is to ask what caused them to have that self-perception. In *Socialism: Utopian and Scientific*, Engels provides a two-part answer to that question.[16]

First, at the time of the early socialists, the contradictions of capitalism were, though sufficiently severe to generate some kind of socialist critique, nevertheless not yet so severe as they were to become. And connectedly—for this first part of Engels' answer has a two-fold character—connected with the fact that the system was not yet manifestly falling apart, it, the system, had not yet so transformed itself that socialism could be seen as a natural outgrowth of it, rather than, as the utopians saw it, as a desirable replacement for it to be instituted not in accordance with but against its own tendencies.

And the second part of the answer to the question about what caused the utopians to be utopian is that, at the time they were writing, the working-class movement was still immature, and the utopians therefore did not see themselves as organically united with it. They could not but see themselves as bringing liberation *to* the workers from a social and intellectual position unambiguously superior to that of those who were to be liberated. And the two parts of the explanation are connected, since the proletarian movement grows stronger as and because the contradictions of capitalism grow more severe *and* it becomes more visible that socialism constitutes their solution.

The utopians did not see that the emancipation of the workers *can* and *must* be the task of the workers themselves. They did not see that it *could* be because the proletariat was still politically weak. And they did not see that it *had* to be because the privileged orders had not yet revealed their remorselessly one-sided class perspective, just because, the proletariat being as yet weak, there was no challenge to privilege which would elicit class selfishness in its full savagery.

11

The contrast between utopian and scientific socialism, together with its causal explanation, is vividly stated by Marx in this splendid passage (I have added explanatory remarks in the passages in brackets):

Just as the *economists* are the scientific representatives of the bourgeois class, so the *Socialists* and the *Communists* are the theoreticians of the proletarian class. So long as the proletariat is not yet sufficiently developed to constitute itself as a class [so long, that is, as proletarians at large do not identify themselves as members of the proletariat as such], and consequently so long as the struggle itself of the proletariat with the bourgeoisie has not yet assumed a political character [so long, that is, as class struggle consists of isolated skirmishes, and is not on a national scale, of class against class], and [so long as] the productive forces are not yet sufficiently developed in the bosom of the bourgeoisie itself to enable us to catch a glimpse of the material conditions necessary for the emancipation of the proletariat and for the formation of a new society, these theoreticians are merely utopians who, to meet the wants of the oppressed classes, improvise systems and go in search of a regenerating science [that is, theory]. But in the measure that history moves forward, and with it the struggle of the proletariat assumes clearer outlines, they no longer need to seek science in their minds; they have only to take note of what is happening before their eyes and to become its mouthpiece. So long as they look for science and merely make systems, so long as they are at the beginning of the struggle, they see in poverty nothing but poverty, without seeing in it the revolutionary, subversive side, which will overthrow the old society [which is to say that they lack the dialectical idea]. From this moment, science, which is a product of the historical movement, has associated itself consciously with it, has ceased to be doctrinaire and has become revolutionary.[17]

Science becomes revolutionary when it unifies itself with the historical process. And once revolutionary scientific socialism appears on the scene, utopian socialism, which, for all its historically unavoidable limitations, was profoundly progressive in its time, becomes instead deeply reactionary in bearing, since the limitations from which it suffered are now avoidable. As Marx wrote: "It is natural that utopianism, which *before* the era of materialist-critical socialism concealed the latter within itself *in nuce,* coming now *post festum* can only be silly—silly, stale, and fundamentally reactionary."[18]

12

Having looked at what makes utopian socialism utopian, let us now ask: What makes scientific socialism scientific, according to Marx and Engels?

The most obvious and least interesting sense, though not therefore the least important sense, in which it is, in their view, scientific, is that it possesses a scientifically defensible theory of history in general and of capitalism in particular.

Rather more interestingly, its very practice is scientific, because it proceeds under the guidance of that theory, and not under the inspiration of ahistorical ideals, or, indeed, as we shall see, of *any* ideals.[19]

But the most interesting claim is about how the movement which possesses the science relates to the social reality which generates the movement and the science—to the "real basis"[20] on which they rest. The movement understands that basis and, consequently, how it itself arises upon it; one may indeed say that it arises through understanding that upon which it arises. It is the consciousness of social reality, in a political form. It is social reality's consciousness of itself.[21]

Recall that what made the utopians utopian was, at root, their inadequate self-perception. They failed, and could not but fail, to understand their own historical significance. The nature of their historical significance ensured that they would not understand it, for their thought and practice were the necessarily immature reflection of an immature proletarian movement, itself necessarily still immature because capitalism itself was not yet thoroughly developed.

Scientific socialism is what it is because of a different self-perception. It understands itself, and it understands utopian socialism as the latter could not understand itself. It understands itself as utopian socialism could not, as the reflex of the stage of development at which it arises, this now being the stage when capitalism's contradictions are acute and the proletarian movement is strong. It understands itself as the consciousness of that movement, rather than as inspired by universally valid ideals. It consequently[22] looks for the solution to the evils of capitalism in the process in which capitalism is transforming itself. So we find Engels, in *Socialism: Utopian and Scientific,* tracing the movement from competitive capitalism to state monopoly capitalism, and from that to socialism. The means of ending the conflict, he says, is to be found within the conflict itself.[23] Capitalism will itself produce socialism, with a little help from socialism's friends.

13

Now, Engels is not here voicing the merely commonsense thought that if you want to solve a problem you must study that problem in its concrete actuality. He means that there is a unique solution to the social problem, to be discovered within the problem, and toward which the development of the problem itself is tending. This solution needs only to be delivered. The obstetric metaphor often invoked by Marx and Engels aptly conveys their meaning. For in the normal (i.e., un-Caesarian etc.) case, the midwife does not consider possible ways of getting the baby out. She does not consider ideals she wants to realize and rank methods of achieving them. The prescribed way forward is dictated by the process of pregnancy itself. *The solution is the consummation of the full development of the problem.*

In a curious, and massively optimistic, argument, Engels proposes that the solution *must* be obstetric in nature, just because the problem is so acutely felt (again, I insert clarifications in brackets):

> The growing perception that existing social institutions are unreasonable and unjust, that reason has become unreason, and right wrong, is only proof that in the modes of production and exchange changes have

silently taken place, with which the social order, adapted to earlier economic conditions, is no longer in keeping. [In short, the popularity of
the attack on the mode of production as unjust and irrational reflects
the fact that the mode is now dysfunctional.] From this [from this
dysfunctionality] it also follows that the means of getting rid of the incongruities that have been brought to light must also be present, in a
more or less developed condition, within the changed modes of production themselves. These means are not to be invented by deduction
from fundamental principles, but are to be discovered in the stubborn
facts of the existing system of production.[24]

Background to the argument of the passage is the general historical
materialist claim that changes in ideas reflect changes in modes of production. And—so Engels no doubt reasoned—*since* changes in ideas
reflect changes in modes of production, a growing perception that the
mode of production is *unjust,* which begins even at the utopian stage of
socialism, reflects a reality in which that mode is becoming *unviable;* and
he *further* infers that the means of establishing a freshly viable mode will
be found within the old mode itself (and not by deduction from basic
principles). Accordingly, the widespread sense of injustice is an infallible
sign both that a *soluble* sociohistorical problem is in being, and that the
solution to it will be found within the developing social reality itself.

Three generalizations are in play here, which we can formulate as follows:

> *p:* Widespread major changes in ideas about society arise in response
> to changes in its mode of production.

Generalization *p* is not stated in the passage, but it is *p* from which *q,*
which is the message (more or less) of the first sentence of the passage,
is inferred:

> *q:* Ideas critical of a mode of production arise on a broad scale only
> when and because that mode is obsolescent—that is, no longer
> suited to the needs of production.[25]

And *r,* which is supposed to follow from *q,* sums up the second and third
sentences of the passage.

> *r:* When the mode of production is obsolescent (and such critical
> ideas therefore arise), the means of transforming the mode of
> production so that suitability to the needs of production will

be restored will be found within that existing mode of production itself.

Engels, so I have supposed, infers q from p, and he appears to infer r from q (I do not think that he intends r as an independent claim). But neither q nor r is evidently true, *even* if p is.

Against the inference from p to q: an oppressed class might develop ideas critical of the mode of production under which they are oppressed, and even secure wide sympathy for their claims, when that mode is *still* functional for production. There was plenty of criticism of industrial capitalism and sympathy for its victims at its inception. That would not contradict p, but it would contradict q. And one can readily deny r even if one affirms both p and q—which is to say that even if it is true both that big ideas about society reflect big changes in its mode of production, and that critical ideas achieve wide currency only when and because the mode of production is dysfunctional, there might yet be no reason to think that a solution to the problem will be found within the dysfunctional structure itself. Indeed, there might be *no* solution discernible, *anywhere*.

Let me nuance that last point. "No longer suited," in q, is ambiguous. It can be taken either absolutely or comparatively. It can mean that the mode of production is absolutely unsuited—that it no longer allows production to proceed as before, that it produces less than it used to. But if the mode of production is *in that (absolute) sense* no longer suited to the needs of production, then it does not follow that a superior mode, which is suited to those needs, must be available (because the old mode is outmoded). If, on the other hand, "no longer suited" means "less well suited than some other mode," then, by definition, a superior mode is possible But on this comparative understanding of "no longer suited," a mode could now be awful, yet *not* "no longer suited," since it might be true that nothing better than it is now feasible.[26]

The obviousness to Engels of r may *partly* depend on the exhibited ambiguity in "no longer suited." If a mode is declared to be unsuited according to the first, *and absolute,* sense distinguished above (that is, because it now fetters production), and irrespective of whether a better mode is available, and one then slides unconsciously to the comparative sense, it will then follow, through illicit equivocation on the two senses, that when a mode is no longer vigorous, a new mode which is more vigorous must be available.

But I said that the equivocation articulated above may (only) *partly* explain Engels' confidence in *r.* And that is because, even if it would be easy to add (to its being available) that the new and better mode would, sooner or later, be discovered, why must that new mode reside *within* the old mode itself? This additional element in *r* comes from Hegelian dialectics, not scientific or even diagnosably (by me anyway) fallacious reasoning.

14

Whether or not the view expressed in Engels' propositions *q* and *r* is defensible, there could not be a more optimistic one with respect to the task of changing society. For *q* and *r* entail that the task will not be undertaken—or not, anyway, on a large scale—until success is guaranteed. The optimistic entailment is that, as Marx said, "mankind always sets itself only such tasks as it can solve; since . . . the task itself arises only when the material conditions for its solution already exist or are at least in the process of formation."[27]

The present optimism is not about how good society can be made to be, though that optimism was also in Marxism, but about how easy it is to find the route to the better society. I am not aware of a rigorous defense of this line of thought in Marxist tradition from beginning to end, but I think it has been a powerful and a dangerous inheritance. I think Marx himself took this line for granted because of his Hegelian background, which in this respect he never transcended. The distinction between utopian and scientific socialism turns out to be profoundly Hegelian. It represents a return of the repressed philosophy, which disfigured the attempt at science.

In the next lecture, I shall try to substantiate that etiological claim.

Hegel in Marx

The Obstetric Motif in the Marxist Conception of Revolution

> History . . . has the fine habit of always producing along with any real
> social need the means to its satisfaction, along with the task simul-
> taneously the solution.
>
> > Rosa Luxemburg, "The Russian Revolution"

1

I have read, somewhere, that Bertrand Russell, having once been a Hegelian, forsook Hegel because, so he said, he was revolted by what Hegel
had said about mathematics. It was Russell's impression, so I seem to recall, that Hegel had disparaged mathematics.

Now, if Russell indeed forsook Hegel, for the stated reason, that was
probably a good thing, but his reason for doing so might not have been
so good.

For it is not clear that Hegel disparaged mathematics itself.[1] What is
clear is that he thought that standard mathematics, as it was commonly
practiced, was a bad model for philosophy. He thought that philosophy
should not imitate the standard mathematical proof procedure, which,
so Hegel thought, demonstrates *that* something is true without displaying *why* it is true. The kind of proof Hegel disliked was one after the provision of which it could remain *mysterious* that the theorem in question
was true, even though it had certainly been *proved* to be true.

Let me present three paragraphs from Hegel's preface to his *Phenomenology of the Spirit*.[2] As you read them, you might bear in mind whatever
you may remember of the proof of the Pythagorean theorem, which says
that the square on the hypotenuse of a right-angled triangle is equal

in area to the sum of the squares on the other two sides. I ask you to bear the theorem in mind, because, *if* Hegel has a point, then, following, as we shall see, Schopenhauer, we may look to the standard Euclidean proof of the Pythagorean theorem for an illustration of his point. (Bracketed insertions in quoted passages, here and elsewhere in this book, are my own.)

> The real defectiveness of mathematical knowledge, however, concerns both the knowledge itself and its content [that is, both the *way* we know it and *what*, therefore, we know]. Regarding the knowledge, the first point is that the *necessity* of the construction is not apprehended. This [that is, the construction] does not issue from the Concept of the theorem; rather it is commanded, and one must blindly obey the command to draw precisely these lines instead of an indefinite number of others, not because one knows anything but merely in the good faith that this will turn out to be expedient for the conduct of the demonstration. Afterward this expediency does indeed become manifest, but it is an *external* expediency because it manifests itself only *after* the demonstration.
>
> Just so, the demonstration follows a path that begins somewhere— one does not yet know in what relation to the result that is to be attained. As it proceeds, these determinations and relations are taken up while others are ignored, although one does not by any means see immediately according to what necessity. An *external* purpose rules this movement.
>
> The evident certainty of this defective knowledge, of which mathematics is proud and of which it also boasts as against philosophy, rests solely on the poverty of its purpose and the defectiveness of its material and is therefore of a kind that philosophy must spurn.—Its purpose or Concept is magnitude. This is precisely the relation that is not essential and is void of Concept.[3] The movement of knowledge therefore proceeds on the surface, does not touch the matter itself, not the essence or the Concept, and is therefore not comprehension.[4]

2

As Walter Kaufmann suggests, a passage from Schopenhauer's *World as Will and Idea* bears comparison with what Hegel says here, and illuminates it.[5] Schopenhauer complains about standard mathematics in the way that Hegel did, but he helps us to understand what Hegel was complaining about by purporting to supply, for the case of the Pythagorean theorem, what Hegel said was missing in standard mathematics.

> What Euclid demonstrates is indeed that way, one has to admit, compelled by the principle of contradiction; but *why* things are that way, one is not told. One therefore has almost the uncomfortable feeling that attends a sleight of hand; and in fact most Euclidean proofs are strikingly similar to that. Almost always truth enters through the back door. . . . Often, as in the Pythagorean theorem, lines are drawn, one knows not why: afterwards it appears that they were nooses that are unexpectedly tightened and captivate the assent of the student who now has to admit, amazed, *what in its inner context remains totally incomprehensible for him*—so much so that he can study all of Euclid without gaining any insight into the laws of spatial relations; instead he would merely learn by heart a few of their results. This really empirical and unscientific knowledge is like that of a doctor who knows disease and remedy, but not their connection. . . . Just so, the Pythagorean theorem teaches us to know a *qualitas occulta* of the right-angled triangle. Euclid's stilted, really crafty proof leaves us when it comes to the *why*, and the accompanying familiar simple figure offers at a single glance far more insight into the matter . . . than that proof:

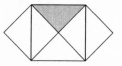

We can recover the insight that Schopenhauer thinks his diagram provides by numbering its parts, as follows:

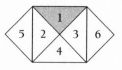

The following proof would, I presume, have satisfied Schopenhauer:

1 is a right-angled triangle.
1 + 2 + 3 + 4 = the square on its hypotenuse.
5 + 2 + 3 + 6 = the sum of the squares on its other two sides.
You can *see* that 1 + 4 = 5 + 6.

So, You can *see* that $1 + 2 + 3 + 4 = 5 + 2 + 3 + 6$.

So, You can *see* that Pythagoras' theorem is true.

(Of course, that demonstration applies to isosceles right-angled triangles only, but Schopenhauer proceeds to add, rather heroically: "In the case of unequal sides, too, it must be possible to achieve such intuitive conviction; indeed this must be so in the case of every possible geometric truth if only because its discovery always was prompted by such an intuitive necessity and the proof was thought out only afterward.")

In the proofs that Hegel and Schopenhauer find wanting, there is no false premise and no invalidity in the derivation of the conclusion. The geometer undoubtedly does prove what he sets out to prove. And Schopenhauer acknowledges that: he does not conceal the anger which the geometer's success induces in him. Schopenhauer is angry because, so he thinks, it remains mysterious *why* what is shown to be true turns out to be true. We are never made to *see* its necessity in the proven proposition itself, as Schopenhauer thinks we do once we are provided with his diagram. And that is why this mathematics represents a bad model for philosophy to emulate. This mathematics provides no *insight,* no *seeing into* the truth it purveys. The unexplanatory proofs of Euclidean geometry are a bad model for philosophy because in philosophy—so Schopenhauer and Hegel insist—we need to be shown not just *that* but *why* the demonstrable truth is true, and not all demonstrations do that for us. The *fundamental* status of philosophy, within the architectonic of knowledge, imposes this demand on philosophers.

We can call this the demand for (full) *comprehensibility.* It is a demand that we be put in a cognitive condition where everything has been made clear. And for Hegel, and indeed for Schopenhauer, this means a *further* thing: that we need to see how the answer resides within the question, how the solution develops out of the problem. Each step toward the solution must be seen to relate naturally to the previous step, the opening step being the exposition of the problem itself. Hence the emphasis both in Hegel and in Schopenhauer on the unsatisfactorily *external* character of Euclid's approach: he is an engineer who applies a scheme of independent design, not a midwife who derives a solution from within. The defect in Euclid's proof is, so Hegel says, that "the construction . . . does not issue from the concept of the theorem."

Now, when I say that for Hegel this *further* thing is required, I call it "further" because one need not agree with Hegel that the demand for comprehensibility implies that the solution must be seen to grow out of the problem. Plato and Descartes, so one might argue, insisted on comprehensibility without giving it that particular dialectical twist. But if one thinks, as Hegel did, that thought is inherently developmental, that it progresses by getting itself into difficulties which induce an endogenous recovery, then it is natural that the demand for comprehensibility should take this form—the form, that is, of an insistence that the answer will become apparent, that it will shine forth from the question, when the question is posed in an especially clear form. So, in the case of the Pythagorean theorem, the answer about the relationship among the squares can be read off the question when the question is posed in its lucid Schopenhauerian form.

3

The distinction between proofs that are, and ones that are not, fully comprehensible *may* not possess the depth that Hegel discerned in it. Maybe it is just certain forms of familiarity, or limits on intelligence, that make the difference between finding a proof comprehensible and not finding it so. Maybe *every* proof is comprehensible for a sufficiently powerful mind. I cannot address that question here. Instead, let me summarize this preamble to my discussion of the obstetric motif in Marxism by noting three theses of strictly increasing strength about problems and their solutions (meaning, here, by "solutions," thoroughly satisfactory solutions): the third thesis entails the second, and the second entails the first. The present interest of the theses is that, as we shall see, they have *both* theoretical readings that fit with the Hegelian critique of the limits of conventional mathematics *and* political readings that fit with the Marxist critique of the limits of utopian socialism.

   (i) If there is a solution to a (genuine) problem, then it will be found if and (only) when the problem is presented in its fully developed form.
   (ii) There always is a solution to a (genuine) problem (but (by (i)) it will be found if and (only) when the problem is presented in its fully developed form.)

(iii) The completion of the development of a (genuine) problem, and only that, provides its solution. Its solution is the consummation of the full development of the problem.

Now, as I said, this doctrine—that the full development of a problem always issues in its solution—has both theoretical and political readings. That is because we can understand "the *development* of a problem" *either* as the development of its exposition, *or* as the development not of its exposition but of the problem itself, of the problematic object, or situation, in the world. In the first case the problem is solved when its *formulation* is consummated; in the second, when the problem *itself* is consummated, when it reaches its highest pitch. (Hegel's idealism might be thought to prejudice this distinction between the development of a problem and the development of its formulation; but, however that may be, *we* can readily make the indicated distinction.)

The political reading of the three theses reads "the development of a problem" as the development of a problematic situation: in this case, a social situation. Consider, for example, the problem posed by capitalism, as Marx and Engels envisaged it—the problem, to describe it simply, of massive power to produce, alongside massive poverty. As that problem deepens, its solution looms, as and because the problem deepens.

Thus, in its political reading, thesis (i) explains why the utopian socialists had no sound solution to the social problem: it was not yet sufficiently developed for a solution to it to be discernible. And thesis (ii) proceeds to reassure us that, now that the problem is acute, a solution to it must be forthcoming. Finally, thesis (iii) adds that the desired solution will come from the development of the problem itself: the solution-providing proletarian revolution is the outgrowth of the problem, of the contradictions of capitalism itself. (Thesis (iii) adds to (ii) the motif that the solution is exposed *within* the problem, when the full development of which (ii) also speaks has been completed.) Thesis (iii) is also the foundation of the Marxist criticism of utopian socialists, who think that they will find a solution to the social problem by turning their backs on existing society and seeking a superior social form, rather than by studying the actual social problem in its depth. All that the socialist theorist has to do is to make the task facing the proletariat more explicit. So we read this in the final paragraph of Engels' *Socialism: Utopian and Scientific:* "To accomplish this act of universal emancipation is the historical mission of the modern proletariat. To thoroughly comprehend the historical conditions and thus the very nature of this act, to impart to the now oppressed proletarian class a full knowledge of the conditions and of the meaning of the momentous act it is called upon to accomplish—this is the task of the theoretical expression of the proletarian movement, scientific socialism."[6] The "momentous act" the proletariat is called upon to accomplish is the revolutionary act that solves the historical problem. The revolution is the problem's resolution.

Notice that (ii) and (iii) are, in their social readings, incredibly optimistic doctrines. Little could be more optimistic than (iii) with respect to the means of effecting social change. The structure of this optimism relates as follows to the structure of the Engelsian optimism which was given in proposition *r* in Lecture 3, section 13. Proposition *r* speaks of a period when critical ideas arise—when, that is, there is a social problem. Thesis (iii) tells us that solutions come with the full development of a problem: the solution comes *out of* the fully developed problematic structure, which, in the case that *r* treats, is a mode of production. So (iii) provides the general doctrine which *r* illustrates.

It follows that the central claim in Marxism's celebration of the supposed scientificity of its politics—namely, that its politics teases solutions out of developing problems—descends from a Hegelian idea which few would now regard as consonant with the demands of rigorous science. And notice how strong that central claim is. Scientific socialism offers no ideals or values to the proletariat. What the communists do (see the second sentence of the passage from Engels quoted two paragraphs back) is simply to tell it like it is, to tell the proletariat how it is.

I now want to indicate how deeply entrenched this obstetric doctrine was in classical Marxism.

4

I begin with the letter of November 10, 1837, which Marx wrote to his father in Trier when he was nineteen, after he had spent just over a year studying law in Berlin.

In this letter Marx reports a turbulent progress that he has undergone. He has left behind a stage of personal development in which he "believed in a complete opposition between what is and what ought to be," and now finds himself at a point where he sees more harmony between what is and what ought to be. Marx summarizes his new viewpoint in this flourish: "If the gods had before dwelt *above* the earth, they had *now* become its center."[7]

The letter is fascinating partly because, a little psychotically, Marx associates his now abandoned world-denying idealism with a particular soaringly yearning way in which he had been missing his sweetheart, Jenny, who remained in Trier when Marx went off to Berlin.[8] Here is part of his analogy between his love for Jenny, whom he experienced as (not Marx's phrase) "out of this world," and his love of world-rejecting ideals: "My heaven and art became a Beyond as distant as my love. Everything real began to dissolve and thus lose its finiteness, I attacked the present, feeling was expressed without moderation or form, nothing was natural, everything was built of moonshine. I believed in a complete opposition between what is and what ought to be."[9]

He proceeds to associate the duality of the rejected idealism with what he calls "the unscientific form of mathematical dogmatism, where one circles round a subject, reasoning back and forth, without letting it unfold its own rich and living content, [which] prevented any *grasp* of the truth."[10]

So Marx here imitates Hegel's disparagement of the duality in standard mathematics, the duality between the problem on the one hand and its exogenously derived solution on the other. And the desired contrast, where the problem "unfold[s] its own rich and living content," and thereby dissolves, and therefore solves itself, also reappears.

The text continues:

> The mathematician constructs and proves the triangle, but it remains a pure abstraction in space and does not develop any further; you have to put it beside something else and then it takes up other positions, and it is the juxtaposition of these different things that gives it different relationships and truths. Whereas in the practical expression of the living world of ideas in which law, the state, nature, and the whole of philosophy consist, the object itself must be studied in its own development, arbitrary divisions must not be introduced [after the fashion of what Hegel calls *Verstand*, the Understanding], and it is the ratio [the rational essence] of the object itself which must develop out of its inner contradictions and find unity within itself.[11]

It is in virtue of this shift of attitude that "the gods" no longer dwell "above the earth" but "become its center," which is to say that Marx has "left behind the idealism . . . of Kant and Fichte, and [come] to seek the idea in the real itself," as Hegel did.[12] Marx too, now, seeks the solution in the problem.

Note that Marx applies this doctrine of radical endogeny—this principle that solutions grow in, and out of, problems—to every *"living"* subject matter. (He does not apply the doctrine to standard mathematics, but that is because it is not alive.) A few years later, in 1842, he expressly applies it to *political* problems and their solutions, although he is not yet a Marx*ist* who thinks of such problems and their solutions in materialist terms. Thus he writes in an article entitled "The Centralization Question" (*Rheinische Zeitung,* May 17, 1842): "It is the fate of a question of the day that the *question,* not the *answer,* constitutes the main difficulty. True criticism, therefore, analyzes not the answers but the questions. Just as the solution of an algebraic question is found the moment the problem is put in its purest and sharpest form,[13] any question is answered the moment it becomes an *actual* question. World history itself has only one method: to answer and settle old questions through new ones."[14]

For a question to be *actual* is for it to be fully developed: the contrast with actuality is potentiality.

A year later, in 1843, Marx wrote a pair of very important letters to Arnold Ruge, a fellow radical—a person, that is, who believed in democracy, freedom of speech, and other liberal reforms, but who was not, any more than Marx himself then was, a full-blooded socialist. In these letters, Marx continues to think of social reform as fundamentally reform of consciousness, and the task of the social reformer is understood obstetrically: he must deliver the new consciousness from the womb of the old.

> The interior difficulties [i.e., "the difficulties within our reform movement"] almost seem to be even greater than the exterior ones [i.e., "the difficulties posed by our enemies"]. For even though the "whence" [i.e., the current problem] is not in doubt, yet all the more confusion reigns over the "whither" [i.e., the solution]. It is not only that a general anarchy has burst out among the reformers. Everyone will have to admit to himself that he has no exact view of what should happen. However, that is just the advantage of the new line that we do not an-

ticipate the world dogmatically but wish to discover the new world by criticism of the old. . . .

On our side the old world must be brought right out into the light of day and the new one given a positive form. The longer that events allow thinking humanity time to recollect itself and suffering humanity time to assemble itself, the more perfect will be the birth of the product that the present carries in its womb. . . .[15]

. . . We do not then set ourselves opposite the world with a doctrinaire principle, saying: "Here is the truth, kneel down here!" It is out of the world's own principles that we develop for it new principles. We do not say to her, "Stop your battles, they are stupid stuff. We want to preach the true slogans of battle at you." We merely show it what it is actually fighting about, and this realization is a thing that it must make its own even though it may not wish to.

The reform of consciousness consists solely in letting the world perceive its own consciousness by awaking it from dreaming about itself, in explaining to it its own actions. Our whole and only aim consists in putting religious and political questions in a self-conscious, human form. . . .[16]

So our election cry must be: reform of consciousness not through dogmas but through the analysis of mystical consciousness that is not clear to itself, whether it appears in a religious or a political form. It will then be clear that the world has long possessed the dream of a thing of which it only needs to possess the consciousness in order really to possess it. It will be clear that the problem is not some great gap between the thoughts of the past and those of the future but the completion of thoughts of the past. Finally, it will be clear that humanity is not beginning a new work, but consciously bringing its old work to completion.

So we can summarize the tendency of our journal in one word: self-understanding (equals critical philosophy) by our age of its struggles and wishes. This is a task for the world and for us. It can only be the result of united forces. What is at stake is a confession, nothing more. To get its sins forgiven, humanity only needs to describe them as they are.[17]

The Hegelian thesis that the solution to a problem comes with its full development can, as I said in section 3 above, be interpreted as applying to the development of the *formulation* of the problem *and* as applying to the development of the problem itself. The recently quoted texts show that these two interpretations of the Hegelian thesis can be joined together, within the obstetric point of view. For it is the political midwife who, in the words of "The Centralization Question," "puts the problem in its purest and sharpest form." It is the political midwife who, in the words of the September letter to Ruge, "shows the world what it is actually fighting about." By advancing "self-understanding," by consummating the formulation of the problem, she brings the problem itself to term.[18] But it is possible for her to do so only when the autonomous development of the problem has reached its penultimate stage—when, that is, the pregnancy is complete.

Now, it is somewhat extraordinary to apply the Hegelian doctrine about conceptual problems to social and political problems, *even* when one thinks, as Marx shows he did in the quoted youthful exuberances, that social consciousness is at the center of historical change. But it is surely even more extraordinary to continue in this vein when one has shifted the site of historical development from a politics of consciousness to a politics centered on modes of production and their revolutionary transformation. Yet, after Marx has irreversibly effected that shift, we find him saying, in *The German Ideology:* "Communism is for us not a *state of affairs* which is to be established, an *ideal* to which reality [will] have to adjust itself. We call communism the *real* movement which abolishes the present state of things."[19]

And the point is not, of course, that the movement is guided by an ideal *other* than communism, but rather that it does not *need* an ideal, a supraterrestrial inspiration, a God "above the earth,"[20] any more than a question requires an answer that comes from beyond the question. A question gets its answer when it is properly put; it develops its answer as it develops itself. Similarly, that by which the movement replaces the present state of things, a state that it "abolishes," just depends on the completion of its movement. "Abolishes" is *aufhebt,*[21] the Hegelian word for dialectical transition, which literally means "raises up," but which in Hegel means "transforms and completes, raises up to a higher form." The movement "abolishes," in that very special sense, the present state of things, but it does not *annihilate* the present state of things: it draws up from it what is growing within it.

There is, be it further noted, a nice ambiguity here in the word "movement" (*Bewegung*), for it can denote both a movement, or process, in history *and* a movement in the organized political sense. The political movement swims with the current and is thereby part of the current. We are moving with history, and that is here assimilated to thinking a problem through to its conclusion. And Marx calls communism a *real* (*wirkliche*) movement because, as he thinks of it, it is a movement in reality itself, not one approaching reality from without. The task of the scientific socialist revolutionary is simply to join that movement in the world, to connect with the changing reality, which is the self-transforming mode of production. To adopt and adapt a slogan of the American 1960s: the duty of every revolutionary is to help make the evolution.[22]

Marx presented his theory of history in systematic fashion in only one place: in the 1859 preface to his book *A Contribution to the Critique of Political Economy*. The obstetric metaphor is deeply impressed on that statement. In a stretch of text part of which I quoted in Lecture 3, section 14, Marx insists that the consciousness of contending groups during periods of social transformation "must . . . be explained . . . from the contradictions of material life, from the existing conflict between the social productive forces and the relations of production"—an insistence which matches propositions *p* and *q* in Lecture 3, section 13. Marx then goes on to say:

> No social order ever perishes before all the productive forces for which there is room in it have developed; and new higher relations of production never appear before the material conditions of their existence have matured in the *womb* of the old society itself. Therefore, mankind always takes up only such problems as it can solve; since, looking at the matter more closely, we will always find that the problem itself arises only when the material conditions necessary for its solution already exist or are at least in the process of formation.[23]

It follows from these statements[24] that whenever a social order has exhausted its progressiveness, has exhausted what it has to give humanity by way of increasing its productive power, then, with wonderful convenience, a new order is available to replace the exhausted order and to take progress further and, moreover, the new order will be found in the old society itself: that confidence confirms Engels' proposition *r* (see Lecture 3, section 13).

And so we get the happy result that, in a phrase from *Capital*, "the problem and the means for its solution arise simultaneously."[25] Social repair—like conceptual repair, as Hegel conceived it—*cannot* come from without and always *will* be found within, *provided* that the thing is really broken.

The utopian project is, therefore, both *impossible* and *unnecessary*. It is impossible to reconstruct society by following a design that comes from without, and it is unnecessary to seek any such design because a broken society is in process of reconstructing itself. Midwifery is needed, not engineering.[26]

What makes Marxian socialism realistic, according to Marx and Engels, is that it is, in Engels' words, "nothing but the reflex in thought of this conflict [i.e., the capitalist contradictions] in fact": "The means of getting rid of the incongruities [in the existing social order] that have been brought to light must also be present, in a more or less developed condition, within the changed modes of production themselves. . . . Modern socialism is nothing but the reflex, in thought, of this [capitalist] conflict in fact; its ideal reflection in the minds, first, of the class directly suffering under it, the working class."[27]

Modern socialism is the ideal reflection of a conflict, *first*, says Engels, in the minds of the workers; but *then*, so we can add, that reflection is perfected by their theoretical representatives. Modern socialism, the socialism of Marx and Engels, is thereby a reflection which knows itself to be a reflection.

This means that there are two successive moments in reality's assertion of itself in consciousness, the first being its manifestation in the proletarian movement, and the second its manifestation in the political completion of that movement in organized form. The second and first moments are, respectively, mentioned when Marx says of the First International that it "has not been hatched by a sect or a theory. It is the spontaneous growth of the proletarian movement, which itself is the offspring of the natural and irrepressible tendencies of modern society."[28]

So on the one hand, "the working class have no ideals to realize but to set free the elements of the new society with which old collapsing bourgeois society is pregnant,"[29] and, on the other, just as the workers do not invent ideals, so their theoretical representatives simply take and perfect the position which the workers have struck in their response to the developing reality, so that "communism now no longer mean[s] the concoction, by means of the imagination, of an ideal society as perfect as possible, but insight into the nature, the conditions, and the consequent general aims of the struggle waged by the proletariat."[30]

I end this parade of texts with a passage from Rosa Luxemburg's 1918 essay "The Russian Revolution," in which she uses the Marxian distinction between utopian and scientific socialism to criticize the *étatiste* designs of Lenin and Trotsky. What she says in the passage is breathtakingly sanguine, but not more so than the parallel passages from the writings of Marx and Engels that were presented above: "History . . .— just like organic nature of which, in the last analysis, it forms a part— has the fine habit of always producing along with any real social need the means to its satisfaction, along with the task simultaneously the solution."[31]

5

Marxism's evolutionary view of the movement toward socialism has an interesting implication for Marxism's attitude to social reform.[32] Marxists are prepared to work for change *within* capitalism because they can view such change as part of capitalism's self-transformation into socialism. Since utopians lack the concept of capitalist self-transformation, they cannot see reform in that way, and they often see no value in it, or regard it as counterproductive.

The point is illustrated by the posture of those highly utopian sects (there are some in Britain) which contemn all change within capitalism (such as successful struggles for higher wages and better working conditions) *because* it is (merely) change within capitalism. Marx could have been referring to such sects when he said, in *The Poverty of Philosophy,* that "the [utopian] socialists want the workers to leave the old society alone, the better to be able to enter the new society which they have prepared for them with so much foresight."[33]

And Engels made a similar point in the brilliant work of his youth, *The Condition of the Working-Class in England in 1844*, when he said that

> the Socialists are thoroughly tame and peaceable, accept our existing order, bad as it is, so far as to reject all other methods but that of winning public opinion. Yet they are so dogmatic that success by this method is for them . . . utterly hopeless. . . . They acknowledge no historic development, and wish to place the nation in a state of communism at once, overnight, not by the unavoidable march of its political development up to the point at which this transition becomes both possible and necessary.[34]

To be sure, Marx and Engels perceived danger to the cause in a political perspective that myopically *limited* itself to reform. Marx warned against such reformism, in the proper sense of that term, in his 1865 address "Wages, Price, and Profit":

The working class ought not to exaggerate to themselves the ultimate working of these everyday struggles. They ought not to forget that they are fighting with effects, but not with the causes of those effects . . . , that they are applying palliatives, not curing the malady. They ought, therefore, not to be exclusively absorbed in these unavoidable guerrilla fights. . . . Instead of the *conservative* motto, "A fair day's wage for a fair day's work" they ought to inscribe on their banner the *revolutionary* watchword, "Abolition of the wages system."[35]

But "Wages, Price, and Profit" was nevertheless written as an attack on "Citizen Weston's" view that the battle for higher wages was pointless. Marx opposed not partial transformations of capitalism, some of which (e.g., the Ten Hours Bill) he described as a "victory of the political economy of labor over the political economy of property,"[36] but *restricting* political activity to a "war against the effects of the existing system, instead of *simultaneously* trying to change it."[37] Nevertheless, the limited-aim "guerrilla fights" were "unavoidable."

Reform movements without a revolutionary dimension were dangerous because they led the proletariat astray. But it does not follow that success in achieving humanizing reforms was to be avoided for fear that it would pacify the proletariat. I cannot think of a text where Marx or Engels affirms this repugnant view, whoever might have held it later.

6

Recall (see Lecture 3, section 12) what, according to Marxism, makes a scientific socialism possible when scientific socialism in fact arises, and also what ensures that the dominant socialism of that time will be scientific: it is that capitalism has reached such a pass that *both* the society which will solve the problems it creates *and* the means of bringing about that society are discernible in capitalism itself. Socialism is now in prospect not because principles warranting it have been discovered but because the socialist revolution is simply the completion of what capitalism has done to itself, a completion which it is in the interest, and within the capacity, of the proletariat to effect.

Utopian socialism did not arise accidentally. Capitalism had to reach a particular stage of its development for the insights of utopian socialism to be possible, a stage sufficiently advanced to generate a kind of socialism, but at which the limitations of utopian socialism were unavoidable, since the stage was not advanced *enough* to generate *scientific* socialism.[38]

For Marx and Engels it was inevitable, in two senses, that socialism should have been utopian *before* it was scientific.

First, only a utopian socialism could have arisen at the actual *time*— that is, roughly speaking, the first third of the nineteenth century— when utopian socialism in fact arose. If there was to be any socialism at that time, then it was fated to be a utopian one. So socialism had to be utopian before it was scientific in the sense that it could only be a utopian socialism that appeared before the time when, as a matter of fact, scientific socialism appeared.

Second—and this, I grant, is a more freely interpretative (of Marx and Engels) suggestion—scientific socialism had to have a utopian precursor. It had to be preceded by utopian socialism because (if I may here put a Marxian dictum to special use) being precedes consciousness, and *scientific socialism is socialism risen to consciousness of itself.*[39] So utopian socialism had to come before scientific in the sense of the *order* in which they appeared, independently of the particular times when either appeared.

Was it also necessary that utopian socialism come to be at all? I cannot cite textual material which bears decisively on this question, but an affirmative answer would follow from the claim that scientific socialism had to have a utopian precursor, together with the proposition, no doubt believed by Marx and Engels, that scientific socialism was bound, sooner or later, to arise, when capitalism had reached the relevant stage.

If scientific socialism is socialism risen to consciousness of itself, it is also history risen to consciousness of itself. In his *Manuscripts* of 1844, Marx described communism as "the solution of the riddle [*das Rätsel*] of history [which] knows itself to be this solution."[40] He is here thinking of communism more as a form of society than as a movement, but he might later be prepared to say the same of the communist movement. For although people have always made history, it is only with the advent of the communist movement that they make history knowing what they are doing. Previous history makers' conceptions of themselves were riddled with illusion.

7

I have put a certain reflexivity at the center of scientific socialism's self-description: it is, in its own account of itself, a socialism that, unlike earlier socialism, understands its own character. It is a socialism that is self-aware, and it counts thereby as history's achievement of self-awareness too. And this reflexivity reproduces, in modified form, a theme in the philosophy of Hegel that I have not thus far mentioned.

Hegel teaches that the mind can understand itself only by understanding its own history, and, moreover, that what *enables* it to understand its history is its having *undergone* that history. Hegel's *Phenomenology* traces the genesis of mind in general in order that the individual reading it can come, through that reading, to an understanding of himself. I quote Jon Elster's splendid formulation of this element in Hegel's outlook: "The process that enables the mind to understand its history is identical with that history."[41] As consciousness widens and deepens, so too grows its capacity to explain its own genesis and content.

Partly analogously, the practice of scientific socialism is governed by its understanding of its place in history. It knows itself and what it must do because it understands that place, and it possesses that understanding only because enough history has unfolded for understanding of history—and thus of the utopians, who could not understand themselves—to be possible.

For Hegel, the science of mind cannot exist until the mind has reached a point when it can develop that science, and then the science of mind is nothing but the mind's exposition of how it reached that point. For scientific socialism, the science of society and history cannot exist until history has reached a stage where such a science is possible, and then the science, if it is not nothing but, at least crucially involves an exposition of how that stage has been reached.

For utopian socialism, theory is developed independently of the world, and practice is the attempt by the subject (thought of as counterposed to the world) to make the world conform to the demands of theory. That is how utopian socialism misconceives its own theory and practice, because it is ignorant of its own worldly character, because it fails to understand where its movement came from and where it is going. For scientific socialism, by contrast, theory develops out of the world, and the practice it animates is therefore part of the world's self-transformation. There is, accordingly, no problem, or not the same problem, of getting the world to conform to the demands of theory, in the scientific socialist conception of the relationship binding world, theory, and practice.

In the usage of *The German Ideology*, a set of ideas qualifies as an ideology not *merely* because it is false, or *even* because the falsehood in it is explained by its service of a class interest. A set of ideas is an ideology *only if* those who have the ideas attach to them a false account of *why* they have those ideas, and of how the ideas they have relate to reality. It is constitutive of ideology that subscribers to it believe that they believe it for purely intellectual reasons, and not because of social developments in which they are engulfed,[42] and they consequently believe that ideas which do not derive *from* social development can give direction *to* social development: they pose as engineers, as masters of history, and not as its midwiving servants. It follows that what makes the utopian socialists utopian also makes them ideologists, in the *German Ideology* sense,[43] and that what makes Marxist socialism scientific ensures that it is not (in that derogatory sense) an ideology.

Not all doctrines need or have a conception of themselves, a subdoctrine about how and why the doctrine of which it is a subdoctrine comes to appear. That Marxism possesses such a doctrine is a deep fact about it, for the subdoctrine is required to vindicate Marxism against the charge that it, too, is an ideology. In its own view of itself, it is *not* an ideology, because it is aware of its own worldly origin, and it can proclaim its envelopment by the world without prejudice to its claim to truth, because it is the voice of the proletariat, and the proletariat's historical emplacement rids it of the need for illusions. The proletariat is the first class in history that can prosecute a world-historical role without wearing a mantle of untruth. It can do so because it need not purvey illusions to gain allies. For unlike feudal and capitalist classes, it needs no allies, since it is by its nature and its numbers the universal class, the representative of humanity as such.[44]

Marxism's (sub)doctrine about itself was a source of epistemic pride and a protection against the embarrassments facing beliefs traceable to nonrational sources that were canvassed in Lecture 1 above.

8

The obstetric conception of political practice is patently false. Whether or not the beliefs about history that sustained it were tenable a hundred years ago and more, no one could defend them now.

One way of seeing why obstetricism is false, and at the same time how it was possible for Marxists to have confidence in it, is by comparing the first and second halves of a long Rosa Luxemburg sentence, the second half of which was quoted at the close of section 4 above. Let us look at the whole of her sentence (I have italicized the word that separates the two halves of the sentence, by introducing a subordinate clause):

> The socialist system of society should only be, and can only be, a historical product, born out of the school of its own experiences, born in the course of its realization, as a result of the developments of living history, *which*—just like organic nature of which, in the last analysis, it forms a part—has the fine habit of always producing along with any real social need the means to its satisfaction, along with the task simultaneously the solution.

The first half of this sentence is true, interesting, and important. Luxemburg probably thought that the second half, which is far stronger, and which, unlike the first half, affirms the obstetric doctrine, follows from, or restates, what is said in the first. But one may believe, against the full utopian doctrine, that socialism can be achieved only through an intervention in history that is sensitive both to history and to what it has wrought—one may, that is, affirm the first part of Luxemburg's sentence—yet steadfastly resist the reassurance offered in its second part. And that is a reassurance which, after the sorry history of the twentieth century, we can no longer enjoy, and which it is, moreover, dangerous to crave.

For I believe not only that the obstetric conception is false but also that it has done a great deal of damage. If you think of politics obstetrically, you risk supposing that what Lenin called "the concrete analysis of a concrete situation"[45] will disclose, transparently, what your political intervention must be, so that you do not expect and therefore do not face the uncertainties and hard choices with which a responsible politics must contend.

It might be objected that a vulgar construal of the obstetric doctrine is required to support the inference from it that political practice is easy. After all, the specific task allocated by Marx to socialist politics, a task which falls within the obstetric metaphor, is that of "shortening and lessening the birth pangs"[46] of the arrival of the new society, and that could be a very difficult, and consequential, operation. One might believe, *consistently* with obstetric doctrine, that we are indeed now in an era of transition to socialism, the birth pangs of which have been rendered immensely more protracted, and more ghastly, than they needed to be, because of unwise political choices of communists in Russia and Germany in the first third of the twentieth century. One might say that obstetricism is consistent with a proper emphasis on the difficulty of political labor, and therefore does not justify a cavalier attitude to politics; but the examples which prompt that thought might also be thought to show how strongly obstetricism *encourages* a cavalier attitude, even if it does not justify it. If you're sure you're *bound* to get the answer, it's easy to think you've already got it.

And whether or not obstetricism justifies and/or encourages a less than appropriately sensitive and circumspect attention to problems of socialist *strategy,* the problem of *how* to overturn capitalism, it certainly appears to justify a criminal inattention to *what* one is trying to achieve, to the problem of socialist design. In the preceding part of the paragraph from which the Luxemburg sentence quoted above is drawn, she criticizes those who see the creation of socialism as the application of a recipe conceived in advance.[47] To be sure, and in virtue of the truth of the first part of Luxemburg's sentence, one must not write inflexible recipes which ignore possible constraining conditions of the kitchen in which the meal is to be cooked. Yet one must write recipes, and thereby reject the obstetric perspective (according to which the baby is what the baby is, not what the midwife designs it to be, so that—to mangle metaphors—midwives indeed don't write recipes for future kitchens).[48] The history of socialist failure shows that socialists do need to write recipes, and not only, as that history suggests, in order to know what to do with power, but also in order to attract the masses of the people, who are, very reasonably, wedded to the devil they know. Unless we write recipes for future kitchens, there's no reason to think we'll get food we like. So if we don't like the heat of the kitchen we're in, we (that is, those of us who remain socialists) had better write recipes for future kitchens.[49]

10

In Lecture 5, I shall examine Marx's dictum that "religion is the opium of the people." We shall see that the opium sentence can be understood within the terms of the obstetric motif.

Lecture 5 ends with a look at Marx's invocation of proletarian agency, and that will prepare the ground for Lecture 6, in which I show that the classical Marxist conception of the proletariat is not (any longer) sustainable, so that, whatever is meant by calling Marxism *scientific* socialism, it cannot now maintain its pretension to that designation without transforming itself radically. The particular ways in which the classic doctrine is false mean that we need to get out of obstetric space, but without, of course, entering utopian space in every sense. We have to work with social forces, if not, perhaps, always in the direction in which they are disposed to go. We have to be guided by the first half of Rosa Luxemburg's overloaded sentence.

5

The Opium of the People

God in Hegel, Feuerbach, and Marx

Without the world, God is not God.
> G. W. F. Hegel, *Lectures on the Philosophy of Religion*

1

In a common but natural misunderstanding of what Marx meant when he said that religion was the opium of the people, he is misrepresented as saying that priests devise religion to keep the suffering and, therefore, potentially rebellious masses quiet. And the misrepresentation of the opium sentence is compounded when its misinterpreter adds that priests are appointed by the ruling class to carry out the stated analgesic mission.

Now, I say that this misrepresentation of the opium sentence expresses a *natural* misunderstanding of that sentence because it provides a natural reading of the opium sentence when the sentence is taken on its own. But the context in which the sentence appears establishes that Marx did not claim that priests devise religion. Let me present the passage in which the opium sentence is embedded. You will gather, from the sentence in the passage that precedes the opium sentence, that priests do not (in the relevant sense) devise religion. It is, rather, the people themselves who create the religion which is their opium:

> *Religious* distress is at the same time the *expression* of real distress and the *protest* against real distress. Religion is the sigh of the oppressed creature, the heart of a heartless world, just as it is the spirit of a spiritless situation. It is the *opium* of the people.
>
> The abolition of religion as the *illusory* happiness of the people is required for their *real* happiness. The demand to give up the illusions

about its condition is the *demand to give up a condition which needs illu-sions.* The criticism of religion is therefore *in embryo the criticism of the vale of woe,* the *halo* of which is religion.[1]

So: the people need religion. They need it because they inhabit a vale of woe. And it is they who create religion, to service their need. Religion is *their* sigh. It may also be good for the ruling class that the people get religion, but that is not what this particular text says. As for the priests, it is not excluded that they play a significant role in *sustaining* religious belief, but their function is secondary to the *creation* of religion by the people. The oppressed creature is disposed to sigh, and the priest gives the creature a language to sigh in. If you call the language in which they express their woe religion, then, to be sure, it may not be the people who create it. But if you call what religious language expresses religion—and what it expresses, not the language of its expression, is, after all, the fun-damental thing—then religion is created by the people.

Now, this returns us to the obstetric motif. Remember Marx's letters of May and September 1843 to Arnold Ruge,[2] which were penned only months before the opium text.[3] Marx said in these Ruge letters that, in order to save the world, "we merely show it what it is actually fighting about." We draw forth from the people, and make explicit, what they themselves are saying:

> We do not then set ourselves opposite the world with a doctrinaire principle, saying: 'Here is the truth, kneel down here!'. . . We do not say to her, 'Stop your battles, they are stupid stuff. We want to preach the true slogans of battle at you.'

> The reform of consciousness consists solely in letting the world per-ceive its own consciousness by awaking it from dreaming about itself, in explaining to it its own actions.

> So our election cry must be: reform of consciousness not through dog-mas, but through the analysis of mystical consciousness that is not clear to itself, whether it appears in a religious or political form. It will then be clear that the world has long possessed the dream of a thing of which it only needs to possess the consciousness in order really to pos-sess it.

Religion is the dream of the better world that will come when people realize that that is what religion is. We show the oppressed creature what its sigh means, and then and thereby comes the revolution. The abolition of religion brings human liberation. Religion is the demand for, the promise of, and the obstacle to that liberation.

The widespread misunderstanding of the opium sentence is a natural misunderstanding, because the sentence lacks the dialectical motif present in the sentence that precedes it, which says (to repeat): "Religion is the sigh of the oppressed creature, the heart of a heartless world, just as it is the spirit of a spiritless situation." That sentence shows that, while religion is indeed the enemy of emancipation, it is also the route through which emancipation must run. Emancipation comes not by proving that religion is false but by revealing the source of religion in a spiritless world that needs to have its spirit returned to it, a world that needs to be humanized. Accordingly, "the criticism of religion ends with the teaching that man is the highest being for man, hence with the categorical imperative to overthrow all relations in which man is a debased, enslaved, abandoned, despicable being."[4] If "the world has long possessed the *dream*," then the way to make the dream come true is to overthrow those debasing relations.

If we take the opium sentence in its context, then we see that its message is not a reductionist one in the sense of reducing spirituality to something material. If it is reductionist, it is so in that, quite differently, it reduces the illusory independent spiritual form to an absence of the spiritual in material life, to a need for, and lack of, spirit there, and not to the material as such.

I should like to go back to Hegel and to his critic Ludwig Feuerbach, in order to trace the source of Marx's view of religion.

2

Actually, let us go back beyond Hegel to the very beginning of human history, or anyway to the beginning of history according to one influential theory of how it all began. Here's the theory, as we find it in verses 26 and 27 of Chapter 1 of Genesis:

And God said, Let us make man in our image, after our likeness; and let them have dominion over the fish of the sea, and over the fowl of the air, and over the cattle, and over all the earth, and over every creeping thing that creepeth upon the earth.

So God created man in his *own* image, in the image of God created he him; male and female created he them.

"God created man in his own image." The sentence is difficult to interpret, but it surely means at least three things. First, quite obviously, that God created man. Second, that He did not produce a perfect replica of himself in creating man: the metaphor of the "image" conveys that man is not on a par with God. But, third, the same metaphor ensures that, however inadequate he may be, man resembles God in some way or other, has *some* share of God's nature. This creature bears the mark of its creator in a way that no other creature does.

3

If we ask, why is there a world, and why are there people, then the Bible's answer, so far as it goes, is entirely clear: God created both. And note that God could not create man without also creating a world for man to be in, for, being what he is, man cannot be without a world to be in. Maybe an angel could *be* without a world. Man cannot.

4

But if we pursue the matter further, we notice a certain silence. That is, having been told that man and the world exist because God created them, if we now ask *why* God created them, then the Book of Genesis supplies no answer. And if we assign to God the customary plenitudes of power, knowledge, beatitude, and so on—if, that is, we think, as tradition requires, that God is entirely perfect and complete—then it can seem a mystery why he should have created anything at all. Why did he bother? What reason could he have had?

Notice that this problem is independent of the more famous problem of evil, which I shall discuss in Lecture 7.[5] The problem of evil is the problem of why, given that God is both omnipotent and completely good, the world that He created has (at least apparently) so much evil in it. That problem has to do with the *character* of God's creation, *given* that He creates; it takes it *as* given that He created—or at least that is the given hypothesis. The present (different) problem is why God should create anything at all, whatever its character may be.[6]

As Hegel put the question: "If God is all-sufficient and lacks nothing, how does he come to release himself into something so utterly unequal to him?"[7] That is, how does he come to release himself into what is not God, into what is sheerly finite, into nature and into man?

5

Some believers accept that the question is difficult, and they respond by saying that it represents a mystery, one of the many insoluble mysteries you must take on board when you commit yourself to the theory under discussion. More interesting (and, indeed, interestingly contrasting) responses to the question are provided by Thomas Aquinas and by Hegel.

6

For Aquinas, God, understood as a separate transcendent God (transcendent in the sense that He transcends His creation), is indeed all-sufficient and lacking in nothing, and He therefore *need* not create anything. But, says Aquinas, and here he is influenced by the neo-Platonism of Plotinus, the world and man issue forth from God by virtue of his superabundant nature. The world is, as it were, God's overflow, not so much part of His nature as an extra emanation from it. One thing God overflows with is love, and the existence of the world and of man are proofs of His overflowing love.

7

Disagreeing with Aquinas, Hegel thinks that, although God is indeed all-sufficient and lacking in nothing, He would *not* be all-sufficient if, as Aquinas thought, He transcended the world. He would be imperfect without His creation—and that is the explanation of the creation: "Without the world," says Hegel, "God is not God."[8] God comes to be perfect, and, therefore, paradoxically—since God *is* perfect, since it is his nature to be perfect—He comes to *be,* only by manifesting Himself in the world. The Hegelian sentence "Without the world God is not God" identifies not a deficiency in God but a deficiency or incompleteness in a *conception* of God which neglects the Spinozistic truth that He is *all* reality.[9]

Immanuel Kant formulated an antinomy regarding the freedom of the will which can be paralleled with an antinomy about God's creation of the world, and Hegel's solution to the latter antinomy is like Kant's to the former.[10] Kant's antinomy of freedom goes like this: Either your act is uncaused, in which case it is an accident, or it is caused, in which case it is unfree; in either case, your act displays no intelligible exercise of freedom. Kant purportedly solves the antinomy through his claim that actions induced by recognition of the moral law are free because they are caused by your own rational nature. The parallel antinomy about God's creation goes like this: Either He doesn't have to create the world, in which case it's just accidental and arbitrary that there is one, or He must create the world, in which case He's unfree. Hegel's solution is that He isn't God unless He creates the world; and since it's in His nature to do so, there is no unfreedom in His doing so.

Hegel's point is *not* that God creates in order to overcome a deficiency that He'd otherwise have, but that He creates because otherwise He'd be deficient, which is impossible. And what He creates is part of Himself. For there cannot be over and above or, better, under and below, and therefore separate from God, a finite reality which He is not; the infinite would be limited if it did not include the finite. Being unlimited, the infinite, so Hegel reasoned, must include the finite. As Lord Gifford specified in his testament, God is "the One and Sole Substance, the Sole Being, the Sole Reality, and the Sole Existence."[11]

The story of the incarnation of God in Jesus is a symbolic rendering of the (supposed) truth that I have been expounding. According to Hegel, the Jewish conception of a God set over and above men is a primitive one. The advent of Christianity signifies great progress, for it brings the realization that God, to *be* God, must express Himself in a world, and in a world of men, of finite spirits. (According to Hegel, Christianity tells the truth about things in the form of images and symbols, and it is the task of philosophy to formulate the same truth in concepts. Hegel claimed that his philosophy just *was* Christianity, in a philosophical form.)

Not only is God not fully God, not fully real, without the world, but the world in turn is unreal, a mere appearance, save to the extent that it is a manifestation of God, and it is a profound mistake of Judaism not to realize that. The Jewish religion is unaware that

God, the absolutely infinite, is not something outside and beside whom there are *other* beings. All else outside God, if separated from him, possesses no being: in its isolation it becomes a mere show or seeming, without stay or essence of its own. . . . God, far from being *a* Being, even the highest, is *the* Being. . . . If we consider God as the Essence only [i.e., apart from His manifestation in the world], and nothing more, we know Him only as the universal and irresistible power; in other words, as the Lord. Now the fear of the Lord is, doubtless, the beginning, but *only* the beginning, of wisdom. To look at God in this light, as the Lord, and the Lord alone, is especially characteristic of Judaism and also of Mohammedanism. The defect of these religions lies in their scant recognition of the finite, which, be it as natural things or as finite phases of mind, it is characteristic of the heathen and (as they also for that reason are) polytheistic religions to maintain intact.[12]

The heathens do see finite things as manifesting the divine, but not a unitary divine. They understand different natural forces as the powers of different gods. The Jews rise to the thought of the unity of the divine; they know that there is only *one* God, but they lose the idea of the manifestation of the divine in the world. The Christian doctrine of the incarnation in the world of a single God provides both divine unity and divine manifestation, thereby uniting the heathen and Jewish truths.[13]

8

But why does Hegel think that "without the world God is not God"? Why is it in God's nature to create a world? At one level, or so I said, it is because the infinite must include the finite in order not to be limited by it. But there is more to be said, at another level.

Here I must say something about Hegel's conception of *Geist*, a term which is usually translated in English as "mind," or "spirit." There are various forms of *Geist*. In its most familiar form *Geist* is embodied in a human being; each of us, for example, has a mind. A second form is the mentality of a community, its national character—that in virtue of which an Italian child grows up to have different kinds of attitude and temperament and intellectual dispositions from, say, a Navajo. And a third form of *Geist* is the mind of God, which Hegel called the world-spirit, at least as that mind relates to the world's doings.

9

There are, of course, important differences among these three kinds of mind, but there are common features too. And a common feature which Hegel thought all minds share is that it is a primary concern of any mind that it should enjoy self-awareness. It is the primacy of that concern which, I hope we shall come to see, explains for Hegel why it belongs to the nature of God to create the world.

10

I shall proceed as follows. First, I explain why, according to Hegel, a mind is interested in self-awareness. Next I show how God, being a mind, and therefore having that interest, satisfies it by creating the world and man. The second matter, which is dealt with in sections 14–17 below, is very much additional to the first, so I ask you for the moment to set aside the question why God created the world, and consider with me just the first question, which is why it is that a mind (and, hence, God) has a special interest in achieving consciousness of itself, according to Hegel.

11

The short answer is that for Hegel self-consciousness is equivalent to freedom, and that *is* an answer, because we can take it for granted that any mind is interested in freedom. But on what basis does Hegel assert a consciousness/freedom equivalence?

Here we must look at a difficult text, perhaps the most difficult text that I shall ask you to examine with me in these lectures. The text gives Hegel's explanation of the identity between freedom and self-awareness, and thereby shows why minds require self-awareness, on the plausible assumption that they require freedom. I shall read the text, and then reconstruct its argument, without defending the fidelity of that reconstruction to the text. I shall then criticize the argument I have constructed.

In the text in question, Hegel speaks of how spirit is to be defined. It is important to realize that, for Hegel, as for Aristotle, the proper definition of a thing describes what it is like when it is fully developed. So when

Hegel says, here, what spirit is, we may take it that he is saying what spirit is when it is fully developed:

> Spirit . . . may be defined as that which has its center in itself. It has not a unity outside itself, but has already found it; it exists in and with itself. . . . Spirit is self-contained existence (*bei-sich-selbst-sein*). Now this is freedom, exactly. For if I am dependent, my being is referred to something else which I am not; I cannot exist independently of something external. I am free, on the contrary, when I am with myself. This self-contained existence of spirit is none other than self-consciousness—consciousness of one's own being.[14]

12

I shall criticize the argument in that text for the identity of freedom and self-consciousness; but, for the sake of advancing our understanding of Hegel, I should first like to motivate the argument as strongly as I can.

So here is my attempt to do so. In a word, the argument is that both the freedom of consciousness and its self-consciousness are its presence to itself and the presence of nothing else to itself; that is why freedom and self-consciousness are identical. Stepwise, the argument runs as follows:

  (i) A mind is a consciousness.
 (ii) Consciousness is always *of* something or other.
(iii) Consciousness depends for its existence on what it is conscious of. (By (ii).)

Now,

 (iv) Consciousness is either of consciousness itself only or (also) of something other than itself. (By (ii) and a truth of logic.)
  (v) Consciousness is free of dependence on something alien if and only if it is conscious of itself alone. (By (iii) and (iv).)
 (vi) A mind is free if and only if it is conscious of itself alone (that is, if and only if the only thing of which it is conscious is itself). (By (i) and (v).)

To explain. A spirit or mind is something which possesses consciousness or awareness, and which we may also refer to as *a* consciousness (premise (i)). And a further premise of the argument in the passage (premise (ii)), which Hegel does not state, but which is plausible, is that there is no such thing as objectless awareness: awareness or consciousness is always *of* something or other. From this premise, (ii), Hegel infers subconclusion (iii), which is that consciousness depends for its existence on being related to something—namely, that of which it is conscious. Now if, as (ii) says, consciousness must be conscious of something, then it follows by mere logic that it must be conscious either only of itself or (also) of something other than consciousness (subconclusion (iv)). And since consciousness depends on what it is conscious of for its existence, it is, if conscious of itself alone, dependent on nothing else for its existence, but, if conscious of something else, then dependent on that other thing for its existence. But then it is free, because not other-dependent, if and only if (subconclusion (v)) it is conscious of itself and nothing but itself. Then and only then will it depend on itself alone. Accordingly, we get Hegel's conclusion, which is that (see (vi)) for a mind to be free, the relation without which it does not exist must be to itself: the mind is free when and only when it is free *of* what is not mind, when it is not trammeled by anything external to itself.

That is why Hegel says, in his *Logic:* "Freedom means that the other thing with which you deal is a second self," and "For freedom it is necessary that we should feel no presence of something else which is not ourselves."[15] Or, again: "We become free when we are confronted by no absolutely alien world, but depend upon a fact which we ourselves are."[16] In the culmination of Hegel's *Phenomenology,* when spirit realizes that the world is its own creation, there is freedom because, finally, "self-consciousness . . . is . . . at home with itself in its otherness as such."[17]

There are various errors in this argument, and I want to point out two of them. First, it is not true that (iii) follows from (ii); and (iii) is, moreover, false. What might be true, and what might follow from (ii) is that

   (iiia) consciousness depends for its existence on its being conscious
          of something.

Proposition (iiia) might be true, but it doesn't imply (iii), which, unlike (iiia), says that consciousness depends for its existence on the *particular* item(s) it happens to be conscious of. Consciousness lacks that dependence simply because, whatever it may actually be conscious of, it is also capable of being conscious of something else.

But the argument suffers from a second error which is independent of that one, and this second error matters more for us, because of our interest in the movement from Hegel to Marx. This further error is Hegel's inference from (iii) and (iv) to (v), an error which is concentrated in the word "depends." For the notion of being dependent on something for its existence, as it is exercised in (iii), must be the notion of *conceptual* dependence, A depending on B in the sense that it *is* not, does not *count* as, A without B; it is attention to the mere *concept* of consciousness which is supposed to satisfy us of the truth of (ii), from which (iii) is derived. Conceptual dependence is, however, an entirely different matter from dependence on something for one's existence in a sense that implies lack of (independence in a sense that implies lack of) freedom. So, for example, the painter's freedom isn't compromised by his dependence on a surface on which to paint. He would not be freer without such a surface; he simply (a conceptual truth, not a truth about his freedom) would not *be* a *painter.* He cannot say: If only I could paint without a surface, then I would be free! Accordingly, even if we waive the first error, we must insist that (v) does not follow from (iii) and (iv). Proposition (v) follows from them only through equivocation on the meaning of the word "dependence." Which means that it *doesn't* follow.

The painter example illustrates a point which Marx made in his reaction to Hegel—the point that, far from my freedom being compromised by the presence to me of a wholly external reality, some wholly external reality must be there for central exercises of freedom, such as the transformation of nature by human beings, to be possible. Marx attacked both the metaphysical idealism of the doctrine that I am free when no reality that is not myself faces me, *and* its consequent passivity toward external reality, its attitude that freedom is achieved through mere recognition of what seems alien as self. Marx's materialism, at least in its early anti-Hegelian form, is not the reducibility of everything to matter, but just the independent existence of matter, its existence independent of mind and self. For Hegel, to assert the independent existence of matter is to affirm the unfreedom of spirit. Hence, he regards empiricism,[18] for which the world is independent of mind, as an epistemological self-enslavement: "so long . . . as this sensible sphere is and continues to be for Empiricism a mere datum, we have a doctrine of bondage."[19] Empiricism contradicts the freedom of thinking, the doctrine that "thinking means that, in the other, one meets with one's self."[20]

One might say that, for Hegel, as for proponents of what is called "negative" freedom, you are free when you are free of external constraint. But, for proponents of negative freedom, you become free when you rid yourself of the constraint, while, for Hegel, you become free when you rid yourself of its externality, when you rise to the thought that what constrains you is not truly external. *Self*-constraint is consistent with freedom, and so, when the state is represented as an elaboration of mind, and therefore as one in substance with me, then being constrained by it does not contradict my freedom. So the totalitarian tendency in Hegel can be developed out of the freedom-is-facing-nothing-but-oneself doctrine. That doctrine does not necessitate totalitarianism,[21] but it makes a Hegelian *form* of totalitarianism possible.

13

I began by saying, in section 11, that, within Hegel's thought, the mind has a special interest in self-awareness because self-awareness is freedom, and that we can take for granted that a mind is interested in freedom. Yet, while all of that is true, it is also potentially misleading. For it suggests that the mind's fundamental aim is freedom, *as opposed to self-awareness*. It would be more apt to say that, according to Hegel, what mind requires is to be, as it were, in full possession of itself, and that its self-possession is *both* its self-awareness *and* its freedom.

14

The passage presented in section 11 above identifies freedom and self-awareness. It does not say how self-awareness is to be achieved. Hegel's prescription for the attainment of self-awareness will prepare us for the answer to the question: Why did God create the world?

Suppose you want to know what you are like. How can you go about finding out? You might try sitting in your study, thinking very hard about yourself. But if that is all you do you will come to know very little, for there will be almost nothing for you to think about, almost nothing for you to reflect upon. You will not be able to think about how you relate to other people, for you will always be in your study, sitting there, without relationships. You won't be able to think about things you have made and actions you have performed, for both imply engagement in the world, and you have been simply sitting in your study. An actress who wants to know what sort of talent she has must enact a role in a play and then reflect on what she has done. A general who wants to know what sort of soldier he is must fight and then reflect on what *he* has done. They must manifest themselves in the world and, through understanding their manifestations, they will understand themselves. There is no other way. As Hegel puts it in the *Phenomenology:* "Consciousness must act solely in order that what it inherently and implicitly [i.e., potentially] is, may be for it explicitly. . . . What it is implicitly, therefore, it knows from its actual reality. Hence it is that an individual cannot know what he is till he has made himself real by action."[22]

You cannot know yourself without objectifying yourself—without, that is, making yourself an *object* of knowledge.

15

We have been talking about individual minds, but Hegel also applies this idea to the minds of whole communities, to the spirits of nations. Just as, by undertaking projects, I am able to perceive the nature and results of my engagement in them, and I thereby learn about myself, so too the aspirations and problems of a community are represented by Hegel as instances of its self-exploration. Speaking of the spirit of a nation, he says that "in its work it is employed in rendering itself an object of its own contemplation."[23] The mind of a society reveals itself to itself in the multiform phenomena of social life. "Its religion, its polity, its ethics, its legislation, and even its science, art, and mechanical skill all bear its stamp."[24] It "erects itself into an objective world that exists and persists in a particular religious form of worship, customs, constitution, and political laws—in the whole complex of its institutions—in the events and transactions that make up its history."[25] Thus, Hegel unites what may seem disparate expressions of the nation by discerning in each a conception of itself which the nation has and which it learns it has through awareness of these its self-expressions.

16

The idea that the mind achieves awareness of itself by expressing itself in an outward form, and then by recognizing itself in its expressions, is also applied to God, and it explains why God creates the world. He creates because He can come to know Himself, and therefore to possess Himself, only in His creation. In order to know Himself, God too must make and act. He makes the world and man, and He acts through people and in and through the communities people compose.

17

It follows that the coming to self-awareness of individuals and communities is not just *parallel* to God's coming to self-awareness. Rather, communities and the individuals comprising them are the *only* vehicles of God's ascent to self-consciousness, so that Hegel can write, in an extraordinary passage in his *Philosophy of Mind,* that "God is God only so far as he knows himself; his self-knowledge is, further, a self-consciousness in man and man's knowledge *of* God, which proceeds to man's self-knowledge *in* God."[26] The passage affirms a fourfold equivalence:

God's knowledge of God =
God's knowledge of man =
man's knowledge of God =
man's knowledge of man.

God comes to know Himself in and through the work of human beings in history. There has to be a *history* of the world because God cannot know Himself immediately; He can do so only in stages, and only in the minds of people. Those stages comprise world history, which is "the exhibition of Spirit in the process of working out the knowledge of that which it is potentially."[27]

18

And now we must leave Hegel. In retrospect, let us recall the relation between man and God in his philosophy. Certainly man is essential to God. But it is also clear that human beings are secondary to God. Human beings exist because God exists, not vice versa. Human beings are manifestations of God, not vice versa. They are vehicles of God's self-development, and they have the value and dignity that they do insofar as they are such. So while in Hegel's perhaps blasphemous construal of Christianity, God does indeed require men and is incomplete without them, the orthodox secondariness and derivativeness of men is nevertheless upheld. Recall (see section 7 above) that there is no reality in anything save insofar as it manifests the divine. This means that the divine does exist here below, but also that nothing here below has any reality of its *own:* it owes its reality to what is divine *in* it.

19

Ludwig Feuerbach set out to invert the relation between God and man which is proposed in Christianity and in Hegel's philosophy. Feuerbach said that while, according to Christianity and to Hegel, God is the subject and man is the predicate, in truth the reverse is the case. The truth is that God is created in *man's* image, by man. (It would, perhaps, be more accurate to say that, for Feuerbach, man creates not God but the *idea* of God; but Feuerbach said "God," and, in expounding him, I shall follow this usage. Perhaps we can justify it by saying that, for Feuerbach, if God is anything, then that is what he is—an idea, a human representation.)

According to Feuerbach, people create God by gathering the best features of their own humanity, glorifying them, and projecting them into a beyond. People do this because they do not recognize that the features which they attribute to God are their *own* features, that goodness and knowledge and power belong to the human race itself, and exist nowhere else.[28] There is, moreover, no limit, in principle, to the power and goodness and knowledge of human beings, considered collectively, as a species; if anything is infinitely good and knowledgeable and powerful, it is, potentially, humanity itself. So the properties Christianity lodges in God are nothing but properties of human beings. Being out of touch with their own properties, people refer them to a deity, and then they suppose that they inherit inadequate copies of them from the deity: "The divine being is nothing else than the human being, or, rather, the human being purified, freed from the limits of the individual man, made objective—that is, contemplated and revered in another, a distinct being."[29]

Feuerbach's "subject/predicate" inversion, his transfer of Hegel's subject (God) into predicate position, and his exaltation of Hegel's predicate (man) into subject position, implies that men are *not* manifestations of God but that God is a manifestation of men. People are not vehicles of God's self-awareness; the idea of God is the vehicle of the confused and alienated self-awareness of humanity. And that self-awareness counts as an *alienated* one for the plain reason that it is an awareness of self only in the form of something other, which means that the human self is cut off from itself in its very awareness of itself. So Feuerbach can endorse the last two elements in the four-fold Hegelian equation given in section 17 above, but he must delete the first two, since God is the subject of those two sentences, and, as Feuerbach expressed his conceptual revolution, Christianity mistakenly treats God, the predicate, the features of humanity, as a subject in its own right. And whereas for Hegel there is no alienation in the fact that people grasp their own nature in their conception of God (since God is what is true and essential in that nature), for Feuerbach the indirect character of the human route to self-awareness of the species' nature proves human estrangement from its own nature. Far from things and people being real only insofar as they are manifestations of God (see, again, section 7 above), God is unreal to the extent that He is not a manifestation of what is human. Here is how Feuerbach develops the point:

> To characterize the consciousness of God as man's self-consciousness does not mean that religious man is directly *aware* that the consciousness of God is the self-consciousness of his own nature. For the lack of this very awareness is in fact the distinctive mark of religion. To avoid this misunderstanding, it is better to say that religion is the earliest and really the indirect form of man's self-consciousness. Therefore, religion always precedes philosophy, both in the history of mankind in general, and in the history of the individual. At first man misplaces his essential nature as if it were outside of himself, before he discovers it in himself. . . . What formerly was taken to be God and was worshiped as such is now recognized to be something *human.* . . . Man is seen to have adored his own nature.[30]

The insight Feuerbach takes himself to be offering is not that there is consequently something wrong with worshiping our own nature, but that we should worship it *as such* and not refer it away to another being. That is why he denied he was an atheist: "He alone is the true atheist to whom the *predicates* of the Divine Being are nothing; not he to whom merely the *subject* of these predicates is nothing."[31]

If people worship as creator of themselves what is in truth their own creation, that can only be because they are estranged from themselves, because their condition is one of alienation. Alienation obtains when something issues forth from men which they do not recognize as their own, and which consequently dominates them. The motif of subjection to what they estrange from themselves is not contained in the very words "alienation" and "estrangement," or in the original German *Entfremdung*, but it is present in both the Feuerbachian and the Marxian uses of those words.

For Feuerbach, liberation would come when people realized what God really was, and he was telling them what God is. They could then reclaim the human essence they had alienated heavenward, and establish a socialist community in which the goodness, knowledge, and power of humanity would be subject to no alien limitation.

20

Karl Marx was a student of philosophy and law at the University of Berlin in the later 1830s, in the period five to ten years after Hegel's death. Hegel had been professor of philosophy at Berlin, and the influence of his philosophy there, and indeed beyond, was enormous. Certainly Marx was intoxicated by it, and his escape from it was a slow process. A major episode in that process was his acceptance of the Feuerbachian and "Young Hegelian" critique of Hegel, the latter following shortly on Hegel's death, notably in David Friedrich Strauss's *Life of Jesus,* which appeared in 1835, and in Bruno Bauer's writings of the late 1830s and early 1840s. Engels recollected later that, in 1841, when Feuerbach's *Essence of Christianity* appeared, so powerful was its impact that "we all became at once Feuerbachians."[32]

It is now widely thought that Engels thereby exaggerated the effect of Feuerbach on Marx in particular. Engels didn't know Marx in 1841, and Marx was in fact more politically oriented than Feuerbach from the start, so that he did not have an unambivalently Feuerbachian phase. In any case, and however Feuerbachian he might ever have been, Marx displayed a decisive break with Feuerbach in the spring of 1845, while traveling on a train in the Rhineland, when he penned eleven momentous paragraphs, conventionally known as the *Theses on Feuerbach,* the last and most famous of which reads: "The philosophers have only interpreted the world; the point, however, is to change it." If any one sentence is the beginning of Marxism, it is that one. I shall explicate it presently, and I shall try to explain how it represents a transcendence of Feuerbach's perspective. But I should like, first, to exhibit the Fourth Thesis on Feuerbach:

> Feuerbach starts out from the fact of religious self-estrangement, of the duplication of the world into a religious, imaginary world and a real one. His work consists in resolving the religious world into its secular basis. He overlooks the fact that after completing this work, the chief thing still remains to be done. For the fact that the secular basis lifts off from itself and establishes itself in the clouds as an independent realm can only be explained by the inner strife and intrinsic contradictori-ness of this secular basis. The latter must itself, therefore, first be un-derstood in its contradiction and then, by the removal of the contradic-tion, revolutionized in practice. Thus, for instance, once the earthly family is discovered to be the secret of the holy family, the former must then itself be criticized in theory and transformed in practice.[33]

The Fourth Thesis denies that religious illusion has its ultimate foun-dation in humanity's lack of clear awareness of itself, a lack that reflects the incomplete development of human self-awareness. It says that the il-lusion and lack of awareness are alike generated by ructions within the real secular life of society. It is because reality itself is inadequate that il-lusions about it flourish, and, more specifically, it is a lack of harmony ("inner strife and intrinsic contradictoriness") in reality which leads to its reproduction in an illusory harmonious form.

So, first, and by contrast with Feuerbach, there is a sociological diag-nosis of religious alienation, and, in the light of that diagnosis, the infer-ence is drawn that philosophical clarity about religion, the state, and all other forms of alienation will not suffice to dispel the illusions which philosophical clarity exposes. They will persist in social consciousness, and even in the theorist's mind so soon as she leaves her study, as long as the reality which generates the illusions rests unrevolutionized. Such a theorist is rather like a person who continues to perceive a mirage even after she knows that it is one, and knows why she mistakes it for reality.[34]

Feuerbach's view of the order of battle in the struggle against illusion was in one way precisely the opposite of Marx's. In a reply to attacks by Max Stirner, Feuerbach, having described his work as intended to "destroy an illusion," proceeds to assure us that it is an illusion "with which all illusions, all prejudices, all unnatural constraints fall away, even though this might not happen immediately; for humanity's primary illusion, primary prejudice, primary constraint, is God as subject. If one therefore devotes one's time and power to the dissolution of the primary illusion, it follows that at the same time one will dissolve the illusions and constraints derived from it."[35] For Marx, this is precisely upside down. Religion is the *third* level of illusion, the basic one being economic and an intermediate one being political (and the philosophical the fourth and highest).[36]

21

Insofar, then, as it is the mission of philosophy to bring clear thinking into the world, to spread the truth, to, as Feuerbach said, "destroy illusion," it is insufficient for the philosopher to discover the truth and publish it. His very commitment as a philosopher will compel him to become a political activist. And that brings us back to Marx's Eleventh Thesis on Feuerbach: "The philosophers have only interpreted the world; the point, however, is to change it."

It is misleading to describe the Eleventh Thesis as a call to abandon theory for practice, as though, ridiculously, we should stop thinking and start doing. For the Eleventh Thesis reflects a viewpoint according to which true theory, an illusionless conception of the world, will not prevail until practice overturns the structures which continually reproduce false theory. But in order that practice may overturn these structures, theory must first deliver an understanding of the world we are in. We should *not*, therefore, cease to interpret the world. (Those who think this was part of Marx's message cannot readily explain why he should have believed that *Capital* was worth writing.)

22

Philosophy harbors a tradition in which it seeks to realize itself in the world. The tradition is at least as old as Plato, whose *Republic* weaves a prescriptive social and political theory around a central strand of metaphysics. For Plato, the ideal perceived by philosophy would have a chance of realization only in the improbable but not impossible event that a philosopher should find himself with political power, or a powerful politician should become a philosopher: "Neither cities nor States nor individuals will ever attain perfection until the small class of philosophers whom we termed useless but not corrupt are providentially compelled, whether they will or not, to take care of the State, and until a like necessity be laid on the State to obey them; or until kings, or if not kings, the sons of kings or princes, are divinely inspired with a true love of true philosophy. That either or both of these alternatives are impossible, I see no reason to affirm."[37] A union between philosophical insight and worldly power was necessary to bring philosophical insight into the structure of the world, to make philosophy real, to real-ize it, as one might say. And that union might come to be, although it was unlikely; its advent would be a matter of pure chance.

Feuerbach's ideal was a free and equal human community. He thought to promote it by propagating an awareness that religious belief was illusory, a projection of human properties onto something nonexistent. Clarity of mind was the route to regeneration of reality. Human consciousness had reached a stage at which Feuerbach's lesson could be seized and absorbed.

Marx reversed Feuerbach's program for rescuing humanity from illusion and alienation. Thought will never correspond to reality, hence be truthful, until reality itself is changed, for it is a distorted reality which generates distortions of thought. Feuerbach demanded that people give up illusions about their condition. He should have demanded that they overthrow the condition which continues to produce illusion, even when the illusions have been exposed theoretically. When social circumstances induce discord between thought and reality, the enemy of illusion must operate on reality itself, not in thought alone. Only what practice achieves can dissipate the mist that clouds clear thinking.

Thus, Marx is *not,* in the Eleventh Thesis, simply expressing an activist's impatience with the analytical response to people's mistakes. He is not announcing his discontent with merely intellectual victories. He is, rather, insisting there will be no secure intellectual victory as long as all that happens is that intellectuals do good intellectual work.

It is false that whereas Feuerbach's concern is theory, Marx's is practice. Their primary interest is the same. Both want to suppress illusion, and Marx's complaint is that theorizing alone will not do so. The goal with respect to which "the chief thing still remains to be done" (see section 20 above) is to secure intelligibility in a transparent world. By bearing in mind that common aim, we can understand the critique of Feuer-bach as motivated by something other than a difference of temper or of circumstance. There is a genuine disagreement with Feuerbach, arising out of a shared desire to destroy illusion and initiate a harmony of reality and thought.

The illusions occupying these thinkers survive theoretical exposé, ac-cording to Marx, because theory does not cure the conditions which produce them. And that is because they are not, in the first instance, er-rors of thought, but distortions in the world (relevantly parallel to those which produce mirages), which theory is impotent to rectify. For Marx, social conditions must themselves be conflicted to generate a conflict between reality and appearance, between how things are and how they seem.

23

In the text in which the opium sentence appears (see section 1 above), Marx said that "you cannot abolish[38] philosophy without making it a re-ality." As long as reality falls short of the philosophical prescription, phi-losophy will persist "as an independent realm . . . in the clouds" (Fourth Thesis). The perennial philosophical elaboration of a world superior to the real one will endure as long as the real world fails to meet the stan-dards of philosophy, and once it does, philosophy will disappear, or unite with life. There will not be two worlds, a deficient real world and a compensating perfect world elaborated by philosophy.

But the philosopher is impotent to change reality acting on his own. Social reality can be subverted only by powers within social reality. And subversive power was to be found only in the most suffering class in that reality: the new industrial proletariat. In the proletariat, said Marx, phi-losophy would find its material weapon, and the proletariat would find its spiritual weapon in philosophy. The Platonic union of philosophy and power (see section 22 above) thereby returns, in a revolutionary and democratic form.

Marx writes: "Philosophy cannot be made a reality without the aboli-tion of the proletariat; the proletariat cannot be abolished without phi-losophy being made a reality."[39] The first is true because the existence of the proletariat proves the woeful inadequacy of reality: as long as there is a proletariat, philosophy has not been realized. And the second is true because, so Marx thought, the proletariat cannot be abolished without a revolution which harmonizes society once and for all. You cannot abolish the working class without abolishing all class divisions.

These reflections, then, give rise to the idea of an extraordinary alliance between the most exalted manifestation of humanity, in the truth-seeking philosopher, and its most debased and deformed manifestation, in the oppressed outcasts. When Engels said that "the German working-class movement is the inheritor of German classical philosophy,"[40] he intended that the movement would realize in practice what the philosophers had vainly sought to realize through theory alone. The Platonic alliance of philosophy and power reappears, but it is not, now, an accident, as the one that Plato projected was (see, again, section 22 above).

According to the *Hegel Critique* Introduction, which is the text from which the opium sentence comes, "the . . . task of philosophy, . . . once the holy form of human self-alienation has been unmasked, is to unmask self-alienation in its unholy forms. Thus, the criticism of heaven turns into the criticism of the earth, the criticism of religion into the criticism of law, and the criticism of theology into the criticism of politics."[41]

To carry through those criticisms, an alliance of philosophy with proletarian agency was required. I shall explain, in Lecture 6, why that alliance has not and will not come to pass, and why too, therefore, socialism, if it is to come at all, cannot come by mere delivery of what is gestating in the womb of capitalism. The obstetric promise has been confounded.

6

Equality

From Fact to Norm

It is we who ploughed the prairies, built the cities where they trade,
Dug the mines and built the workshops, endless miles of railroad laid;
Now, we stand outcast and starving, 'mid the wonders we have made.
Ralph Chaplin, "Solidarity Forever,"
in Hille, ed., The People's Song Book

In August 1964, I spent two weeks in Czechoslovakia, in Prague, in what was then the home of my father's sister, Jennie Freed, and her husband, Norman. They were there because Norman was at the time an editor of *World Marxist Review,* the now defunct Prague-based theoretical journal of the also now defunct international communist movement. Daytimes I wandered around Prague, speaking with whoever would speak to me. Evenings I spent with Jennie and Norman, and sometimes we argued.

One evening, I raised a question about the relationship between justice, and indeed moral principles more generally, and communist political practice. The question elicited a sardonic response from Uncle Norman. "Don't talk to me about morality," he said, with some contempt. "I'm not interested in morals." The tone and context of his words gave them this force: "Morality is ideological eyewash; it has nothing to do with the struggle between capitalism and socialism."

In response to Norman's "Don't talk to me about morals," I said: "But, Uncle Norman, you're a life-long communist. Surely your political activity reflects a strong moral commitment?"

"It's nothing to do with morals," he replied, his voice now rising in volume. "I'm fighting for my class!"

We then turned from the problem of the relationship between morals and politics to the problem of identifying Norman's class. Our exchange about that was stormy, but I draw a veil across it, since it is not germane to my theme.

In his depreciation of morality, Uncle Norman was expressing, in vernacular form, a venerable, deep, and disastrously illuded Marxist self-conception. There were several reasons why questions of moral principle were brushed aside in the Marxist tradition. Some were better than others, and some of the relatively good ones are presented in sections 1–4 and 7 here. But the most distinctive reason was that, as we have seen, Marxism presented itself to itself from its inception as the consciousness of a struggle within the world, rather than as a set of ideals proposed to the world to which the world was required to adjust itself. The consciousness of the world's struggle would induce the world to consummate its struggle. As we have also seen, that conception of practice appeared in the thought of Marx himself even before he became a Marxist, on anyone's understanding of when that was. Recall, in particular, his letters of 1843, excerpts from which were presented in section 4 of Lecture 4, above.

1

In striking the posture that he did, Uncle Norman was, therefore, faithful to classical Marxism.[1] Classical Marxism distinguished itself from what it condemned as the socialism of dreams by declaring a commitment to hard-headed historical and economic analysis: it was proud of what it considered to be the stoutly factual character of its central claims.[2] The title of Engels' book *Die Entwicklung des Sozialismus von der Utopie zur Wissenschaft* (The Development of Socialism from Utopia to Science)[3] articulated that piece of Marxist self-interpretation. Socialism, once raised aloft by airy ideals, would henceforth rest on a firm foundation of fact. It had been utopian, but now, as a result of Marx's work, it had become a science.

Marxism's heroic self-description was *in part* justified. For its founders and followers did distinguish themselves from socialist forerunners like Charles Fourier and Robert Owen by forsaking the detailed depiction of imaginary perfect societies, and they did achieve a great leap forward in realistic understanding of how the social order functions. But the favored classical Marxist self-description was also *in part* bravado. For values of equality, community, and human self-realization were undoubtedly integral to the Marxist belief structure. All classical Marxists believed in some kind of equality, even if many would have refused to acknowledge that they believed in it and even if none, perhaps, could have formulated with any precision a principle of equality that he believed in.

Yet Marxists were not preoccupied with, and therefore never examined, principles of equality, or indeed any other values or principles. Instead, they devoted their intellectual energy to the hard factual carapace surrounding their values, to bold explanatory theses about history in general and capitalism in particular—the theses which gave Marxism its commanding authority in the field of socialist doctrine, and even, indeed, its moral authority, because its heavy intellectual labor on matters of history and economic theory proved the depth of its political commitment.

And now Marxism has lost much or most of its carapace, its hard shell of supposed fact. Scarcely anybody defends it in the academy, and there are no more apparatchiki who believe that they are applying it in Communist Party offices. To the extent that Marxism is still alive—and one may say that a sort of Marxism is alive in, for example, the work of scholars like John Roemer in the United States and Philippe Van Parijs in Belgium—it presents itself as a set of values and a set of designs for realizing those values. It is therefore, now, far less different than it could once advertise itself to be from the utopian socialism with which it so proudly contrasted itself. Its shell is cracked and crumbling, its soft underbelly exposed.

Let me illustrate Marxism's loss of factual carapace with respect to the value of equality in particular. Whatever one may think, in general terms, of the obstetric perspective, it presupposed, in its Marxist form, factual beliefs about equality that are no longer sustainable.

Classical Marxists believed that material equality, equality of access to goods and services, was both historically inevitable and morally right. They believed the first entirely consciously, and they believed the second more or less consciously, and exhibited more or less evasion when asked whether they believed it. It was partly because they believed that equality was historically inevitable that classical Marxists did not spend much time thinking about *why* equality was morally right, about exactly what made it morally binding. Equality was coming, it was welcome, and it would be a waste of time to theorize about why it was welcome, rather than about how to make it come as quickly and as painlessly as possible—for the precise date at which equality would be achieved and the cost of reaching it were, unlike equality itself, not themselves inevitable, and obstetric wisdom would therefore find its application here.

Two supposedly irrepressible historical trends, working together, guaranteed the future material equality. One was the rise of an organized working class, whose social emplacement, at the short end of *inequality*, directed it in favor of equality. The workers' movement would grow in numbers and in strength, until it had the power to abolish the unequal society which had nurtured its growth. And the other trend helping to ensure an eventual equality was the development of the productive forces, the continual increase in the human power to transform nature for human benefit. That growth would issue in a material abundance so great that anything anyone needed for a richly fulfilling life could be taken from the common store at no cost to anyone. The guaranteed future abundance served as a source of rebuttal to the suggestion that inequality might reemerge, in a new form, *after* the revolution—peaceful or bloody, legal or illegal, fast or slow—which the proletariat could and would accomplish. Following that revolution, there would be an interim period of limited inequality: although class division would no longer exist, more productive people would still be better rewarded than less productive. But when "all the springs of cooperative wealth [came] to flow more abundantly,"[4] even that limited inequality would disappear, because everyone could have everything they might (in all sanity) want to have.

History has shredded each of the predictions that I have just sketched. The proletariat did, for a while, grow larger and stronger, but it never became, as the "Communist Manifesto" foretold, "the immense majority,"[5] and it was ultimately reduced and divided by the increasing technological sophistication of the capitalist production process, which had been expected to continue to expand the proletariat's size and augment its power. And the development of the productive forces now runs up against a resource barrier. Technical knowledge has not stopped, and will not stop growing, but productive power, which is the capacity (all things considered) to transform nature into use-value—that is, into sources of utility for human beings—cannot expand *pari passu* with the growth of technical knowledge, because planet Earth rebels: its resources turn out to be not lavish enough for continuous growth in technical knowledge to generate unceasing expansion of use-value.

2

Let us look more closely at the two leading Marxist inevitabilitarian claims that were distinguished above.

The first claim is false because the proletariat is in process of disintegration, in a sense that I shall shortly try to make precise. As a result—and a very discouraging result it is for those of us who remain egalitarians—the struggle for equality is no longer a reflex movement on the part of an agent located at a strategic point in the capitalist industrial process;[6] socialist values have lost their mooring in capitalist social structure. Accordingly, and as I shall now explain, issues arise for socialist philosophy that did not have to be faced in the past. And Marxists or semi-Marxists, or ex-Marxists, like Roemer and Van Parijs and me, find themselves engaged by questions in moral and political philosophy which did not, in the past, attract the attention of Marxists, and which very often earned their disdain.

The sharp shift of attention is explained by profound changes in the class structure of Western capitalist societies, changes which raise normative problems which did not exist before, or, rather, which previously had little political significance. Those normative problems have great political significance now.

As a way into the normative problems, I shall begin by repeating the epigraph of this chapter, which is from the second verse of "Solidarity Forever,"[7] an old American socialist song:

> It is we who ploughed the prairies, built the cities where they
>   trade,
> Dug the mines and built the workshops, endless miles of
>   railroad laid;
> Now we stand outcast and starving, 'mid the wonders we have
>   made. . . .

"Solidarity Forever" was sung not only by revolutionary communists but also by social democrats whose socialist aspiration did not go beyond a demand for welfare state provision in a capitalism that, initially, did nothing for those who were thrown out of work in hard times. The part of the exhibited verse that merits special attention here is its third line: "Now we stand outcast and starving, 'mid the wonders we have made." As these words suggest, the campaigns for socialism, and for the welfare state, were seen as a struggle on behalf, centrally, of *working* people; the outcast and starving people who needed socialism, or at least the welfare state, were the very people who created the wealth of society. More or less extensive public provision of the necessities of life was regarded as a rectification of the wrongs done to labor with respect to the product of its own activity, its products being the wonders it had made. Compare the famous American lamentation of the 1930s, "Brother, Can You Spare a Dime?"—a song which was, for a while, at the top of the hit parade. The man says, "Once I built a railroad, Made it run . . . Once I built a tower, To the sun"; and those creations are supposed to show that he should have at least a dime.[8]

In the lines of these songs, people do not demand relief from starvation on the ground that they cannot produce, because, for example, they are disabled, or because they are permanently unemployed, or because they are carers who have no time for paid work. The people who demand relief in these songs demand it on the ground that they *have* produced and should therefore not be left to starve. Two claims to recompense, *need* and *entitlement through labor,* are fused, in a fashion typical of the old socialist rhetoric, in the "Solidarity" line. It was possible to fuse such claims at the time the song was written because socialists saw the set of exploited producers as roughly coterminous with the set of those who needed socialism's benefits. Accordingly, they did not sense any conflict between the producer entitlement doctrine implied by the second part of the third line ("'Mid the wonders we have made") and the more egalitarian doctrine suggested in its first part ("Now we stand outcast and starving"), when it is read on its own. For it does not require much argument to show that there is indeed a difference of principle between the appeals in the two parts of the line. Starving people are not necessarily people who have produced what starving people need; and if what people produce belongs by right to them, the people who have produced it, then starving people who have *not* produced it have no claim on it. The old image of the working class, as a set of people who *both* make the wealth *and* have very little of it, conceals, in its fusion of those characteristics, the poignant and problematic truth that the two claims—namely, "I made this and I should therefore have it" and "I need this, I will die or wither if I do not get it"—are not only different but potentially contradictory pleas.[9]

3

That they created the wonders and that they were outcast and starving were two of four characteristics which Marxists perceived in the working class in the heyday of the socialist movement. The four features never belonged to any single set of people anywhere, but there used to be enough convergence among them for an impression of their coincidence to be sustainable, given a dose of enthusiasm and a bit of self-deception. The communist impression of the working class was that its members

1. constituted the majority of society;
2. produced the wealth of society;
3. were the exploited people in society; and
4. were the needy people in society.

There were, moreover, in the same impression, two further characteristics consequent on those four. The workers were *so* needy that they

5. would have nothing to lose from revolution, whatever its upshot might be;

and, because of 1, 2, and 5, it was within the capacity (1, 2) and in the interest (5) of the working class to change society, so that it

6. could and would transform society.

We can use these names to denote the six features: *majority, production, exploitation, need, nothing-to-lose,* and *revolution.*

However one chooses to apply the much contested labels "working class" and "proletariat," there is now no group in advanced industrial society which unites the four characteristics of: (1) being the producers on whom society depends, (2) being exploited, (3) being (with their families) the majority of society, and (4) being in dire need. There certainly still exist key producers, exploited people, and needy people, but these are not now, as they were in the past, even roughly coincident designations, nor, still less, alternative designations of the great majority of the population. And, as a result, there is now no group with both (because of its exploitation, and its neediness) a compelling interest in, and (because of its productiveness, and its numbers) a ready capacity to achieve, a socialist transformation. In confidently expecting the proletariat to become such a group, classical Marxism failed to anticipate what we now know to be the natural course of capitalist social evolution.

It is necessary to emphasize that the point I am laboring has nothing to do with the scholastic question about what is the correct way to use the phrases "working class" or "proletariat." Under some orthodox definitions of these terms, where, for example, the essential condition for inclusion in their denotation is that one must sell one's labor power to get one's living, the overwhelming mass of the population is, some would argue, now proletarian. But that, if indeed a fact,[10] is an entirely boring fact, in face of the nonverbal, and politically fateful, truth that the four features I listed have come apart. That truth has nothing to do with the proper meaning of the expression "proletariat" (or "working class"), and is therefore not refutable on the basis of whatever anyone thinks its proper meaning is.

Many of the present problems of socialist theory, and of socialist and communist parties, reflect the increasing lack of coincidence of the first four characteristics. Particularly problematic, from the point of view of a socialist political philosopher, is the coming apart of the exploitation and need features. It forces a choice between the principle of a right to the product of one's labor embedded in the doctrine of exploitation and a principle of equality of benefits and burdens which negates the right to the product of one's labor and which is required to defend support for very needy people who are not producers and who are, *a fortiori*, not exploited. This is the central normative problem which Marxists did not have to face in the past.[11]

If you can get yourself to believe that the features cohere, you then have a very powerful political posture.[12] You can say to democrats that they should embrace socialism, because workers form the immense majority of the population. You can say the same to humanitarians, because workers suffer tremendous need. And, very importantly, you are under less pressure than you otherwise would be to worry about the exact ideals and principles of socialism, and that is so for two reasons. The first is that, when the features are seen to cohere, several kinds of moral principle will justify a struggle for socialism, and there is then no practical urgency about identifying which principle or principles are essential; from a practical point of view, such discussion will appear unnecessary, and a waste of political energy. And the second reason for not worrying too much about principles, when the features (seem to) cohere, is that you do not then need to recruit people to the socialist cause by articulating principles which will draw them to it. Success of the cause is guaranteed, by the majority, production, and nothing-to-lose features.

It is partly because there is now patently no group which has those features, and therefore the will to and capacity for revolution, that Marxists, or what were Marxists, are increasingly impelled into normative political philosophy. The disintegration of the characteristics produces an intellectual need to philosophize, which is related to a political need to be clear as never before about values and principles, for the sake of socialist advocacy. Normative socialist advocacy is less necessary when the features coincide. You do not have to justify a socialist transformation as a matter of principle when people are driven to make it by the urgencies of their situation, and in a good position to succeed. And you do not have to decide what principle justifies socialism to recommend it to all people of good will when you think that so many principles justify it that any person of good will would be moved by at least one of them. For when the group whose plight requires the relief supplied by socialism is conceived as having the four features that I have listed, socialism will then present itself as a demand of democracy, justice, elementary human need, and even of the general happiness.

All non-self-serving politics proceeds under the inspiration of ideals. The Marxist declaration that scientific socialists needed no ideals was, paradoxically, buoyed up by a sense that all ideals favored them: they thought they needed no ideals because they had all of them. This powerful sense depended entirely, as I have explained, on a conception of the proletariat which is now unsustainable. If that conception had remained sustainable, the collapse of world communism would not have disoriented socialists as much as it has. Had world communism, moreover, persisted, socialists would not then be much less disoriented than they actually are, given the defeating transformation of the Western proletariat.

4

Each of the first four characteristics listed at the beginning of section 3 is now the leading motif in a certain kind of left-wing or post-left-wing politics in Britain. First, there is "rainbow" majority politics, adopted by socialists who recognize the disintegration and look to generate a majority for egalitarian social change out of heterogeneous elements: badly paid workers, the unemployed, oppressed races, people oppressed because of their gender or their sexual preference, neglected old people, single-parent families, the infirm, and so forth. A producer politics with reduced emphasis on exploitation characterized the Harold Wilsonian rhetoric of 1964, which promised a melting away of reactionary British structures in the "white heat" of a technological transformation of the country in which an alliance of proletarian and highly educated producers would overcome the power of City and landed and other drones; and there are similar strains in Tony Blair's emphasis on hooking Labour up to the computer revolution. Producer politics projects a Saint-Simonian alliance of workers and high-tech producers with greater emphasis on the parasitism of those who do not produce than on the exploitation of those who do (since some of the high fliers who fall within the Saint-Simonian inclusion could hardly be regarded as exploited). An exploitation politics, with a degree of pretense that the other features are still there, characterizes various forms of obsolescent laborism. And, finally, there is the need-centered politics of welfare rights action, a politics of those who think that current suffering has the first claim on radical energy and who devote their efforts to new organizations such as Shelter, the Child Poverty Action Group, Age Concern, and the panoply of groups which confront worldwide deprivation, hunger, and injustice. Such organizations did not exist when the disintegration was less advanced and the labor movement and the welfare movement were pretty well identical. (Philanthropic activity on behalf of deprived children, the homeless, and the indigent old long predates the founding of the organizations named above, but the new organizations pursue their aims in a new spirit—not the old one of providing charity, but a new spirit of rectifying injustice; injustice, moreover, which cannot be brought under the concept of exploitation.)

When those who suffer dire need can be conceived as coinciding with, or as a subset of, the exploited working class, then the socialist doctrine

of exploitation does not cause much difficulty for the socialist principle
of distribution according to need. But once the really needy and the exploited producers no longer coincide, then the inherited doctrine of exploitation is flagrantly incongruent with even the minimal principle of
the welfare state. And tasks are thereby set for socialist political philosophy that did not have to be addressed in the past.

5

Sometimes, when I present the foregoing reflections about the disintegration of the working class at a seminar, or to some more political audience, someone accuses me of forgetting that, from the start, Marxism
conceived the revolution in international terms: the closing sentence of
the "Communist Manifesto" was, after all, "Working men of all countries, unite!"[13] If I widen my focus, so it is urged, I shall see that the features listed in section 3 remain integrated, but, now, on a world scale. I
am said to show blindness, in the foregoing, to the fact that a classically
featured *international* proletariat has emerged, or is emerging.

But that is instructively false. It is no doubt true that, across the countries which form the bulk of the world's population, there are producers,
previously cut off from capitalism, who amply realize the exploitation
and need characteristics—in Indian steel mills, in Korean electronic as-
sembly factories, and so on. But they do not form a majority within or
across the societies in question,[14] which remain largely agrarian, and
they do not represent producers on whose labor capitalism is dependent,
in the traditional projected sense. For the engine of production in today's world is the transnational corporation, which absorbs and expels
sets of workers at will. No group of its workers has substantial clout, because so many other groups form a kind of industrial reserve army vis-à-
vis any one of those groups. The actual and potential proletariats of In-
dia and China are ready to displace the workers of Birmingham, Detroit,
and Lille, and of Manila and São Paolo and Capetown.

Unification of capital historically precedes unification of labor. Capital coagulates in joint stock oligopolies before it faces a unionized work-
force, and the capitalist interest is asserted at the level of the nation-state
long before labor achieves any kind of national voice. But, for combined
cultural and economic reasons, it is far more difficult for labor to emulate capital at the international level, where, increasingly, the action is.

The problem does not lie in the dimension Marx and Engels would have focused on: that of transport and communication. Communication is now easy, and cheap. But the cultural diversity across nations and the huge gulfs between them in actual and expected living standards make mutual identification of their working classes difficult.

The final verse of one of the socialist songs that expressed the sentiments of the old working class-movement runs as follows:

> I've seen my brothers working
> Throughout this mighty land
> I prayed we'd get together,
> And together make a stand.[15]

This getting together, this transcendence of cultural and economic difference, was more or less attainable, and was sometimes in good measure achieved, within a single country. But it is a daunting project on a world scale. How can a Boeing technician in Seattle envisage "getting together" with a laborer on an Indian tea plantation? If there is to be any form of solidarity linking such people, it needs, once again, the moral leavening which seemed so unnecessary[16] for proletarian solidarity in the past. The hugely better off in the world's proletariat must become highly sensitive to moral appeals for there to be any progress along these lines.

6

So much on the consequences for the prospects of equality of the fact that the proletariat did not, and will not, gain the unity and power anticipated for it in Marxist belief. Capitalism does not produce its own gravediggers.[17] The old (partly real, partly imagined) agency of socialist transformation is gone, and there is not, and never will be, another one like it. Socialists have to settle for a less dramatic scenario, and they must engage in more moral advocacy than used to be fashionable. And I now want to discuss, in the spirit of those acknowledgments, an aspect of the present predicament which brings to the fore a basis for demanding equality which is new, relative to traditional Marxist, and also to mainstream liberal, expectations. As we shall see, this new basis is connected with the falsehood of Marxism's abundance prediction, which was the basis, in the past, not for *demanding* equality but for believing it to be inevitable.

The new basis of a demand for equality relates to the ecological crisis. The scale of the threat to humanity which that crisis poses is a matter of controversy among the experts, and so is the shape of the required remedy, if indeed it is not too late to speak of remedies. But two propositions seem to me to be true: that our environment is already severely degraded, and that, if there is a way out of the crisis, then it must include much less aggregate material consumption than what now prevails, and, as a result, unwanted changes in lifestyle, for hundreds of millions of people.

Let me distinguish between what is certain and what is conjectural in that uncongenial assessment. It is beyond dispute that Western consumption, *measured in terms of use of fossil fuel energy and natural resources,* must, on average, fall drastically, and that non-Western consumption, considered in the aggregate, will never reach current Western levels, *so measured.* But the qualification carried by the italicized phrases is important. It is certain that we cannot achieve Western-style goods and services for humanity as a whole, nor even sustain them for as large a minority as has enjoyed them, by drawing on the fuels and materials that we have hitherto used to provide them. It is less certain that the desired consumption satisfactions themselves, the goods and services considered in abstraction from the customary means of supplying them, cannot be secured, by new means, on the desired scale. But I believe that the second claim, about goods and services as such, is also true,[18] and the following remarks proceed under that assumption.

When aggregate wealth is increasing, the condition of those at the bottom of society, and in the world, can improve, even while the distance between them and the better off does not diminish, or even grows. Where such improvement occurs (and it has occurred, on a substantial scale, for many disadvantaged groups), egalitarian justice does not cease to demand equality, but that demand can seem shrill, and even dangerous, if the worse off are steadily growing better off, even though they are not catching up with those above them. When, however, progress must give way to regress, when average material living standards must fall, then poor people and poor nations can no longer hope to approach the levels of amenity which are now enjoyed by the world's well off. Sharply falling average standards mean that settling for limitless improvement, instead of equality, ceases to be an option, and huge disparities of wealth become correspondingly more intolerable, from a moral point of view.

Notice the strong contrast between the foregoing ecologically grounded case for reduced tolerance of inequality and traditional Marxist belief. The achievement of Marxist equality ("From each according to his ability, to each according to his needs")[19] is premised on a conviction that industrial progress will bring society to a condition of such fluent abundance that it is possible to supply what everyone needs for a richly fulfilling life. There will then no longer be any occasion for competition for precedence, either across individuals or between groups. A (supposedly) inevitable future plenty was a reason for *predicting* equality. Persisting scarcity is now a reason for *demanding* it.

We can no longer sustain Marx's extravagant, pre-Green, materialist optimism. At least for the foreseeable future, we have to abandon the vision of abundance. But, if I am right about the straitened choices posed by the ecological crisis, we also have to abandon, on pain of giving up socialist politics, a severe pessimism about *social* possibility which accompanied Marx's optimism about *material* possibility. For Marx thought that material abundance was not only a sufficient but also a necessary condition of equality, and not only of equality, but of a reasonably decent society. He thought that anything short of an abundance so complete that it removed all major conflicts of interest would guarantee continued social strife, a "struggle for necessities . . . and all the old filthy business."[20] *It was because he was so uncompromisingly pessimistic about the social consequences of anything less than limitless abundance that Marx needed to be so optimistic about the possibility of that abundance.*[21]

7

And that amplifies the explanation of traditional Marxism's failure to bring questions of distributive justice into close focus. Under conditions of scarcity, so traditional Marxism maintains, class society is inescapable, its property structures settle questions of distribution, and discussion of the nature of justice, in general terms, is therefore futile, for a political movement whose task must be to overturn class society, rather than to decide which of the many criteria by which it comes out unjust is the right one to use to condemn it. Nor is it necessary to inquire into what, precisely, will be demanded by justice in the future condition of abundance. For communism, in which everyone has what she wants, will then supervene effortlessly (with a little help from its obstetric friends, such as Tim Buck)[22] and justice will thereby be achieved, on any conception of it, from utilitarian through egalitarian to libertarian. Devoting energy to the question "What is the right way to distribute?" is futile with respect to the present and unnecessary with respect to the future.[23]

We can no longer believe the factual premises of those conclusions about the practical (ir)relevance of the study of norms. We cannot share Marx's optimism about material possibility, but we therefore also cannot share his pessimism about social possibility, if we wish to sustain a socialist commitment. Marx's optimism allowed him to maintain a pessimism that we must give up, because we must give up the optimism that made that pessimism safe.

We cannot rely on technology to fix things for us; if they can be fixed, then *we* have to fix them, through hard theoretical and political labor. Marxism thought that equality would be delivered to us, by abundance, but we have to seek equality for a context of scarcity, and we consequently have to be far more clear than we were about what we are seeking, why we are justified in seeking it, and how it can be implemented institutionally. That recognition must govern the future efforts of socialist economists and philosophers.

Ways That Bad Things Can Be Good

A Lighter Look at the Problem of Evil

Lecture 7 could not be reproduced here. That is because it was a multimedia exercise: the audience accepted my invitation to sing with me, to the accompaniment of tapes, a set of American popular songs that illustrate how bad things can be good. Persons familiar with baseball will know about the seventh-inning stretch, when the crowd is asked to rise and sing "Take Me Out to the Ball Game," usually to the strains of a loud organ. Ten lectures are, I considered, more demanding than nine baseball innings, partly because they are ten, but mainly because they are lectures. So I thought my audience would, like baseball fans, appreciate a moment of respite; but the respite that I laid on cannot, alas or otherwise, be embodied in mere print.

8

Justice, Incentives, and Selfishness

"My back's broad enough and strong enough; I should be no better than
a coward to go away and leave the troubles to be borne by them as aren't
half so able. 'They that are strong ought to bear the infirmities of those
that are weak, and not to please themselves.' There's a text wants no
candle to show't; it shines by its own light. It's plain enough you get
into the wrong road i' this life if you run after this and that only for the
sake o' making things easy and pleasant to yourself. A pig may poke his
nose into the trough and think o' nothing outside it; but if you've got a
man's heart and soul in you, you can't be easy a-making your own bed
an' leaving the rest to lie on the stones. Nay, nay, I'll never slip my neck
out o' the yoke, and leave the load to be drawn by the weak uns."

George Eliot, *Adam Bede*

1

I have explained why the disintegration of the proletariat induces persons of Marxist formation to turn to normative political philosophy, and
how the loss of confidence in a future unlimited abundance reinforces
their tendency to take that turn.[1] In my own case, the turn has produced
a sustained engagement with the work of three leading American political philosophers: Robert Nozick, Ronald Dworkin, and John Rawls, to
name them in the temporal order in which they have occupied my attention. The work of Rawls is now at the center of my research, and this lecture and the next are largely given over to an extended critique of Rawls.

Before beginning to mount this critique, I should like to contrast how
certain matters that are relevant to it appeared to me once with how they
appear to me now. Having been raised in a family devoted to the Canadian Communist Party,[2] I was, in my teens, a pretty orthodox Marxist; I
had enthusiastically embraced the theory that was offered to me. From

the perspective of that theory, as I then understood it, I was contemptuous of various then current and now still familiar apologies for, or defenses of, economic inequality. Some of those defenses of economic inequality can be called *normative,* and the others can be called *factual.* The normative defenses *endorse* inequality. They represent it as just. The factual ones, by contrast, do not deny (or affirm) that inequality is unjust. They say that inequality, whether it be just, unjust, or neither, is unavoidable.

A prominent factual defense of inequality traces it to a supposedly ineradicable human selfishness. This defense says that inequality is ensured by something as original to human nature as sin is, on the Christian view of original sin: people are by nature selfish, whether or not that is, like being a sinner, a bad thing to be, and inequality is an unavoidable result of that selfishness, whether or not inequality is unjust.

Being "selfish," here, means desiring things for oneself, and for those in one's immediate circle, and being disposed to act on that desire, even when the consequence is that one has (much) more than other people do, and could otherwise have had. In a strong version of the selfishness hypothesis, it is in the very nature of the relevant desire that it is a desire to have more than other people—that is, it is a desire *both* that I be on one of the higher rungs of the ladder of inequality *and* that others be on lower rungs. If I am (in this sense) strongly selfish, then I want to have more than another does, *not* (merely) because I'll then have more than I otherwise would, but because I (at least also) *fundamentally* want to be above him. In a weaker version of the selfishness hypothesis, what a person desires to have will merely as a matter of fact (in virtue, that is, of the fact that resources are finite) put her above others. Being above, as such, is not, as it is in the stronger version, the goal of our self-seeking, but it remains the outcome of that quest, for those who are gifted enough or lucky enough to enjoy success in the pursuit of self-interested desire.

The selfishness defense of inequality has two premises. First, a *human-nature* premise: that people are by nature selfish. And, second, a *sociological* premise: that *if* people are selfish (whether by nature or otherwise), then equality is impossible to achieve and/or to sustain.

Now, I used to reject both premises of the selfishness defense of inequality. But I have become sympathetic to the sociological premise. On that, more in a moment. First, let me explain why I rejected both premises in the past.

I rejected the human-nature premise for the Marxist reason that, as I believed, social structures extensively shape the structure of motivation. There exists, so I thought, no underlying human nature which could be qualified as *straightforwardly* unselfish or selfish, or selfish in some fixed degree. I do not mean that I thought there was no underlying human nature at all; I would have considered that to be a heretically unmaterialist proposition.[3] (We are, after all, animals, with a particular biology, and a psychology induced by it.) But I did think that human nature was quite plastic with respect to motivation. There were, in a sense, I nevertheless recognized, truths about how selfish human beings are by nature—such as, for example, the truth as to how propitious circumstances would have to be for humans to be unselfish in their attitude and behavior. Or, more generally, the truth about selfishness and human nature would be disclosed by the (variable) height of a line on a graph with circumstances on the horizontal and degrees of manifested selfish orientation on the vertical. The right way to characterize human nature would be as a function, with circumstances as arguments and forms of behavior as values. And all you needed to believe, in order to deny that human nature was selfish in a sense that threatened the egalitarian project, was what I indeed believed: that people would be relevantly unselfish in propitious circumstances, and that such circumstances were accessible.[4]

So I rejected the human-nature premise of the selfishness defense of inequality. But I independently rejected its sociological premise. I thought that even *if* people were by nature selfish, the conclusion that inequality was inescapable would not follow—and was, in fact, false—because, just as social structure was sovereign over motivation, to the detriment of the first premise of the selfishness argument, so, too, structure was sovereign over the *upshot* of motivation: even if and when people were indeed selfish, be it in virtue of their unvarying nature or otherwise, the rules governing their interaction could nevertheless prevent their selfishness from issuing in inequality.[5] Such rules might, for example, be enforced by a great majority, who were themselves selfishly or at any rate not altruistically motivated, and who would be at the short end of inequality in the absence of such rules.

I remain skeptical of the human-nature premise of the selfishness defense of inequality, for something like the old reasons. But I am no longer so skeptical of the sociological premise. I no longer think that, even granting selfishness in motivation, structure can block inequality in upshot.[6] And this change of view is highly consequential. Thus, for example, if people are by now *irreversibly* selfish (not by nature but) as a result of capitalist history, then, so I now think, structure alone could not suffice to deliver equality, in the face of that selfishness.[7] Even on reasonably sunny views about the limits of human nature itself, capitalist history would have thrown us into a cul-de-sac from which we could not exit and regain the road to socialism.

2

In keeping with my changed attitude to the venerable doctrine that equality requires a relevant absence of selfishness, I now find myself less contemptuous of another old nostrum, one which is not (except, sometimes, indirectly) an apology for inequality, but a recipe for eliminating it. This nostrum says that, *for inequality to be overcome, there needs to be a revolution in feeling or motivation, as opposed to (just) in economic structure.* I do not now think that just plain *true,* but I think there is *more* truth in it than I was once prepared to recognize. And the reason it sometimes constitutes, as I said, an indirect apology for inequality is that, short of a second coming of Jesus Christ, or (if Jesus was not the Messiah) of a first coming of the Messiah, there will never *be,* many people would think, the needed change in motivation.

My present greater friendliness to the claim of the italicized nostrum, which we can call the Christian social nostrum, is supported by reflection on work that I have done in the past few years on the Rawlsian justification of economic inequality. Rawls says that inequality is justified when it has the effect that those who are worst off are better off than they would be if the inequality were removed. Inequality is (not only justified but) just, for Rawls, when and because it is necessary to enhance the position of the worst off, and he thinks it typically *is* necessary to that end, in virtue of the benign influence on productive motivation of the material incentives associated with economic inequality.

Rawls presents that as a normative justification of inequality—the sort of justification of it, that is, which seeks to present (certain forms of) inequality as just. But, so I shall argue, a close investigation of the principal mechanism that makes it true, when it is true, that economic inequality benefits the badly off, reveals that the Rawlsian case for inequality is better characterized as a merely factual defense of it. Despite what Rawls himself says, he does not show that incentive-based inequality is just, on his own conception of justice, but, at most, that it is regrettably unavoidable, if not *tout court*,[8] then at least if we do not want to depress everyone's condition.[9] Rawls's purportedly normative defense of inequality exposes itself, on properly insistent interrogation, as a merely factual defense of it. That is because, as we shall see, an anti-egalitarian selfishness must be attributed to the more productive, as part of the explanation for why inequality is necessary, to the extent that it is indeed necessary.

3

I should like to remark on a change of formulation by Rawls, across two otherwise substantially identical texts—a change which is of the first importance in relation to the contrast between factual and normative defenses of inequality.

In his early essay "Justice as Fairness," we find the following passage:

> If, as is quite likely, these inequalities work as incentives to draw out better efforts, *the members of this society may look upon them as concessions to human nature:* they, like us, may think that people ideally should want to serve one another. But, as they are mutually self-interested, their acceptance of these inequalities is merely the acceptance of the relations in which they actually stand, and a recognition of the motives which lead them to engage in their common practices.[10]

There are, in my view, a number of obscurities and infelicities in this passage, and further ones in the paragraph from which it is drawn.[11] But I am, at present, concerned only to remark on the extremely interesting fact that Rawls deleted the clause I have placed in italics when, fourteen years later, he published an otherwise substantially (and nearly verbally) identical paragraph in *A Theory of Justice*. The *Theory* sentence that corresponds to the first sentence in the passage above reads as follows: "If, for example, these inequalities set up various incentives which succeed in eliciting more productive efforts, a person in the original position may look upon them as *necessary* to cover the costs of training and to encourage effective performance."[12] It will follow from my argument against Rawls that *if* unequalizing incentives are truly necessary from the point of view of the interests of the badly off,[13] then they are necessary only because of infirmities in human nature that are more or less affirmed in the "Justice as Fairness" passage but which gain no mention, as such, in the corresponding *Theory* passage.[14]

It is as though both the Rawls of 1957 and the Rawls of 1971 agree with Bernard Mandeville (and Adam Smith) that "private vices" make for "publick benefits"—that (in other words) human selfishness can be made to benefit everyone—but that the Rawls of 1971 is unwilling to acknowledge that it is *indeed* vices which are in question.[15] I agree with Mandeville—and Adam Bede[16]—that that's what they are.

4

If, as I now believe, how selfish people are affects the prospects for equality and justice, then that is partly because, as I now also believe, justice cannot be a matter only of the state-legislated structure in which people act but is also a matter of the acts they choose within that structure, the personal choices of their daily lives. I have come to think, in the words of a recently familiar slogan, that *the personal is political.*

Now, that slogan, as it stands, is vague, but I mean something reasonably precise by it here: that principles of distributive justice—principles, that is, about the just distribution of benefits and burdens in society— apply, wherever else they do, to people's legally unconstrained choices. Those principles, so I claim, apply to the choices that people make *within* the legally coercive structures to which, so everyone would agree, principles of justice (also) apply. (In speaking of the choices people make *within* coercive structures, I do not include the choice whether or not to comply with the rules of such structures—to which choice, once again, so everyone would agree, principles of justice (also) apply). I mean, rather, the choices left open by those rules because neither enjoined nor forbidden by them.)

The italicized slogan that I have appropriated here is widely used by feminists.[17] More importantly, however, the idea itself, which I have here used the slogan to formulate, and which I have tried to explicate above, is a feminist idea. Notice, however, that, in briefly explaining the idea that I shall defend, I have not mentioned relations between men and women in particular, or the issue of sexism. We can distinguish between the substance and the form of the feminist critique of standard ideas about justice, and it is the form of it which is of prime concern to me here,[18] even though I also endorse its substance.

The substance of the feminist critique is that standard liberal theory of justice, and the theory of Rawls in particular, unjustifiably ignore an unjust division of labor, and unjust power relations, within families (whose legal structure *may* show no sexism at all). That is the key point of the feminist critique, from a political point of view. But the (often merely implicit) form of the feminist critique, which we get when we abstract from its gender-centered content, is that choices not regulated by the law fall within the primary purview of justice, and that is the key lesson of the critique, from a theoretical point of view.

Because I believe that the personal is political, in the specified sense, I reject Rawls's view that principles of justice apply only to what he calls the "basic structure" of society. Feminists have noticed that Rawls wobbles, across the course of his writings, on the matter of whether or not the family belongs to the basic structure and is therefore, in his view, a site at which principles of justice apply. I shall argue that Rawls's wobble on this matter is not a case of mere indecision, which could readily be resolved in favor of inclusion of the family within the basic structure; that is the view of Susan Okin,[19] and, in my opinion, she is wrong on this count. I shall show (in section 2 of Lecture 9) that Rawls cannot admit the family into the basic structure of society without abandoning his insistence that it is to the basic structure only that principles of distributive justice apply. In supposing that he could include family relations, Okin shows a failure to grasp the *form* of the feminist critique of Rawls.

5

I reach the conclusion announced above at the end of a trail of argument that runs as follows. Here, in section 5, I restate a criticism that I have made elsewhere of Rawls's application of his difference principle,[20] to wit, that he does not apply it in censure of the self-seeking choices of high-flying marketeers, choices which induce an inequality that, so I claim, is harmful to the badly off. In section 6, I present an objection to my criticism of Rawls. The objection says that the difference principle is, by stipulation and design, a principle that applies only to social institutions (to those, in particular, which compose the basic structure of society), and therefore not one that applies to the choices, such as those of self-seeking high fliers, that people make *within* such institutions. Sections 1 and 2 of Lecture 9 offer independent replies to that *basic-*

structure objection. I show, in section 1, that the objection is inconsistent with many statements by Rawls about the role of principles of justice in a just society. I then allow that the discordant statements may be dropped from the Rawlsian canon, and, in section 2, I reply afresh to the basic-structure objection, by showing that no defensible account of what the basic structure *is* allows Rawls to insist that the principles which apply to it do not apply to choices within it. I conclude that my original criticism of Rawls rests vindicated, against the particular objection at issue here. (Section 3 of Lecture 9 comments on the implications of my position for the moral blameability of individuals whose choices violate principles of justice. Section 4 explores the distinction between coercive and noncoercive institutions, which plays a key role in the argument of section 2.)

My criticism of Rawls is of his application of the difference principle. The principle says, in one of its formulations,[21] that inequalities are just if and only if they are necessary to make the worst off people in society better off than they would otherwise be. I have no quarrel here with the difference principle itself,[22] but I disagree sharply with Rawls on the matter of *which* inequalities pass the test for justifying inequality that it sets and, therefore, about how *much* inequality passes that test. In my view, there is hardly any serious inequality that satisfies the requirement set by the difference principle, when it is conceived, as Rawls himself proposes to conceive it,[23] as regulating the affairs of a society whose members themselves accept that principle. If I am right, affirmation of the difference principle implies that justice requires (virtually)[24] unqualified equality itself, as opposed to the "deep inequalities" in initial life chances with which Rawls thinks justice to be consistent.[25]

It is commonly thought, for example by Rawls, that the difference principle licenses an argument for inequality which centers on the device of material incentives. The idea is that talented people will produce more than they otherwise would if, and only if, they are paid more than an ordinary wage, and some of the extra which they will then produce can be recruited on behalf of the worst off.[26] The inequality consequent on differential material incentives is said to be justified within the terms of the difference principle, for, so it is said, that inequality benefits the worst off people: the inequality is necessary for them to be positioned as well as they are, however paltry their position may nevertheless be.

Now, before I mount my criticism of this argument, a caveat is necessary with respect to the terms in which it is expressed. The argument focuses on a *choice* enjoyed by well-placed people who command a high salary in a market economy: they can choose to work more or less hard, and also to work at this occupation rather than that one, and for this employer rather than that one, in accordance with how well they are remunerated. These well-placed people, in the foregoing standard presentation of the argument, are designated as "the talented," and, for reasons to be given presently, I shall so designate them throughout my criticism of the argument. Even so, these fortunate people need not be thought to be talented, in any sense of that word which implies something more than a capacity for high-market earnings, for the argument to possess whatever force it has. All that need be true of them is that *they are so positioned that, happily for them, they do command a high salary and they can vary their productivity according to exactly how high it is.* But, as far as the incentives argument is concerned, their happy position could be due to circumstances that are entirely accidental, relative to whatever kind of natural or even socially induced endowment they possess. One need not think that the average dishwasher's endowment of strength, flair, ingenuity, and so forth falls below that of the average chief executive to accept the argument's message. One no doubt does need to think some such thing to agree with the different argument which justifies rewards to well-placed people in whole or in part as a fair return to exercise of unusual ability, but Rawls's theory is built around his rejection of such desert considerations. Nor does Rawls believe that the enhanced rewards are justified because extra contribution warrants extra reward on grounds of proper reciprocity. They are justified, in his view, purely because they elicit more productive performance.

I nevertheless persist in designating the relevant individuals as "the talented," because to object that they are not actually especially talented *anyway* is to enter an empirical claim which is both contentious and, in context, misleading, since it would give the impression that it should matter to our assessment of the incentives argument whether or not well-placed people merit the contestable designation. The particular criticism of the incentives argument that I shall develop is best understood in its specificity when the apparently concessive word "talented" is used; it does not indicate a concession on the factual question of how top people in a market society get to be where they are. My use of the argument's own terms shows the strength of my critique of it: the critique stands even if we make generous assumptions about how well-placed people secured their powerful market positions. It is, moreover, especially appropriate to make such assumptions here, since the Rawlsian difference principle is lexically secondary to his principle that fair equality of opportunity has been enforced with respect to the attainment of desired positions; if anything ensures that those who occupy them possess superior creative endowment, that does. (Which is not to say that it indeed ensures that. It is consistent with fair equality of opportunity that what principally distinguishes top people is superior cunning and/or prodigious aggressivity, and nothing more admirable.)

Now, for the following reasons, I believe that the incentives argument for inequality represents a distorted application of the difference principle, even though it is its most familiar and perhaps even its most persuasive application. Either the relevant talented people themselves affirm the difference principle or they do not. That is, either they themselves believe that inequalities are unjust if they are not necessary to make the badly off better off, or they do not believe that to be a dictate of justice. If they do not believe it, then their society is not just in the appropriate Rawlsian sense, for a society is just, according to Rawls, only if its members themselves affirm and uphold the correct principles of justice. The difference principle might be appealed to in justification of a government's toleration, or promotion, of inequality in a society in which the talented do not themselves accept it, but it then justifies a public policy of inequality in a society some members of which—the talented—do not share community with the rest.[27] Their behavior is then taken as fixed or parametric, a datum vis-à-vis a principle applied to it from without, rather than as itself answerable to that principle. That is not how principles of justice operate in a just society, as Rawls specifies the concept: within his terms, one may distinguish between a just society and a just government—one, that is, which applies just principles to a society whose members may not themselves accept those principles.

So we turn to the second and only remaining possibility, which is that the talented people do affirm the difference principle—that, as Rawls says, they apply the principles of justice *in their daily life* and achieve a sense of their own justice in doing so.[28] But they can then be asked why, in the light of their own belief in the principle, they require more pay than the untalented get, for work which may indeed demand special talent but which is not specially unpleasant (for no such consideration enters the Rawlsian justification of incentives-derived inequality). The talented can be asked whether the extra they get is *necessary* to enhance the position of the worst off, which is the only thing, according to the difference principle, that could justify it. Is it necessary *tout court*—that is, independently of human will, so that with all the will in the world, removal of inequality would make everyone worse off? Or is it necessary only insofar as the talented would *decide* to produce less than they now do, or to not take up posts where they are in special demand, if inequality were removed (by, for example, income taxation which redistributes to fully egalitarian effect)?[29]

Talented people who affirm the difference principle would find those questions hard to handle. For they could not claim, *in self-justification,* at the bar of the difference principle, that their high rewards are necessary to enhance the position of the worst off, since, in the standard case,[30] it is they themselves who *make* those rewards necessary, through their own unwillingness to work for ordinary rewards as productively as they do for exceptionally high ones, an unwillingness which ensures that the untalented get less than they otherwise would. High rewards are, therefore, necessary only because the choices of talented people are not appropriately informed by the difference principle.[31]

Apart, then, from the very special cases in which the talented literally *could* not—as opposed to the normal case where they (merely) would not—perform as productively as they do without superior remuneration, the difference principle can justify inequality only in a society where not everyone accepts that very principle. It therefore cannot justify inequality in the appropriate Rawlsian way.

Now, this conclusion about what it means to accept and implement the difference principle implies that the justice of a society is not exclusively a function of its legislative structure, of its legally imperative rules, but is also a function of the choices people make within those rules. The standard (and in my view misguided) Rawlsian application of the difference principle can be modeled as follows. There is a market economy in which all agents seek to maximize their own gains, and there is a Rawlsian state that selects a tax function on income that maximizes the income return to the worst off people, within the constraint that, because of the self-seeking motivation of the talented, a fully equalizing taxation system would make everyone worse off than one which is less than fully equalizing. But this double-minded modeling of the implementation of the difference principle, with citizens inspired by justice endorsing a state policy which plays a tax game against (some of) them in their manifestation as self-seeking economic agents, is wholly out of accord with the (sound) Rawlsian requirement on a just society that its citizens themselves willingly submit to the standard of justice embodied in the difference principle. A society that is just within the terms of the difference principle, so we may conclude, requires not simply just coercive *rules*, but also an *ethos* of justice that informs individual choices. In the absence of such an ethos, inequalities will obtain that are not necessary to enhance the condition of the worst off: the required ethos promotes a distribution more just than what the rules of the economic game by themselves can secure. And what is required is indeed an ethos, a structure of response lodged in the motivations that inform everyday life, not only because it is impossible to design rules of egalitarian economic choice conformity with which can always be checked,[32] but also because it would severely compromise liberty if people were required forever to consult such rules, even supposing that appropriate applicable rules could be formulated.[33]

To be sure, one might imagine, in the abstract, a set of coercive rules so finely tuned that universally self-interested choices within them would raise the worst off to as high a position as any other pattern of choices would produce. Where coercive rules had and were known to have such a character, agents could choose self-interestedly and be confident that the results of their choices would satisfy an appropriately uncompromising interpretation of the difference principle. In that (imaginary) case, the only ethos necessary for difference-principle justice would be willing obedience to the relevant rules, an ethos which Rawls expressly requires. But the vast economics literature on incentive-compatibility teaches that rules of the contemplated perfect kind cannot be designed. Accordingly, as things actually are, the required ethos must, as I have argued, guide choice within the rules, and not merely direct agents to obey them. (I should emphasize that this is not so because it is *in general* true that the point of the rules governing an activity must be aimed at when agents pursue that activity in good faith. Every competitive sport represents a counterexample to that generalization. But my argument for the conclusion stated above did not rest on the stated false generalization.)[34]

6

There is an objection which friends of Rawls's *Theory of Justice* would press against my argument in criticism of his application of the difference principle. The objection is that my focus on the posture of talented producers in daily economic life is inappropriate, since their behavior occurs within, and does not determine, *the basic structure* of society, and it is only to the latter that the difference principle applies.[35] Whatever people's choices within it may be, the basic structure is just provided that it satisfies the two principles of justice. To be sure, so Rawls acknowledges, people's choices can themselves be assessed as just or unjust, from a number of points of view. Thus, for example, capriciously appointing candidate A rather than candidate B to a given post might be judged unjust, even when it occurs within the rules of a just basic structure (since those rules could not feasibly be designed to outlaw the variety of caprice in question).[36] But such injustice in choice is not the sort of injustice that the Rawlsian principles are designed to condemn. For, *ex hypothesi,* that choice occurs within an established basic structure; it therefore cannot affect the justice of the basic structure itself, which is what, according to Rawls, the two principles govern. Nor, similarly, should the choices with respect to work and remuneration that talented people make be submitted for judgment at the bar of the difference principle. So to judge those choices is to apply the principle at the wrong point. The difference principle is a "principle of justice for institutions."[37] It governs the choice of institutions, not the choices made within them. Accordingly, the development of the second horn of the dilemma argument in section 5 above misconstrues the Rawlsian requirement that citizens in a just society uphold the principles that make it just. By virtue of the stipulated scope of the difference principle, talented people do count as faithfully upholding it, as long as they conform to the prevailing economic rules *because* that principle requires those rules.

Call that "the basic-structure objection." Now, before I develop it further, and then reply to it, I wish to point out that there is an important ambiguity in the concept of the basic structure, as that is wielded by Rawlsians. The ambiguity turns on whether the Rawlsian basic structure includes only coercive aspects of the social order or, also, conventions and usages that are deeply entrenched but not legally or literally coercive. I shall return to that ambiguity in section 2 of Lecture 9, and I shall show that it shipwrecks not only the basic-structure objection but also the whole approach to justice that Rawls has taught so many to pursue. But, for the time being, I shall ignore the fatal ambiguity, and I shall take the phrase "basic structure," as it appears in the basic-structure objection, as denoting *some* sort of structure, be it legally coercive or not, but whose key feature, for the purposes of the objection, is that it is indeed a structure—that is, a framework of rules within which choices are made, as opposed to a set of choices and/or actions. Accordingly, my Rawlsian critic would say, whatever structure, precisely, the basic structure is, the objection stands that my criticism of the incentives argument misapplies principles devised for a structure to individual choices and actions.

In further clarification of the polemical position, let me make a background point about the difference between Rawls and me with respect to the site or sites at which principles of justice apply. My own fundamental concern is neither the basic structure of society, in any sense, nor people's individual choices, but the pattern of benefits and burdens in society—that is neither a structure in which choice occurs nor a set of choices, but the upshot of structure and choices alike. My concern is *distributive justice,* by which I uneccentrically mean justice (and its lack) in the distribution of benefits and burdens to individuals. My root belief is that there is injustice in distribution when inequality of goods reflects not such things as differences in the arduousness of different people's labors, or people's different preferences and choices with respect to income and leisure, but myriad forms of lucky and unlucky circumstance. Such differences of advantage are a function of the structure *and* of people's choices within it; so I am concerned, secondarily, with *both* of those.

Now, Rawls could say that his concern, too, is distributive justice, in the specified sense, but that, for him, distributive justice obtains just in case the allocation of benefits and burdens in society results from actions which display full conformity with the rules of a just basic structure.[38] When full compliance with the rules of a just basic structure obtains, it follows, on Rawls's view, that there is no scope for (further) personal justice and injustice which affects *distributive* justice, whether it be by enhancing it or by reducing it. There is, Rawls would of course readily agree, scope within a just structure for distribution-affecting meanness and generosity;[39] but generosity, though it would alter the distribution, and might make it more equal than it would otherwise be, could not make it more *just* than it would otherwise be, for it would then be doing the impossible—to wit, enhancing the justice of what is already established as a (perfectly) just distribution by virtue merely of the just structure in conformity with which it is produced. But as I have indicated, I believe that there is scope for relevant (relevant, that is, because it affects justice in distribution) personal justice and injustice *within* a just structure, and, indeed, that it is impossible to achieve distributive justice by purely structural means.

In discussion of my claim (see section 5 above) that social justice requires a social *ethos* which inspires uncoerced equality-supporting choice, Ronald Dworkin suggested[40] that a Rawlsian government might be thought to be charged with a duty, under the difference principle, of promoting such an ethos. Dworkin's suggestion was intended to support Rawls, against me, by diminishing the difference between Rawls's position and my own, and thereby reducing the reach of my criticism of him. I do not know what Rawls's response to Dworkin's proposal would be, but one thing is clear: Rawls could not say that, to the extent that the indicated ethos-promoting policy failed, society would, as a result, be less just than if the policy had been more successful. Accordingly, if Dworkin is right that Rawlsian justice requires government to promote an ethos friendly to equality, it could not be for the sake of making society more distributively just that it was doing so, *even* though it would be for the sake of making its distribution more *equal*. The following threefold conjunction, which is an inescapable consequence of Rawls's position, on Dworkin's not unnatural interpretation of it, is strikingly incongruous: (1) the difference principle is an egalitarian principle of distributive justice; (2) it imposes on government a duty to promote an egalitarian ethos; (3) it is not for the sake of enhancing distributive justice in society that it is required to promote that ethos. Dworkin's attempt to reduce the distance between Rawls's position and my own threatens to expose the former as incoherent.

Now, before I mount my two replies to the basic-structure objection, a brief conceptual digression is required, in clarification of the relationship between a just *society,* in Rawls's (and my own) understanding of that idea, and a just *distribution,* in my (non-Rawlsian) understanding of that different idea. A just society, here, is one whose citizens affirm and act upon the correct principles of justice, but justice in distribution, as here defined, consists in a certain egalitarian profile of rewards. It follows that, as a matter of logical possibility, a just distribution might obtain in a society that is not itself just.

To illustrate this possibility, imagine a society whose ethos, though not inspired by a belief in equality, nevertheless induces an equal distribution. An example of such an ethos would be an intense Protestant ethic, which is indifferent to equality (on earth) as such, but whose stress on self-denial, hard work, and investment of assets surplus to needs somehow (despite the asceticism in it) makes the worst off as well off as it is possible for them to be. Such an ethos achieves difference-principle justice in distribution, but agents informed by it would not be motivated by the difference principle, and they could not therefore themselves be accounted just, within the terms of that principle.[41] Under the specifications that have been introduced here, this Protestant society would not be just, despite the fact that it displays a just distribution. We might say of the society that it is accidentally, but not constitutively, just. But whatever phrasings we may prefer, the important thing is to distinguish "society" and "distribution" as candidate subjects of the predicate "just." (And it bears mentioning that, in contemporary practice, an ethos that achieves difference-principle equality would almost certainly have to be equality-inspired; the accident of a non-equality-inspired ethos producing the right result is, at least in modern times, highly unlikely. The Protestantism I have described in this paragraph is utterly fantastic, at least for our day.)

Less arresting is the opposite case, in which people strive to govern their behavior by (what are in fact) just principles, but ignorance, or the obduracy of wholly external circumstance, or collective action problems, or self-defeatingness of the kinds studied by Derek Parfit,[42] or something else which I have not thought of, frustrates their intention, so that the distribution remains unjust. It would perhaps be peculiar to call such a society *just,* and neither Rawls nor I need do so: justice in citizens was posited, above, as a *necessary* condition of a just society.

However we resolve the secondary, and largely verbal, complications raised in this digression, the point will stand[43] that an ethos which informs choice within just rules is necessary in a society committed to the difference principle. My argument for that conclusion relied not on aspects of my conception of justice which distinguish it from Rawls's, but on our shared conception of what a just society is. The fact that distributive justice, as I conceive it, (causally) requires an ethos (be it merely equality-promoting, such as our imaginary Protestantism, or also equality-inspired) that goes beyond conformity to just rules was not a premise in my argument against Rawls. The argument of section 5 turned essentially on my understanding of Rawls's well-considered requirement that the citizens of a just society are themselves just. The basic-structure objection challenges that understanding.

Where the Action Is

On the Site of Distributive Justice

Only when the actual, individual man has taken back into himself the
abstract citizen and in his everyday life, his individual work, and his individual relationships has become a *species-being,* only when he has
recognized and organized his own powers as *social* powers so that social power is no longer separated from him as *political* power, only then
is human emancipation complete.

Karl Marx, "On the Jewish Question"

1

I now present a preliminary reply to the basic-structure objection. It is
preliminary in that it precedes my interrogation, in section 2, of what
the phrase "basic structure" denotes, and also in that, by contrast with
the fundamental reply that will follow that interrogation, there is a certain way out for Rawls, in face of the preliminary reply. That way out is
not costless for him, but it does exist.

Although Rawls says often enough that the two principles of justice
govern only justice in basic structure, he also says three things which
tell against that restriction. This means that, in each case, he must either
uphold the restriction and repudiate the comment in question, or maintain the comment and drop the restriction.[1]

First, Rawls says that, when the difference principle is satisfied, society displays *fraternity,* in a particularly strong sense: its citizens do not
want "to have greater advantages unless this is to the benefit of others
who are less well off. . . . Members of a family commonly do not wish to
gain unless they can do so in ways that further the interests of the rest.
Now, wanting to act on the difference principle has precisely this conse-

quence."[2] But fraternity of that strong kind is not realized when all the justice delivered by the difference principle comes from the basic structure, and, therefore, whatever people's motivations in economic interaction may be. Wanting not "to gain unless they can do so in ways that further the interests of the rest" is incompatible with the self-interested motivation of market maximizers, which the difference principle, in its purely structural interpretation, does not condemn.[3]

Second, Rawls says that the worst off in a society governed by the difference principle can bear their inferior position with dignity, since they know that no improvement of it is possible, that they would lose under any less unequal dispensation. Yet that is false, if justice relates to structure alone, since it might then be necessary for the worst off to occupy their relatively low place only because the choices of the better off tend strongly against equality. Why should the fact that no purely structurally induced improvement in their position is possible suffice to guarantee the dignity of the worst off, when their position might be very inferior indeed, because of unlimited self-seekingness in the economic choices of well-placed people?[4] Suppose, for example, that (as politicians now routinely claim) raising rates of income taxation with a view to enhancing benefits for the badly off would be counterproductive, since the higher rates would induce severe disincentive effects on the productivity of the better off. Would awareness of that truth contribute to a sense of dignity on the part of the badly off?

Third, Rawls says that people in a just society act with a sense of justice *from* the principles of justice in their daily lives; they strive to apply those principles in their own choices. And they do so because they "have a desire to express their nature as free and equal moral persons, and this they do most adequately by acting *from* the principles that they would acknowledge in the original position. When all strive to comply with these principles and each succeeds, then individually and collectively their nature as moral persons is most fully realized, and with it their individual and collective good."[5] But why do they have to act *from* the principles of justice, and "apply" them "as their circumstances require,"[6] if it suffices for justice that they choose as they please within a structure designed to effect an implementation of those principles? And how can they, without a redolence of hypocrisy, celebrate the full realization of their natures as moral persons, when they know that they are out for the most that they can get in the market?

Now, as I said, these inconsistencies are not decisive against Rawls. For, in each case, he could stand pat on his restriction of justice to basic structure, and give up, or weaken, the remark that produces the inconsistency. And that is indeed what he is disposed to do, at least with respect to the third inconsistency that I have noted. He said[7] that *A Theory of Justice* erred by in some respects treating the two principles as defining a *comprehensive* conception of justice;[8] he would, accordingly, now drop the high-pitched homily which constitutes the text to note 5 above. But this accommodation carries a cost: it means that the ideals of dignity, fraternity, and full realization of people's moral natures can no longer be said to be delivered by Rawlsian justice.[9]

2

I now provide a more fundamental reply to the basic-structure objection. It is more fundamental in that it shows, decisively, that justice requires an ethos governing daily choice which goes beyond one of obedience to just rules,[10] on grounds which do not, as the preliminary reply did, exploit things that Rawls says in apparent contradiction of his stipulation that justice applies to the basic structure of society alone. The fundamental reply interrogates, and refutes, that stipulation itself.

A major fault line in the Rawlsian architectonic not only wrecks the basic-structure objection but also produces a dilemma for Rawls's view of the subject[11] of justice—a dilemma from which I can imagine no way out. The fault line exposes itself when we ask the apparently simple question: What (exactly) *is* the basic structure? For there is a fatal ambiguity in Rawls's specification of the basic structure, and an associated discrepancy between his criterion for what justice judges and his desire to exclude the effects of structure-consistent personal choice from the purview of its judgment.

The basic structure, the primary subject of justice, is always said by Rawls to be a set of institutions, and, so he infers, the principles of justice do not judge the actions of people within (just) institutions whose rules they observe. But it is seriously unclear *which* institutions are supposed to qualify as part of the basic structure. Sometimes it appears that coercive (in the legal sense) institutions exhaust it, or, better, that institutions belong to it only insofar as they are (legally) coercive.[12] In this widespread interpretation of what Rawls intends by the "basic structure" of a society, that structure is legible in the provisions of its constitution, in such specific legislation as may be required to implement those provisions, and in further legislation and policy which are of central importance but which resist formulation in the constitution itself.[13] The basic structure, in this first understanding of it, is, so one might say, the *broad coercive outline* of society, which determines in a relatively fixed and general way what people may and must do, in advance of legislation that is optional, relative to the principles of justice, and irrespective of the constraints and opportunities created and destroyed by the choices that people make within the given basic structure, so understood.

Yet it is quite unclear that the basic structure is *always* to be so understood, in exclusively coercive terms, within the Rawlsian texts. For Rawls often says that the basic structure consists of the *major* social institutions, and he does not put a particular accent on coercion when he announces *that* specification of the basic structure.[14] In this second reading of what it is, institutions belong to the basic structure whose structuring can depend far less on law than on convention, usage, and expectation; a signal example is the family, which Rawls sometimes includes in the basic structure and sometimes does not.[15] But once the line is crossed, from coercive ordering to the noncoercive ordering of society by rules and conventions of accepted practice, then the ambit of justice can no longer exclude chosen behavior, since, at least in certain cases, the prescriptions that constitute informal structure (think, again, of the family) are bound up with the choices that people customarily make.

"Bound up with" is vague, so let me explain how I mean it here. One can certainly speak of the structure of the family, and it is not identical with the choices that people customarily make within it; but it is nevertheless impossible to claim that the principles of justice which apply to family structure do not apply to day-to-day choices within it. For consider the following contrast. The *coercive* structure, let us provisionally accept,[16] arises independently of people's quotidian choices: it is formed by those specialized choices which legislate the law of the land. But the noncoercive structure of the family has the character it does only because of the choices that its members routinely make. The constraints and pressures that sustain the noncoercive structure reside in the dispositions of agents which are actualized as and when those agents choose to act in a constraining or pressuring way. With respect to coercive structure, one may, perhaps, fairly readily distinguish the choices which institute and sustain a structure from the choices that occur within it.[17] But with respect to informal structure, that distinction, though conceptually intelligible, is compromised extensionally. When A chooses to conform to the prevailing usages, the pressure on B to do so is reinforced; and no such pressure exists, the very usages themselves do not exist, in the absence of conformity to them. Structure and choice remain distinguishable, but not from the point of view of the applicability to them of principles of justice.

Now, since that is so, since appropriately conforming behavior is (at least partly) *constitutive* of *non*coercive structure, it follows that the only way of sustaining the basic-structure objection against my claim that the difference principle condemns maximizing economic behavior (and, more generally, of sustaining the restriction of justice to the basic structure against the insistence that the personal, too, is political) is by holding fast to a purely coercive specification of the basic structure. But that way out is not open to Rawls, because of a further characterization that he offers of the basic structure: this is where the discrepancy adverted to in the second paragraph of this section appears. For Rawls says that "the basic structure is the primary subject of justice because its effects are so profound and present from the start."[18] Nor is this further characterization of the basic structure optional: it is needed to explain why it *is* primary, as far as justice is concerned. Yet it is false that only the *coercive* structure causes profound effects, as the example of the family once again reminds us:[19] if the "values [that] govern the basic [political] framework of social life" thereby govern "the very groundwork of our existence,"[20] so too do the values that govern our nurture and conduct in the family. Accordingly, if Rawls retreats to coercive structure, he contradicts his own criterion for what justice judges, and he lands himself with an arbitrarily narrow definition of his subject matter. So he must let other structure in, and that means, as we have seen, letting chosen behavior in. What is more, even if behavior did not, as I claim it does, partly constitute the noncoercive structure, it will come in by direct appeal to the profundity-of-effect criterion for what justice governs. So, for example, we need not decide whether or not a regular practice of favoring sons over daughters in the matter of providing higher education forms part of the *structure* of the family to condemn it as unjust, under that criterion.[21]

Given, then, his stated rationale[22] for exclusive focus on the basic structure—and what *other* rationale could there be for calling it the *primary* subject of justice?—Rawls is in a dilemma. For he must either admit application of the principles of justice to (legally optional) social practices, and, indeed, to patterns of personal choice that are not legally prescribed, *both* because they are the substance of those practices, *and* because they are similarly profound in effect, in which case the restriction of justice to structure, in any sense, collapses; or, if he restricts his concern to the coercive structure only, then he saddles himself with a purely arbitrary delineation of his subject matter. I now illustrate this dilemma by reference to the two items that have already figured in Lectures 8 and 9: the family and the market economy.

Family structure is fateful for the benefits and burdens that redound to different people, and, in particular, to people of different sexes, where "family structure" includes the socially constructed expectations which lie on husband and wife. And such expectations are sexist and unjust if, for example, they direct the woman in a family where both spouses work outside the home to carry a greater burden of domestic tasks. Yet such expectations need not be supported by the law for them to possess informal coercive force: sexist family structure is consistent with sex-neutral family law. Here, then, is a circumstance, outside the basic structure, as that would be coercively defined, which profoundly affects people's life-chances, *through the choices people make in response to the stated expectations, which are, in turn, sustained by those choices.*[23] Yet Rawls must say, on pain of giving up the basic-structure objection, that (legally uncoerced) family structure and behavior have no implications for justice in the sense of "justice" in which the basic structure has implications for justice, since they are not a consequence of the formal coercive order. But that implication of the stated position is perfectly incredible: no such differentiating sense is available.

John Stuart Mill taught us to recognize that informal social pressure can restrict liberty as much as formal coercive law does. And the family example shows that informal pressure is as relevant to distributive justice as it is to liberty. One reason why the rules of the basic structure, when it is coercively defined, do not by themselves determine the justice of the distributive upshot is that, by virtue of circumstances that are relevantly independent of coercive rules, some people have much more power than others to determine what happens *within* those rules.

The second illustration of discrepancy between what coercive structure commands and what profoundly affects the distribution of benefits and burdens is my own point about incentives. Maximinizing legislation,[24] and, hence, a coercive basic structure that satisfies the difference principle, are consistent with a maximizing ethos across society which, under many conditions, will produce severe inequalities and a meager level of provision for the worst off; yet both have to be declared just by Rawls, if he stays with a coercive conception of what justice judges. And that implication is, surely, perfectly incredible.

Rawls cannot deny the difference between the coercively defined basic structure and that which produces major distributive consequences: the coercively defined basic structure is only an instance of the latter. Yet he must, to retain his position on justice and personal choice, restrict the ambit of justice to what a coercive basic structure produces. But, so I have (by implication) asked: Why should we *care* so disproportionately about the coercive basic structure, when the major reason for caring about it, its impact on people's lives, is *also* a reason for caring about informal structure and patterns of personal choice? To the extent that we care about coercive structure because it is fateful with regard to benefits and burdens, we must care equally about the ethic that sustains gender inequality, and inegalitarian incentives. And the similarity of our reasons for caring about these matters will make it lame to say: Ah, but only the caring about coercive structure is a caring about *justice,* in a certain distinguishable sense. That thought is, I submit, incapable of coherent elaboration.[25]

My response to the basic-structure objection is now fully laid out; but before we proceed, in the sections that follow, to matters arising, it will be useful to rehearse, in compressed form, the arguments that were presented in the foregoing four sections of this book (including, that is, sections 5 and 6 of Lecture 8).

My original criticism of the incentives argument ran, in brief, as follows:

(1) Citizens in a just society adhere to its principles of justice.

But

(2) They do not adhere to the difference principle if they are acquisitive maximizers in daily life.

Therefore

(3) In a society that is governed by the difference principle, citizens lack the acquisitiveness that the incentives argument attributes to them.

The basic-structure objection to that criticism is of this form:

(4) The principles of justice govern only the basic structure of a just society.

Therefore,

(5) Citizens in a just society may adhere to the difference principle whatever their choices may be within the structure it determines, and, in particular, even if their economic choices are entirely acquisitive.

Therefore,

(6) Proposition (2) lacks justification.

My preliminary reply to the basic-structure objection says:

(7) Proposition (5) is inconsistent with many Rawlsian statements about the relationship between citizens and principles of justice in a just society.

And my fundamental reply to the basic-structure objection says:

(8) Proposition (4) is unsustainable.

Let me emphasize that my rebuttal of the basic-structure objection does not *itself* establish that the difference principle properly evaluates not only state policy but everyday economic choice. The argument for that conclusion is given in my "Incentives" lectures, and summarized in section 5 of Lecture 8 above. I do not say that *because* everyday choice cannot be, as the basic-structure objection says it is, beyond the reach of justice, simply because it *is* everyday choice, it then follows that everyday economic choice is indeed within its reach; that would be a non sequitur. I say, rather, that it is no objection to my argument for the claim that justice evaluates everyday economic choice that everyday choice is (in general) beyond the reach of justice, since it is not.

This point about the structure of my argument is easily missed, so let me explain it in a different way. I have not tried to show that a robust structure/choice distinction cannot be sustained in the case of the economy—that claim is false. What I argued is that choices within the economic structure cannot be placed outside the primary purview of justice *on the ground* that the only thing (quite generally) which is within its primary purview is structure. The family case refutes that *argument*. That refutation doesn't, I would agree, exclude treating economic choices like the choices of a game player who obeys the rules (and therefore plays not unjustly), while trying to score as many points as he can.[26] What excludes that, what defeats that analogy, is the argument summarized in section 5 of Lecture 8 above.

3

So the personal is indeed political: personal choices to which the writ of the law is indifferent are fateful for social justice.

But that raises a huge question, with respect to *blame*. The injustice in distribution which reflects personal choices within a just coercive structure can plainly not be blamed on that structure itself, nor, therefore, on whoever legislated that structure. Must it, then, be blamed, in our two examples, on men[27] and on acquisitive people, respectively?

I shall presently address, and answer, that question about blame; but before I do so, I wish to explain why I could remain silent in the face of it—why, that is, my argument in criticism of Rawls's restricted application of the principles of justice requires no judgment about blaming individual choosers. The conclusion of my argument is that the principles of justice apply not only to coercive rules but also to the pattern in people's (legally) uncoerced choices. Now, if we judge a certain set of rules to be just or unjust, we need not add, as pendant to that judgment, that those who legislated the rules in question should be praised or blamed for what they did.[28] And something analogous applies when we come to see that the ambit of justice covers the pattern of choices in a society. We can believe whatever we are inclined to do about how responsible and/or culpable people are for their choices, and that includes believing that they are not responsible and/or culpable for them at all, while affirming the view on which I insist: that the pattern in such choices is relevant to how just or unjust a society is.

That said, let me now face the question of how blameable individuals are. It would be inappropriate to answer it here by first declaring my position, if indeed I have one, on the philosophical problem of the freedom of the will. Instead, I shall answer the question about blame on the prephilosophical assumptions which inform our ordinary judgments about when, and how much, blame is appropriate. On such assumptions, we should avoid two opposite mistakes about how culpable chauvinistic men and self-seeking high fliers are. One is the mistake of saying: there is no ground for blaming these people *as individuals,* for they simply participate in an accepted social practice, however tawdry or awful that practice may be. That is a mistake, since people do have choices: it is, indeed, *only* their choices that reproduce social practices; and some, moreover, choose *against* the grain of nurture, habit, and self-interest. But one also must not say: look how each of these people shamefully decides to behave so badly. That, too, is unbalanced, since, although there exists personal choice, there is heavy social conditioning behind it and it can cost individuals a lot to depart from the prescribed and/or permitted ways. If we care about social justice, we have to look at four things: the coercive structure, other structures, the social ethos, and the choices of individuals; and judgment on the last of those must be informed by awareness of the power of the others. So, for example, a properly sensitive appreciation of these matters allows one to hold that an acquisitive ethos is profoundly unjust in its effects, without holding that those who are gripped by it are commensurately unjust. It is essential to apply principles of justice to dominant patterns in social behavior—that, as it were, is where the action is—but it doesn't follow that we should have a persecuting attitude to the people who display that behavior. We might have good reason to exonerate the perpetrators of injustice, but we should not deny, or apologize for, the injustice itself.[29]

On an extreme view, which I do not accept but need not reject, a typical husband in a thoroughly sexist society—one, that is, in which families in their overwhelming majority display an unjust division of domestic labor—is literally incapable of revising his behavior, or capable of revising it only at the cost of cracking up, to nobody's benefit. But even if that is true of typical husbands, we know it to be false of husbands in general. It is a plain empirical fact that some husbands are capable of revising their behavior, since some husbands have done so, in response to feminist criticism. These husbands, we could say, were moral pioneers. They made a path which becomes easier and easier to follow as more and more people follow it, until social pressures are so altered that it becomes harder to stick to sexist ways than to abandon them. That is a central way in which a social ethos changes. Or, for another example, consider the recent rise in environmental awareness. At first, only a few people bother to save and recycle their paper, plastic, and so forth, and they seem freaky because they do so. Then, more people start doing that, and, finally, it becomes not only difficult not to do it but easy to do it. It is pretty easy to discharge burdens that have become part of the normal round of everybody's life. Expectations determine behavior, behavior determines expectations, which determine behavior, and so on.

Are there circumstances in which a similar incremental process could occur with respect to economic behavior? I do not know. But I do know that universal maximizing is by no means a necessary feature of a market economy. For all that much of its industry was state-owned, the United Kingdom from 1945 to 1951 had a market economy. But salary differentials were nothing like as great as they were to become, or as they were then, in the United States. Yet, so I hazard, when British executives making five times what their workers did met American counterparts making fifteen times what their (anyhow better paid) workers did, many of the British executives would *not* have felt: *we* should press for more. For there was a social ethos of reconstruction after war, an ethos of common project, that moderated desire for personal gain. It is not for a philosopher to delimit the conditions under which such—and even more egalitarian—ethi can prevail. But a philosopher can say that a maximizing ethos is not a necessary feature of society, or even of a market society, and that, to the extent that such an ethos prevails, satisfaction of the difference principle is prejudiced.

In 1988, the ratio of top-executive salaries to production-worker wages was 6.5 to 1 in West Germany and 17.5 to 1 in the United States.[30] Since it is not plausible to think that Germany's lesser inequality was a disincentive to productivity, since it *is* plausible to think that an ethos which was relatively friendly to equality[31] protected German productivity in the face of relatively modest material incentives, we can conclude that the said ethos caused the worst paid to be better paid than they would have been under a different culture of reward. It follows, on my view of the matter, that the difference principle was better realized in Germany in 1988 than it would have been if its culture of reward had been more similar to that of the United States.[32] But Rawls cannot say that, since the smaller inequality that benefited the less well off in Germany was a matter not of law but of ethos. I think that Rawls's inability to regard Germany as having done comparatively well with respect to the difference principle is a grave defect in his conception of the site of distributive justice.

4

I should like, now, to modify the distinction drawn in section 2 above between coercive and other social structure. The modification will strengthen my argument against the basic-structure objection.

The legally coercive structure of society functions in two ways. It *prevents* people from doing things by erecting insurmountable barriers (fences, police lines, prison walls, and so forth), and it *deters* people from doing things by ensuring that certain forms of unprevented behavior carry an (appreciable risk of) penalty.[33] The second (deterrent) aspect of coercive structure may be described counterfactually, in terms of what would or might happen to someone who elects the forbidden behavior: knowledge of the relevant counterfactual truths motivates the complying citizen's choices.

Not much pure prevention goes on within the informal structure of society; not none, but not much. Locking errant teenagers in their rooms would represent an instance of pure prevention, which, if predictable for determinate behavior, would count as part of a society's informal structure: it would be a rule in accordance with which that society operates. That being set aside, informal structure manifests itself in predictable sanctions such as criticism, disapproval, anger, refusal of future cooperation, ostracism, beating (of, for example, spouses who refuse sexual service), and so on.

Finally, to complete this conceptual review, the ethos of a society is the set of sentiments and attitudes in virtue of which its normal practices, and informal pressures, are what they are.

Now, the pressures that sustain the informal structure lack force save insofar as there is a normal practice of compliance with the rules they enforce. That is especially true of that great majority of those pressures (beating does not belong to that majority) which have a moral coloring: criticism and disapproval are ineffective when they come from the mouths of those who ask others not to do what they do themselves. To be sure, that is not a conceptual truth, but a social-psychological one. Even so, it enables us to say that what people ordinarily do supports and partly constitutes (again, not conceptually, but in effect) the informal structure of society, in such a way that it makes no sense to pass judgments of justice on that structure while withholding such judgment from the behavior that supports and constitutes it; that point is crucial to the anti-Rawlsian inference presented in section 2 above.[34] Informal structure is not a behavioral pattern but a set of rules, yet the two are so closely related that, so one might say, they are *merely* categorially different. Accordingly, so I argued, to include (as one must) informal structure within the basic structure is to countenance behavior, too, as a primary object of judgments of justice.

Now, two truths about legally coercive structure might be thought to cast doubt on the contrast that I allowed between it and informal structure in section 2 above. First, although the legally coercive structure of society is indeed discernible in the ordinances of society's political constitution and law, those ordinances count as delineating it only on condition that they enjoy a broad measure of compliance.[35] And, second, legally coercive structure achieves its intended social effect only in and through the actions which constitute compliance with its rules.

In light of those truths, it might be thought that the dilemma I posed for Rawls (see section 2 above), and by means of which I sought to defeat his claim that justice judges structure *as opposed to* the actions of agents, was misframed. For I said, against that claim, that the required opposition between structure and actions works for coercive structure only, with respect to which a relevantly strong distinction can be drawn between structure-sustaining and structure-conforming action, but that coercive structure could not reasonably be thought to exhaust the structure falling within the purview of justice. Accordingly, so I concluded, justice must also judge (at least some) everyday actions.

The truths rehearsed two paragraphs back challenge that articulation of the distinction between coercive structure and action within it. They thereby also challenge the contrast drawn in section 2 between two relationships: that between coercive structure and action, and that between informal structure and action. And to the extent that the first relationship is more like the second, the first horn of the dilemma I posed for Rawls becomes sharper than it was. It is sharp not only for the reason I gave, namely, the consideration about "profound effect," but also for the same reason that the second horn is sharp, namely, that everyday behavior is too germane to the very existence of (even) coercive structure to be immune to the principles of justice that apply to the coercive structure.

The distinction, vis-à-vis action, between coercive and informal structure, so I judge, is more blurred than section 2 allowed—not, of course, because informal structure is more separable from action than I originally claimed, but because coercive structure is less separable from it than I originally allowed. Accordingly, even if the dilemma constructed in section 2 was for the stated reasons misframed, the upshot would hardly be congenial to Rawls's position—that justice judges structure rather than actions—it would, rather, be congenial to my own rejection of it. But I wish to emphasize that this putative strengthening of my argument is not essential. In my opinion, the argument was strong enough already.[36]

10

Political Philosophy and
Personal Behavior

If You're an Egalitarian, How Come You're so Rich?

There may be coarse hypocrites, who consciously affect beliefs and emotions for the sake of gulling the world, but Bulstrode was not one of them. He was simply a man whose desires had been stronger than his theoretic beliefs, and who had gradually explained the gratification of his desires into satisfactory agreement with those beliefs. If this be hypocrisy, it is a process which shows itself occasionally in us all, to whatever confession we belong.

George Eliot, *Middlemarch*

1

According to John Rawls, and to liberals quite generally, the fundamental principles of justice apply to the rules of the basic structure of society, and not to the choices people make within that structure, beyond their choices about whether or not to promote, support, and comply with the rules of a just basic structure. (For a fuller statement of that Rawlsian view, see Lecture 8, section 6.)

It follows that some aims which are rightly pursued by government, whose legislation and policy decide the character of at least a large part of the basic structure, are not aims that citizens themselves can and/or should be expected to pursue (apart from the pursuit of them in which citizens engage when they support those aims politically). According to Rawls, the demands placed by justice on government do not belong on the backs of individuals, as such; individuals discharge those demands collectively, through the government that represents them. Thus, while government should indeed seek to make the worst off as well off as possible, the right way for it to do so is to enforce rules (of, for example, property and taxation) which are such that, when individuals behave as they please, and therefore as self-seekingly as they like, within those rules, then the outcome is better for the worst off than what would come from behavior under any alternative set of rules.

Lecture 9 argued, against that position, that justice in personal choice (under the influence of a just ethos) is necessary for a society to qualify as just. But the question "What does justice demand of individuals in a just society?" is not the same as the question "What does justice demand of individuals in an *unjust* society?" And, in the present lecture, I raise a question related to that second one: I ask whether egalitarians who live in an unequal society (one, that is, whose government, for whatever reason, fails to enforce, and will continue to fail to enforce, whatever equality it is that these egalitarians favor) are committed to implementing, so far as they can, in their own lives, the norm of equality that they prescribe for government.[1] There is one thing egalitarians within an unequal society cannot say, in the light of what was shown in Lecture 9. They cannot say that equality is not a goal for individuals to pursue in their own lives in *any* society (be it just or unjust) and, therefore, more particularly, not something for individuals to pursue in their own lives in an unequal society. But they might, and do, advance other reasons for not pursuing it in an unequal society—reasons which I propose to examine here.

In asking what conduct egalitarians are committed to in an unequal society, I am interested, more particularly, in the conduct of *rich* egalitarians in an unequal society; it's not so hard for a poor egalitarian to be true to her egalitarianism in an unequal society.[2] Or, if you prefer, I am interested in the conduct of rich *professed* egalitarians, since many people would say that they can't *be* egalitarians, that they can't *really* believe in equality, if they're rich[3]—if, that is, they keep their money. (For the principal challenge to them is not that these egalitarians—or "egalitarians"—*earn,* or otherwise receive, a lot. It's not their gettings[4] but their keepings that raise the hard questions, since it would seem possible for them to use their excessive—from an egalitarian point of view—proceeds to promote equality.) Most people find the posture of rich folk who profess a belief in equality peculiar, and my anti-Rawlsian conception of the just society might be thought to make it look more peculiar still. And *their* posture includes *my own* posture, since I am myself a relatively high earner, and, as you will not be surprised to learn, I give away only a fraction of the money that I earn. (By which I don't mean that I give away something like, for example, three quarters of it; I mean a different, more fractional, sort of fraction.)

By way of prelude, I should like to express an embarrassment about the question that frames this lecture. There are two sharply opposite reasons why the topic of the lecture embarrasses me, and I'm not sure what their relative weights are in the genesis of my embarrassment. One reason why I am embarrassed is that I was raised as a Marxist, in a working-class communist home, and it goes against my inherited Marxist grain to place wealthy individuals under what the Marxists of my childhood would have regarded as an unduly *moralistic* focus. I was taught, as a child, to concentrate my judgment on the unjust structure of society, and away from the individuals who happen to benefit from that injustice. I did begin to go against that teaching (albeit on the quiet) in a moralizing direction, when I was very young, and I don't believe it now, yet it still has a place within my feelings. But the other reason why I am embarrassed is that, although I am not as rich as Croesus, or as a Rothschild, I am, like most professors, much richer than the average person in my society, even though, for various reasons that need not be laid out here, I am quite poor, *as professors go.*

Now those are, as I said, sharply *opposite* reasons for being embarrassed. Marxists of the sort that once surrounded me regarded moralizing about an individual's wealth as obviously foolish. They would have said that I am obviously entitled, or not unentitled, to my reasonably comfortable life; they would have said that the topic of this lecture is a silly fuss. I find that I cannot purge my feelings of that attitude, but I also think that there *is* something peculiar about being a rich egalitarian, and that my own posture *is*, therefore, questionable.[5]

So I face embarrassment *both* if I affirm *and* if I deny that I should give away more money than I do.

My topic is not, however, *as* moralistic as it may appear to be, since we must distinguish between, on the one hand, the obligations laid on someone by a conception to which she is committed and, on the other, how severely she is to be blamed for failing to meet those obligations. I do not address that quantitative question here, but my approach to it would be informed by the considerations in mitigation of blame for failure to behave justly that I reviewed in section 3 of Lecture 9. That section shows that I am less moralistically judgmental than some of my views might wrongly lead you to suppose.

2

I shall not reach a definite answer to the question raised in this lecture—the question, that is, whether the posture of rich egalitarians is sustainable. I shall simply present considerations which bear on the question. But I don't feel very apologetic about this incompleteness, because the issue mooted here has not been addressed much by philosophers, and I've therefore had to start pretty well from scratch. I have not been able to build on, or to react to, a body of literature.[6]

It might be objected, to my dearth-of-literature claim, that Shelly Kagan's *Limits of Morality,* and the works prompting it and prompted by it, do address my question, in its appropriately generalized form, when they consider whether or not a person is obliged to make the world as good as possible. But the answer to my question is not necessarily settled by the answer to Kagan's, principally because he is not discussing what *belief* in a principle commits you to in a world where the principle is *not observed* and will for some time go on being not observed, and also because he is not addressing the special question why people who favor state enforcement of a certain sacrifice from them (here, expropriating a substantial portion of their money) nevertheless feel justified in making no equivalent sacrifice on their own. Kagan is discussing what the good's being thus and so requires from you regardless of your beliefs and regardless of how compliant with or transgressive of morality others are. To be sure, if Kagan is right, such qualifications make no fundamental difference to what a person's obligations are, but few think he is right (I, for example, do not);[7] and even if he is right, it may be useful to investigate my more specific question without supposing that he is right.

It is curious that philosophers have not been attracted to the present issue, in its properly specialized form, since it's such a familiar one in everyday life. Virtually everybody, whether rich or poor, whether educated or not, experiences a certain cynicism, or at least a certain reservation, when presented with the spectacle of a rich person who declares a belief in equality. It looked ridiculous, for instance, whenever a rich egalitarian would express indignation at the latest Margaret Thatcher or John Major government policy, while sipping fine wine with fine friends in her fine expensive home.[8] Why has no egalitarian philosopher addressed this issue? Is it because the posture of a rich egalitarian is too obviously indefensible to be worth investigating? Or is it because it is too obviously innocent to require defending? Or is it because egalitarian philosophers divide without substantial remainder into ones who think the rich egalitarian posture obviously indefensible and ones who think it obviously innocent? I believe the last hypothesis to be true, and it follows that there is intellectual work to do in this region, which I try to begin to do here.

Let me recall three relevant incidents in my own life, all of which occurred within my decades-long ambivalent relationship to the British Labour Party. I've joined that party three times, and I've also left it three times. In the 1960s and 1970s the British Labour Party could still have been styled an egalitarian party, by virtue of its ideology, if not by virtue of the policies of its governments. But I remember, when I was a young lecturer in London, on a low salary, campaigning, in 1964, for the millionaire incumbent MP George Strauss in the safe Labour seat of Lambeth, which was a place full of poverty—I remember how uncomfortable I felt when Strauss arrived one evening at local party headquarters in the Kennington Road sporting a silk scarf, beautiful coat, and other sartorial and behavioral accoutrements of opulence. Yet George Strauss was a Labour hero: he had played a central role in the nationalization of the steel industry under Clement Attlee. More poignantly still, I remember the late Harold (eventually Lord) Lever, a Manchester millionaire and right-hand man to Harold Wilson, replying to callers on a phone-in show in the Seventies, when the topic, momentarily, was the Labour Party's then danger of insolvency. One caller asked Lever what I thought was a good question, whatever its answer should have been. Why, Lever was asked, did he not personally wipe out Labour's debt, by giving it the few millions that it needed, after which he'd still have plenty left? What struck me was that Lever did not answer the question, and that his talk-show host did not think that he should. They treated the question as ridiculous and its poser as impertinent. To be sure, those might have been reasonable responses to make *after* some answer had been given to the question, and in the light of that answer; but no answer was given.[9] Finally, I recall being asked by a multimillionaire novelist friend both of mine and more so of the then leader of the Labour Party, Neil Kinnock, to donate money to the party on the eve of the 1992 election campaign. I remember how I felt huffy when my friend responded huffily to my pledge to give (what he considered to be a paltry) fifty pounds.

There's a fine representation of this issue in David Lodge's excellent (and, in my view, deep) satirical novel *Small World*. Lodge depicts an encounter between Maurice Zapp, a Jewish American professor of English at "Euphoric State University" (it's really Berkeley), and Fulvia Morgana, an Italian revolutionary intellectual of enormous wealth. Zapp and Morgana meet for the first time on a flight from London to Milan. He interrupts her reading of the French Marxist Louis Althusser, and she invites him to her sumptuous home for the night. I quote the stretch of text in which Fulvia responds to Zapp's puzzlement about the conjunction between her Marxism and her wealth:

"There's something I must ask you, Fulvia," said Morris Zapp, as he sipped Scotch on the rocks poured from a crystal decanter brought on a silver tray by a black-uniformed, white-aproned maid to the first-floor drawing-room of the magnificent eighteenth-century house just off the Villa Napoleone, which they had reached after a drive [from the airport in Fulvia's Maserati coupé]. . . . "It may sound naive, and even rude, but I can't suppress it any longer. . . . I just want to know . . . how you manage to reconcile living like a millionaire with being a Marxist."

Fulvia, who was smoking a cigarette in an ivory holder, waved it dismissively in the air. "A very American question, if I may say so, Morris. Of course I recognize the contradictions in our way of life, but those are the very contradictions characteristic of the last phase of bourgeois capitalism, which will eventually cause it to collapse. By renouncing our own little bit of privilege"—here Fulvia spread her hands in a modest proprietorial gesture which implied that she and her husband enjoyed a standard of living only a notch or two higher than that of, say, a Puerto Rican family living on welfare [on] the Bowery [in Manhattan]—"we should not accelerate by one minute the consummation of that process, which has its own inexorable rhythm and momentum, and is determined by the pressure of mass movements, not by the puny actions of individuals. Since in terms of dialectical materialism it makes no difference to the 'istorical process whether Ernesto and I, as individuals, are rich or poor, we might as well be rich, because it is a role that we know 'ow to perform with a certain dignity. Whereas to be poor with dignity, poor as our Italian peasants are poor, is something not easily learned, something bred in the bone, through generations."[10]

Now, the average Anglophone egalitarian political philosopher is neither as left-wing nor as wealthy as Fulvia is. He—and it is usually a he—is nevertheless both on the left of the political spectrum and high up the earnings ladder. Academics, or, at any rate, academics in Britain and North America, frequently complain that they make much less money than lawyers, architects, dentists, executives, and so forth do, but they certainly make much more than most people do in the societies in which they live, and leading egalitarian political philosophers are not exceptions; being leading, they make a lot, even as academics go. So some version of Morris Zapp's puzzlement about Fulvia seems to be in order with respect to them.

I began to feel an analogous puzzlement long before I came to know egalitarian philosophers, and long before I encountered the British Labour Party. For I was surrounded by Communist Party members in my childhood, and, while most of them were poor, or, anyway, not particularly well off, there were some fabulously rich ones, and a few of them were actually capitalists. I remember one wealthy and dedicated communist, whom I'll call David B., telling me about his recent trip to the Soviet Union, and how wonderful it was to see efficient factories being run for the welfare of the people, with no capitalist in sight. This exchange occurred in David B.'s plush office in the plush office building that he owned in the center of Montreal; David B. was a big man in real estate. Another dedicated communist was a big man in the garment industry, and reputed to be a pretty tough boss.

Given all that I knew about them, and having strained the resources of my youthful imagination, I found that I could not attribute a consistent set of ideas to these comrades. I don't think they could have looked me in the eye and said that, in being capitalist, they were doing their bit to exacerbate the contradictions of capitalism, or, a shade less extravagantly, that, like everyone else, they were merely playing their assigned role in the capitalist class structure, that they really had no choice in the matter. Those recourses, which occur to academics familiar with Marxism, require too much (contestable and ultimately implausible) theoretical orchestration to be usable in real life; and it is noticeable, and part of his admirable subtlety, that David Lodge doesn't make Fulvia say precisely those things, but something rather different—and part of what she says is not at all contemptible, as I shall have occasion to indicate in section 14 below.

3

I still see no prospect of reconciling a commitment to communism with being tough on your very own workers. Let's not look for an unexpected consistency in this extreme instance of the phenomenon under inspection here. Instead, let's look at the question of consistency, or inconsistency, in its milder because more general form—not, that is, between communist egalitarian belief and wealth through tough bosshood, but just between egalitarian belief as such and wealth as such.

We are navigating close to those familiar philosophical rocks that surround the question whether people may truly believe in principles on which they do not act. This is the ancient problem of *akrasia,* on which Socrates and Aristotle had opposed views. Socrates thought it was impossible to do intentionally what you think it wrong to do, and Aristotle held a view which is harder to summarize but which was certainly not the Socratic view. The *akrasia* problem, or one part of it, is whether this dyad is inconsistent:

1. A believes that he ought (all things considered) to do X.
2. A does not intend to do X.

Not just philosophers, but people in general, are divided in their answer to that question. In the early 1960s, the Oxford philosopher Alan Montefiore asked a lot of people whether they thought it possible that a person might deliberately do what she believes to be wrong. Around half of his sample said yes and the other half said no. More interestingly still, on each side people thought that the opinion they themselves held was *obviously* true.

For my part, I side with those who think that 1 and 2 are consistent. I think it's as easy as pie to do what you believe to be the wrong thing to do. You might do it because you succumb to temptation, and you can succumb to temptation without being overcome by it—your will need not be *weak* for it to be *bad,* by your own lights. We have to distinguish between *moral* weakness (that is, failure, for whatever reason, to meet a moral standard) and weakness of *will,* which is a common excuse for moral weakness, and, quite commonly, a false one. As the late British philosopher J. L. Austin memorably said: "We often succumb to temptation with calm and even with finesse."[11]

R. M. Hare is, by contrast, on Socrates' side. He is convinced that 1 and 2 can be rendered consistent only by attributing some kind of inability to do X to agent A.[12] For, so Hare asks, if A believes that he *can* do X, yet doesn't intend to, then what more could show that he doesn't really believe that he ought to? His mere say-so is hardly counterevidence: anyone can say anything. But I disagree with Hare. Even if behavioral proofs of belief are required, acting as a professed belief directs is not the only type of behavior to be considered. Behavior other than conformity to a given norm can display belief in that norm—manifestly sincere criticism of other agents, behavior that manifests sincere regret about your own behavior, and so on. (The sincerity of the relevant declarations and other expressive behaviors might be indicated by the costs of engaging in them in the relevant contexts.) Such behaviors are evidence that you believe that you ought to do X, even when you regularly fail to do X.

But the *akrasia* dyad does not state my problem. The issue I've raised concerns the consistency of a triad, which I'll reach through two sets of modifications to the exhibited dyad. First, add 3 to it:

1. A believes that he ought (all things considered) to do X.
2. A does not intend to do X.
3. (A believes that) A's behavior is not out of line with his own principles.

Now, that triad undoubtedly represents an inconsistency. If you leave out what's in the parentheses in 3, the inconsistency is a logical one: it's logically impossible for all that to be true of A. And if you include what's in the parentheses, then all of 1 through 3 might be all too true, but there's then an inconsistency in A herself, between her beliefs and her behavior. Or, if there is a subtle consistency in the triad that I'm failing to see, then I'm sure it could be eliminated through a (nontendentious) tightening of one or more of the triad's constituent formulations.

That is not, however, the triad that exercises me. The 1-2-3 triad is relatively uninteresting, because the behavior reported in 2 is the very behavior that is condemned in 1; there can be no question about that. But an analogous question is more difficult to answer when we confront the triad which formulates what is indeed the problem that exercises me:

4. A believes in equality.
5. A is rich (which means that A does not give a relevant amount of his money away).

3. (A believes[13] that) A's behavior is not out of line with his own principles.

It *is* an interesting question whether the behavior reported in 5 is incongruent with the belief reported in 4.

The rich communists that I knew satisfied the full form of 3. They were not people who lamented their own moral weakness or moral insufficiency. They really thought that a principled commitment to an egalitarian society did *not* imply giving away most of their own money, and most egalitarian political philosophers believe the same. How can such a posture be defended?

Before I address that question, let me once more underline that it does not ask how the people under inspection can credibly claim to *believe* in equality. I *know* they believe in it. My question is how they can think it not inconsistent to believe both that *and* that their behavior is unobjectionable. I'm not asking how they can say, given their behavior, "I believe in equality," but how they can say, in light of that behavior, "I believe in equality *and* I am true to that principle in my life."[14] To clarify the difference between the two questions, here is an answer which has some mileage with respect to the question I am *not* asking but which manifestly fails as an answer to the question I *am* asking.

The rich professed egalitarian, challenged by a questioner who does not accept that he really believes in equality, might say: "Look, I'm no saint, but I'm also not particularly sinful. I'm an averagely good person. I became rich not because I was worse than averagely good but because of fortunate circumstances, and, as rich people go, I'm pretty generous with my wealth. The fact that I am lucky enough to have ampler choices than the average nonrich person does not mean that I'm *worse* than the average nonrich person, since I handle my choices in a reasonably decent fashion. (And I at least have the right *belief*. Would it be better if I not only allowed myself to benefit from inequality but also believed that was OK?)"[15]

That, I submit, is a decent answer in vindication of the sincerity of the man's belief. But the answer does not address my question. This man confesses to failure. He confesses that his behavior fails to live up to his principles, while insisting that he does believe in those principles. He offers an *excuse* for his behavior—to wit, that it is not worse than that of people at large—rather than a *justification* of it, since he does not claim that his behavior is justified. (The distinction I here invoke between excuses and justifications runs as follows: When you are excused for not having done X, X remains what you should have done; it was the right thing to do, but your excuse renders you less vulnerable to criticism or to penalty for not having done it. When, by contrast, you have a justification for not having done X, then that justification shows that X was not, as it might first have appeared to be, and/or as it would otherwise have been, the thing that you ought to have done.)

The people I'm interested in do not confess failure to live up to their principles; they do not ask that their behavior be excused. That's what puzzles me here. And, to recall the point made at the end of section 1 above, I am not asking how bad the people under inspection are, or how guilty they should feel. I am asking how they can think that their stance is consistent. I am not asking how bad it is to *be* inconsistent, in the particular way that they putatively are.

4

They might argue that there is no case to answer. They might say that, while egalitarians prefer a society of an egalitarian type, preferring that type of society has no implications for behavior in a society of a different type, and is therefore consistent with their acceptance of rich pickings within the different type of society that they now inhabit.

Well, logical consistency is no doubt there, but logical consistency is a very thin thing, as is shown by the fact that the following position, which a strange (supposed) egalitarian might embrace, is logically consistent: I favor an equal society—one, that is, in which *everyone* lives by an egalitarian norm. But if all but two people live by that norm, of whom I am one and the other is a rich and obdurate anti-egalitarian, then my egalitarianism does not commit me to living by the egalitarian norm, since my society would remain an unequal one even if I did so.

What matters is not bare logical consistency, but a consistency which incorporates the *reason* the egalitarian would give in support of her belief in equality. Everything depends on *why* she favors it. If she favors it because she thinks that inequality is unjust, then it is hard to agree that her behavior is principled. If you hate inequality because you think it is unjust, how can you *qualmlessly* accept and retain money your retention of which embodies that injustice—money which you could give to others, or donate to an egalitarian cause, and thereby diminish, or hope to diminish, the amount of injustice that prevails, by benefiting sufferers of that injustice?

5

But not everybody who believes in equality says that she believes in it as a matter of justice.[16] So, for example, the rich egalitarian might say: "I want a society of equality because I hate the division between rich and poor that disfigures this one. Inequality destroys community; it alienates people from one another. But that is no reason whatsoever for giving away my money and joining the poor side of the division. It's the division that I hate, and extravagant charity on my part might do nothing to eliminate it. There are eighty million poor people in my society and twenty million rich ones. Society would not plainly become less divided—it might even, by some measures, become more divided—if I made myself and some of the eighty million poor slightly less poor than each of the eighty million now is.[17] And I myself would remain divided off from other people. It's clear that an appropriate comprehensive restructuring of society would reduce division, but it's not clear how I can use my own wealth to reduce it."[18]

One can agree that hatred of the division between rich and poor is indeed a reason for desiring equality. But what *makes* the distinction between rich and poor a hateful one, in the way that the distinction between redheads and brunettes, or between beer-lovers and wine-drinkers, is not? What makes the distinction between rich and poor a hateful division? *I* think the rich/poor division is hateful in part because the poor have *intelligible* sentiments of injustice when they contemplate that division. But the antidivision egalitarian who eschews the discourse of justice says that such sentiments are, or (supposing that the poor have no such sentiments) would be, misplaced. He denies that (at least part of) his reason for hating inequality is its injustice. If, as may well be the case, that denial is sincere, then, so far as I can see, his posture is not inconsistent.

6

Still other believers in equality think that egalitarian redistribution is required not by justice, or even to overcome division as such, but because it is desirable that every person be provided with resources that are needed to live a good life,[19] or, failing which, that as many people as possible be so provided,[20] and that, as things are in our society, comprehensive state egalitarian redistribution is required to promote that desideratum: you can't promote it on your own.

One might challenge such a person as follows: Why don't you top up the holdings of some of those who are very near the bottom line of what you consider necessary to have a good life, until you are yourself just above that line?

To this he might offer two replies, one relating to practicality and one relating to principle.

He might say, on the side of practicality, that it is not feasible to make one's charity work in the fine-tuned fashion that the challenge contemplates: one could never be sure that the lives one is targeting are, precisely, nearly good. Epistemic difficulties mean that he could end up bringing no one above the line, and, for good measure, thrusting himself below it, so that the net effect of his intervention would be negative, from the point of view of there being as many good lives as possible.

That answer might justify nongiving on the part of the somewhat rich, but not on the part of those who are so rich that they can give a lot, to each of a number of people with bad lives, and still have quite a bit left, and thereby (because of "a lot") avoid the "targeting problem," and, too (because of "quite a bit"), without making their own lives ungood. (A rich person might, for example, pay for the expensive (but not too expensive, for him) operation of someone whose life, while now unquestionably a misery, is almost certainly destined to be good once the operation has been performed.) So, while the practicality reply might save egalitarian professors of the stated persuasion who, like me, are not *especially* wealthy, it does little to exonerate *very wealthy* egalitarians.[21]

The reply of principle distinguishes between what states of affairs a person thinks are good and what obligations he believes he has to promote those states of affairs. Thus, for example, I might think that London's appearance would benefit if more of its prospective new architecture were neo-Gothic rather than postmodern, but it does not follow that I must think myself obliged to join, or to form, a bring-back-the-Gothic society. More generally, it is only act consequentialists who believe that one has a duty to maximize the good, and that is a minority position in philosophy. Egalitarians who regard equality as desirable, but not as required by justice, have, then, a ready answer to the challenge about why they do not give their money away. This answer is also available to those antidivision egalitarians (see section 5 above) who deny that at least part of what makes social division repugnant is that it reflects injustice.

7

Let us now look at the hard form of our problem, as it arises for egalitarians who believe in equality because they think that inequality is unjust. Their problem is harder. One may indeed deny that one is (even slightly) obliged to strive to produce what one regards as (merely) good, and one can also deny that one is obliged to do whatever one can to right an injustice, just because it is an injustice. But how can one deny, without ado, that one is obliged to forgo the benefits one enjoys as a result of what one regards as injustice,[22] when one can forgo them in a fashion that benefits sufferers of that injustice?[23] There may be good excuses and/or justifications[24] for not taking up the stated task, but how can it be thought that no justification or excuse is needed for not shouldering it?

The questions here put to egalitarians who acknowledge that their egalitarian beliefs are inspired by justice run as follows: Why don't you pursue equality by donating the extra that you would lack in a just society to poor people, and/or to organizations that promote equality? Since you don't do these things (on the relevant scale), you don't believe in doing them (on that scale), if, as you claim (see the 4-5-3 triad in section 3 above), your behavior matches your beliefs.

It would be amazing if wealthy egalitarians of the stated persuasion gave nothing to either of those causes, both to those which attenuate the worst results of current inequality and to those which fight for a more egalitarian society, and I've certainly never known a rich communist who professed to be inspired by justice, or a rich egalitarian political philosopher, who gave, or gives, nothing to either. Since they give what they do with a sense of obligation, they cannot say that their egalitarian beliefs have *no* implications for how they should act in an unequal society. So how come they give away such a small portion of their surplus?

They might say that even if they were to give to such causes on a scale that reduced their own lives to a merely average standard of amenity, that would still be only a drop in the ocean; it wouldn't make enough difference to the global position. But there are at least two replies to that.

One is: Why should you expect single-handedly to make a massive global difference? You are in a position to make a huge difference to many people, and that is surely enough. And the other reply is: You do, after all, give something. At present, you give a smaller drop in the ocean than the one you affect to deride as negligible. So how can you justify giving *only* that even smaller drop?

There are further points to be made about the drop-in-the-ocean defense, but, before I make them, some remarks are needed by way of background to them.

I have not, thus far, offered a precise specification of the principle of equality that those here on trial are to be supposed to be affirming.[25] Precision in the statement of that principle would, for the most part, be inappropriate here, partly because many rich egalitarians are not political philosophers, whose trade requires that they work their egalitarian beliefs into a (relatively)[26] precise form, and partly because those rich egalitarians who are indeed philosophers defend different forms of egalitarian principle. We are investigating those whose lives are powered by resources evidently in excess of what they know they could expect to get in the egalitarian society they profess to favor. The challenge we put to them therefore applies across the different ways they might or do render their beliefs in equality precise.

But the cogency of *some* defensive *responses* to that challenge does depend on the precise form of egalitarianism our egalitarians do or would adopt, and the drop-in-the-ocean response is a case in point. Accordingly, I offer herewith one large distinction between forms of egalitarian principle that our defendants might affirm, a distinction that is pertinent to the "drop" defense.

One may distinguish, broadly, between egalitarian principles which locate value in equality properly so called, which is a relation between what different people get and which is strictly indifferent to how much they get, and egalitarian principles (like Rawls's difference principle) which affirm not, strictly speaking, equality itself, but a policy of rendering the worst off people as well off as possible. We can call the first sorts of egalitarians "relational egalitarians" and the second "prioritarians," since they assign priority to improving the condition of the worst off.[27]

Now, the "drop" defense works better on behalf of relational egalitarians than it does on behalf of prioritarians. For although even a very rich person cannot make society much more equal than it is, he can certainly make some among the very worst off palpably better off than they now are, and thereby, if he is a prioritarian, significantly advance what he regards as the just cause: it is the plight of the badly off that arouses his sense of justice. Accordingly, the "drop" defense looks pretty pale when it is used by prioritarians, whatever it may do for those who endorse equality as such. And there are, I hazard, many more prioritarian egalitarians than there are pure egalitarians. Most egalitarians are egalitarian *because* they think equality would benefit the badly off.[28]

Recall the two replies to the drop-in-the-ocean defense which I offered earlier: that one rich egalitarian can do a great deal for a decently large number of people, and that those rich egalitarians (that is, almost all of them, of whatever specific persuasion) who give something can hardly describe giving much more than what they in fact give as too negligible a sum to be worth giving. The first of those replies works better against that majority of egalitarians who are prioritarian than it does against pure egalitarians. The second reply, the inconsistency it exposes, works well against both, and the factual premise of the second reply, which is that the person under inspection does (after all) give a little something, casts doubt on the self-description of those who profess that they value equality as such, since the very little that they do give can indeed do almost nothing for equality, even though it might benefit some individuals a lot.

Before I leave the drop-in-the-ocean defense, a final point, about negligibility. "Negligible" can mean "numerically small, relative to the total picture," but it can also mean "unimportant," and negligibility in the first of these senses does not entail negligibility in the second sense. Notice, now, that this nonentailment evidently bears against rich prioritarian egalitarians: getting twenty people out of dire straits is a negligible effect in the first, numerical, sense, when five million are in such straits, but it is not plausible to say that it is negligible in the sense of unimportant, especially for someone whose egalitarianism focuses on how badly off the badly off are. (Whether the exhibited ambiguity in "negligible" has a bearing against rich relational egalitarians who employ the "drop" defense is a subtle question that I shall not address.)

8

Once the goal of equality proper is clearly distinguished from a policy of favoring the worst off, many people come to doubt whether there is anything to be said for equality itself. But one important egalitarian view, that propounded by Ronald Dworkin, not only endorses equality itself but also supplies a particularly challenging treatment of the topic of this lecture.

Within Dworkin's theory of equality, the locus of the norm of equality proper (as opposed to, for example, norms governing duties of compassion to the unfortunate, be they at home or abroad) is in the relationship between the state and those whom it claims the right to govern. Because it claims that right, the state must treat its citizens with equal respect and concern, on pain of being a tyranny, and it must *therefore* distribute resources equally to its members. But if the state fails to do so, then no analogous duty falls on individuals. It is not the individual's duty to treat everyone (relatives, friends, and strangers alike) with equal respect and concern.

It does not follow that no related duty falls on the individual when the state fails to be just. For Dworkin, it is then the individual's duty to promote equality by trying to change the state's policy. For, insofar as government is unjust, the citizens whom it represents are, Dworkin thinks, *collectively* responsible for that injustice. Each therefore has a duty to seek to rectify the state's injustice. So there is indeed a tension between professing egalitarianism and not doing anything to promote equality, by, for example, contributing money and/or time to an egalitarian political party. But there is no obligation to contribute so that one ends up as one would in an egalitarian society. Exactly what the size and shape of one's political duty are is a hard question, but it is not the duty to do what the state should be doing. There is no particular reason why one should spend on politics what would reduce one to the level that equality would impose.

According to Dworkin, the state, when properly constituted, is the authoritative agent of the citizenry as a whole, upon whom the state's obligations ultimately lie. So, for example,[29] if the state fails in its distributive duty, but excessively wealthy people happen to be magically good at coordinating their actions with one another, then they would indeed be obliged to coordinate so as to secure equality. So it's not quite true that, for Dworkin, where the state fails, the *only* relevant duty of the individual is to promote equality by working for better state policy. But it remains true that her duty is *as* a member of a collective on whom the duty primarily falls. If I know that others won't cooperate appropriately, then equality *per se* gives me no reason to open my purse, just as I have no reason to open it, based on equality, if I know that no political party or movement is disposed to promote equality, or can be caused to be disposed to do so.

Dworkin does not, of course, think that we owe nothing to starving people as such, whether they be within our own state or outside it; but, so he insists, our duty to them is one of human compassion, not one that derives from a principle of equality. To the extent that the world becomes subject to international governance, a duty of equality would fall on the relevant government; but that is consistent with, and indeed a consequence of, Dworkin's view. It would be a mistake to think that globalization of authority, or the nascent forms of it that we now witness, represent a challenge to his view. The claim that a norm of equality goes with subjection to a common authority allows for shading in the stringency of the demand for equality that matches shading in the extent to which transnational authority obtains.

If Dworkin's "statocentric" view of equality is sustainable, then it follows that the rich egalitarian need not structure his life as the state should structure it, in conformity with an egalitarian norm. But it is, of course, an independent question whether Dworkin's view is indeed sustainable, and I should like, here, to express some doubts about it.

First, it seems quite unclear that a state which forthrightly refuses to pursue a norm of strict distributive equality *ipso facto* shows failure to treat its subjects with equal respect and concern. If the government believes strongly in, and implements, certain nonegalitarian distributive norms—such as, for example, a high guaranteed minimum, with the rest of distribution being determined by laissez-faire—it seems false that it stands convicted, on that basis alone, of disrespect and/or callousness toward at least some of its citizens. But if distributive equality proper does not follow from Dworkin's premise about the duty of the state, then rich egalitarians cannot say that Dworkin has given the right account of their egalitarian beliefs, and they therefore cannot use Dworkin's theory to argue that the duty to promote equality falls on the state (or on the people collectively) and not on individuals as such.

But even if that first doubt is misplaced, and a state which fails to institute distributive equality indeed stands convicted of a form of political tyranny, it still seems implausible that the only point of distributive justice, the only reason for avoiding distributive injustice, is that distributive injustice implies political tyranny. The norm of distributive equality surely stands (if it stands at all) independently of any kind of political equality, even if political equality requires it. And Dworkin himself betrays agreement with that view. For the "immigrants" on the island that he describes in "Equality of Resources" "accept the principle that no one is antecedently entitled to any of [the island's] resources, but that they shall instead be divided equally among them." It is not because they think of the egalitarian auctioneer, whom they proceed to appoint, as their *ruler* that these egalitarian immigrants institute equality of resources. It is, on the contrary, expressly left open whether or not "they might create" a "state."[30] Having received their equal shares, they might, following the auction, go their separate ways.

Finally, I doubt that the motif of collective responsibility for distributive justice can be so readily integrated with the rest of Dworkin's theory as I tried to make it seem in my sympathetic exposition of that theory. If an obligation to enforce equality comes from assertion of a right to rule, why should that obligation lie on the people as a whole, who might not, after all, assert any such right?

9

Another rationale for not giving away what one has in excess of what equality would allow, a rationale that is popular with persons influenced by Marxism, is that such giving does not touch the *fundamental* injustice, which is the structured inequality of power between the rich and the poor. A rich person's charity does nothing to eliminate unequal power. It is but a particular use of the unequal income that reflects unequal power.

In reply:

Even if the power inequality really is the fundamental injustice, it hardly follows that the unequal distribution of income which derives from it is not *also* unjust; the Marxisant defendant must surely agree that this, too, is unjust. So why should he not reduce the injustice that he can reduce, even if it is a secondary one, by distributing his surplus income in an appropriate way? It would be grotesque for him to say to those who lose from the unjust power division: "I won't succour you, since what I deplore is, at root, not your poverty but the system that makes you poor."

It is, moreover, false that the power difference is the fundamental injustice, in every relevant sense. It is, of course, the *causally* fundamental injustice, but it is not, in a certain relevant sense, the *normatively* fundamental injustice,[31] since it is plausible to say that the power difference qualifies as unjust *because* it (standardly) generates an unjust income distribution, and, therefore, unjustly contrasting opportunities to enjoy the good things in life. To be sure, the power difference remains an independent injustice: it's false that there would be *no* injustice if all powerful people were extravagantly charitable. But the distinction between causal and normative fundamentality nevertheless constitutes a strong objection to the stated Marxifying position.

In reply, the Marxist might say: "All right. But even if the income difference is a separate injustice, or even the fundamental injustice, there is nothing productive that I can do about it. What I favor is a society whose basic structure is such that every able-bodied person earns roughly the same income. I don't want the poor to depend on the good will of the rich, and also, perhaps, to experience a wholly misplaced sense of gratitude to them. I want them to have the self-respect that comes from their earning a decent living."

To that attempt at repair I would reply as follows: I can accept your preference for their earning a decent living over their receiving charity. But that first, preferred, condition is not at present feasible, and there is a third condition which is all too feasible: their neither earning a decent living nor receiving charity, but continuing to live in misery. Is that, too, preferable to their living much better, on charity?

10

Yet another putative rationale for not expecting people to pursue privately the norms that would prevail in what they regard as a just society is that each person has the right to a private space into which social duty does not intrude.

But the prosecutor hounding the rich egalitarian need not deny that private spaces are legitimate. In a society with a state-imposed egalitarian income distribution, there is plenty for everyone to decide without regard to social duty about the shape of their own lives, and the same goes for prodigious donors in an unequal society. Inspired by different conceptions of the good, they can eat fish or fowl, go to synagogue or church, play football or chess, and so on; private spaces exist, but, because the egalitarian principle is fulfilled, they are more similar in size than they otherwise would be, and some are bigger than they would otherwise be. In an alternative formulation of my question, it asks the rich who believe in equality as a matter of justice why they do not shrink their private spaces in an unequal society. That question is not answered by the truth (for I think it is one) that everyone has the right to (some sort of) private space.

The real question, for both contexts—that is, for both our unjust and a just society—is not whether a person has a right to a private space, but what its shape should be. In what is perhaps its most persuasive form, the private-space objection says that one's private space should be so shaped that one's life is not *oppressive,* and that it *would* be oppressive to require the rich to have continual regard to the condition of the poor (which no one need have in a society with routinized procedures for producing equality).[32] Whether or not the point is best made in terms of *rights,* to have to keep the demands of the poor before or at the back of one's mind means an oppressive existence. That is the *mental-burden* rationale against extravagant voluntary philanthropy in an unequal society.

11

I shall assess the mental-burden rationale by examining Thomas Nagel's response to a claim made by Robert Nozick. Nagel's response bears directly on our question, even though he and Nozick were not discussing the special problem of how an egalitarian should behave in a society whose government fails to induce equality. They were discussing this more general question: Why should *whatever* redistribution is called for be a matter for the state in particular, as opposed to something that individuals have a duty to carry out by themselves?

Nozick said that, if it was of compelling moral concern that the badly off be assisted, then private charity could achieve that. He claimed that the *only* reason for preferring to assist them through state-imposed redistribution was that people who do not *want* to give are thereby *forced* to give[33] (a coercion that Nozick would forbid, but whether he is right about that has nothing to do with the aspect of the Nozick/Nagel debate on which I invite focus here).

In reply to Nozick, Nagel claimed that there are good grounds for state redistribution[34] of the holdings of those who want to contribute, because a person who is willing and, indeed, eager to contribute through taxation might reasonably be unwilling to give off her own bat. And Nagel's justification of that unwillingness would, if sound, apply to our case, the case of the rich egalitarian who is asked why he does not contribute massively in a society whose state will not force him to do so. I quote Nagel (again, interpolations in brackets are my own):

> Most people are not generous when asked to give voluntarily, and it is unreasonable to ask that they should be. Admittedly there are cases in which a person should do something although it would not be right to force him to do it [for example, to keep an ordinary promise, or to refrain from ordinary lying]. But here I believe the reverse is true. Sometimes it is proper to force people to do something even though it is not true that they should do it without being forced. It is acceptable to compel people to contribute to the support of the indigent by automatic taxation, but unreasonable to insist that in the absence of such a system they ought to contribute voluntarily. The latter is an excessively demanding moral position because *it requires voluntary decisions that are quite difficult to make*. Most people will tolerate a universal system of compulsory taxation without feeling entitled to complain, whereas they would feel justified in refusing an appeal that they contribute the same amount voluntarily. This is partly due to *lack of assurance* that others would do likewise and fear of relative disadvantage; but it is also a sensible rejection of *excessive demands on the will,* which can be more irksome than automatic demands on the purse.[35]

There are two elements in Nagel's reply to Nozick; they are separately indicated in the final sentence of the quoted passage. First, before the semicolon, there is the "assurance problem," which I shall address in section 12. It is not essentially a matter of the contrasting burdens of voluntary and forced giving. Here I take up a distinct supposed advantage of redistribution through the state—to wit, that it relieves the "excessive" burden on a person's will. For Nagel, people might want to be forced by the state to give, so that they can thereby avoid "voluntary decisions that are quite difficult to make." When government justifiably (as Nagel thinks) appropriates some of my resources, it reduces the scope of my choice, but, precisely because I now have no choice in the matter, I am spared the burden of *making* a choice about it. So, even though I'd gladly accept a very high tax on my income, I should not therefore be expected to give away corresponding amounts off my own bat. (Note that the mental-burden argument is unaffected by whether or not *other* people are contributing voluntarily, because their (different) makeup is such that for them the relevant voluntary decisions are easy to make, or because they are acting in a supererogatory manner—that is, undertaking more burden than one can reasonably be asked to under-take.)

Before I respond to the mental-burden argument, two preliminary re-marks.

First, I must set aside a misinterpretation of Nagel to which some have shown themselves drawn. He is *not* saying: "I want to be forced to give because I know (or fear) that I might otherwise not give." That is quite different from what I have supposed Nagel to mean. A person who expresses anxiety as to whether she'd give voluntarily need not believe that it is *unreasonable* to expect her to give (because of the stress on her will that giving would require). She might simply be avowing that she is not good enough (as opposed to: not strong enough)[36] to do what's right. It is not a plausible interpretation of the Nagel passage to represent him as striking that self-critical posture; and if that were what he means, then what he says would be irrelevant to our project, which is to see whether 4, 5, and 3 (see section 3 above) are consistent, since, on this (unlikely) interpretation of Nagel, their inconsistency is not denied. That I know or fear that I would not give off my own bat is indeed a reason for me to prefer redistribution through the state, but it is not what we are looking for, which is a *justification for not giving* if the state does not force me to. It can't be a justification for not giving when the state does not force me to that I *would* not give unless the state forces me to.

Note, secondly, that Nagel is making more than the undeniable com-parative claim that donating voluntarily can be *more* onerous than yield-ing to coerced transfer, for those, that is, who regard a coerced transfer as justified. (To be sure, many people who regard coerced giving as justified might nevertheless prefer to give voluntarily, because of the satisfactions associated with that, but such people are irrelevant here, since they would not press Nagel's case.) That claim may suffice to refute the con-tention of Nozick against which Nagel is arguing; but Nagel is also claiming, more strongly, that people are *justified* in refusing to give vol-untarily, when such giving imposes "excessive" demands on their wills.

It is that noncomparative claim which we must examine here, because, if it is true, it reconciles 4, 5, and 3.

What are we to make of Nagel's claim that problems to do with the will justify a refusal to give voluntarily on the part of those who believe in extensive state-imposed redistribution? Suppose that it would indeed be a heavy burden to have to get myself to give, each month, when my salary comes in, whatever is the amount that I think should be taken from me for the sake of the poor. Even so, Nagel appears to ignore the individual's ability to avoid such recurrent difficult voluntary decisions: I can bind my own will, once and for all, or once in a long while, by sign-ing an appropriate banker's order.[37] I do not need the state to make me give, since, through various contractual devices, I can make myself give. Giving then becomes a relatively unoppressive routine. (I do, of course, lose the money, and that is, other things equal, regrettable. But other things *aren't* relevantly equal here, since I think I shouldn't keep the money. And it is, in any case, similarly regrettable when the state taxes it away.)

In considering the present question, we must distinguish between the *cost* of doing something and how *difficult* it is to do that thing. The cost of an action for me is what I lose (but would have preferred to keep) as a result of performing it, and also whatever pain or other unpleasantness attends the act of performing it, whereas its difficulty for me is a func-tion of how my capacities measure up to the challenge it poses.[38] So, for example, it is difficult, but not necessarily (commensurately) costly, for me to put the thread into the needle's tiny hole, or to return a well-placed tennis serve. But I do not necessarily suffer pain, or lose any-thing, if I manage to pull off these feats: I might find these *difficult* activi-ties enjoyable.[39] Contrariwise, it is easy to make out a check for a large amount. Just a few strokes of the pen are needed, but the cost of those strokes is large. And it is less difficult[40] to make out a check for $5,000 than one for $3,445.66, although the cost of the first signing is mani-festly greater.

Now it isn't clear, from the passage on exhibit, whether Nagel is urg-ing that it's much more difficult or, differently, much more costly, to give money away off your own bat than to have it appropriated willy-nilly by the state. But either way, so I shall argue, his case is weak. I believe that, if it is perceived to have some strength, that is because of a failure to distinguish appropriately between cost and difficulty. It's true that it is *in some sense(s)* "*hard*" to give away money, but we have to nail down the exact senses in which that is, and is not, true; and, once we've done so, Nagel's plea fails as a justification for the egalitarian's inertia (however well or otherwise it might function as an excuse for that inertia).

Nagel does not win his point if we take him to mean difficulty, as such. For even if we grant that the required mental effort is indeed difficult, provided that it is not also costly, we have not been supplied with a reason for not giving off our own bat what we would be willing for the state to take. Its difficulty, as such, is no reason for not performing an action that (although difficult) is possible, and the voluntary giving that Nagel has in mind is undeniably possible. Nagel is not invoking the prospect of a pathological *paralysis* of the will. It's of course unreasonable to ask someone to do something impossible, but it's not unreasonable to ask someone to do something difficult, provided that it does not carry too high a cost.

For sufficiently high cost certainly is a good reason for refusing to perform an action. So we must now ask just how considerable the relevant cost, of getting oneself to give, can be thought to be,[41] and we must avoid polluting our assessment of that with thoughts about the substantial *resulting* cost, the cost of losing the money in question, for that is the same whether I offer it up myself or the state takes it willy-nilly. The present justification for not giving off my own bat turns entirely on the *extra* cost of doing it by myself.

In my opinion, the costs of the two procedures—that is, of giving off one's own bat and the state's just taking—are indeed different, for the sort of person Nagel contemplates, but they are not dramatically different. Let me explain the structure of what I believe to be the modest extra cost that attaches to voluntary giving in the case in question.

Difficulty and cost, though distinct, do interact: they to some extent track, and otherwise affect, each other, which is why, indeed, they are so commonly confused.[42] And a particularly intricate connection between cost and difficulty obtains in the present context. For the cost *consequent* on the required decision—the cost, that is, of losing all that money—may add to the difficulty of making it. It may create mental resistance, and it may, in turn, be painful, or, as Nagel says, "irksome," to have to overcome that resistance. So the difficulty which comes from contemplating the consequent cost can generate a cost in the throes of decision itself,[43] and that might be what Nagel means. It is anyway, so I suggest, the best thing around here for him to mean. But I would still maintain that the costs of voluntary and state-imposed giving are, nevertheless, pretty similar, because it isn't terrifically difficult, or, therefore, terrifically *additionally* costly, to get oneself to sign the check, or the standing order, and I think it can be thought to be so only when one misprojects the enormous cost which *results* from the decision, the cost of what comes *after* it, onto the cost that comes from the difficulty of making the decision itself.

I know that's pretty complicated; it took me a long time to work it out. So I think it will be useful to set forth an analogy that illuminates my point.

Suppose we are on the battlefield and a comrade will die unless my foot is cut off. (Never mind how that's supposed to help him. This is a philosophy lecture, not a commentary on interpersonal surgery.) Nagel is saying the analogue of this: I might recognize that it would be right for someone forcibly to cut my foot off, but I can nevertheless protest that it is asking too much to expect me to cut it off myself. Let me elaborate my doubt about Nagel's case through closer focus on this analogy.

Suppose that the foot is to be removed by a knife, and that there is no anesthetic available. We need to compare the case in which someone else cuts my foot off—someone who, like the taxing state, operates independently of my will—with the case in which I myself have to cut it off. The cost that *results* from the cutting is the same in both cases: pain, and loss of the foot. But, because much pain comes immediately with the cutting, it is fiendishly difficult, will-wise, for me to do the cutting myself, for me to keep myself applied to that grisly task, so difficult that substantial extra costs of struggle and strain supervene if I do. Contrast, now, a case where my foot will be severed by an electrically powered knife five minutes after a button is pressed, and I do agree that the button should be pressed: I recognize the validity of my comrade's claim to my foot. Perhaps there is, in addition to the other costs, an extra burden, on the will, if I have to press the button myself, but that extra burden is surely inconsiderable. It will not be a *great* relief to discover that you are determined to push the button, so that I need not do so. And, so I submit, this second case, not the manual cutting one, is the right analogy here. The rich egalitarian wants the state to press the tax button. It may be a bit easier for him if the state does that than if he has to press the standing-order button when e-mailing his bank, but Nagel's dramatic presentation of the difficulty of deciding to give convinces me that he is mistreating that minor contrast as though it resembled the contrast between my cutting my foot off and your doing it (with, in each case, a nonelectric knife).

I have allowed throughout this section that giving voluntarily is indeed more difficult and more costly for persons of a certain disposition than having the money taken away by the state. But the relevant subset of such persons, here, are those who, like Nagel, favor egalitarian action by the state, and who are, presumably, therefore committed to voting for it. But why should casting such a vote be easier, as Nagel must think it is, than signing a relevant banker's order?

Is it because, unlike that signing, voting doesn't guarantee that you have to pay, since your side might lose? But people of Nagel's persuasion presumably also think that you should vote in favor of equality even when you know that yours will be the casting vote. How could *that* be less difficult and/or costly than signing a banker's order to the same effect?

To drive this point home, consider a device whose design is partly due to Martin Wilkinson, who urged me to consider the comparison with voting. Suppose there's a standing-order form next to the ballot paper and you are to decide whether or not to sign each. But, unusually, both the vote and the standing order are conditional: your vote in favor of the Equality Party will take effect only if it is the casting vote, and your standing order will take effect only if the Equality Party loses. (The Equality Party is irreversibly committed to taking from you in tax exactly what the standing order would cost you.) If you profess yourself in favor of (more) equality, then you cannot credibly refuse to sign the order on the ground that doing so is much more demanding than voting for equality (which, *ex hypothesi*, you are prepared to do), since the two actions impose identical demands in the present case.

This, as it seems to me, devastating point against Nagel's "cost-of-willing" argument does not touch the other argument he offers, to which I now turn.

12

A distinct Nagelian defense of the rich egalitarian that we need to consider relates to the "fear of relative disadvantage" which he mentions at the end of the passage quoted in section 11 above, or, more precisely, to confident expectation of "relative disadvantage," since, in our context (that is, the real world) the desired "assurance" (that others will give as I do) is known to be unforthcoming. In our world, very few rich people (even) profess egalitarianism; society is, and will for the foreseeable future continue to be, unequal, whatever I may give. The "relative-disadvantage" defense is that the consequences for me if I give when others don't are intolerably oppressive.[44] Accordingly, to return to the device introduced at the end of section 11, even though I am committed to pressing the conditional voting button, I can reasonably refuse to press the conditional standing-order button (although not because of the considerations about the difficulty of "willing" that were canvassed in section 11).

Rich egalitarian people might be willing to give generously only if similarly situated people would in general be ready to do the same. But, as they well know, those others are not similarly disposed. And because others will not give, giving severely prejudices their self-interest and, more poignantly, the interest of members of their families. If Johnny's dad buys him a new bicycle, how can Molly's dad explain why he doesn't buy one for Molly? The rich person should not be asked to depart from the observable norm of his peer group—a peer group to which, importantly for present purposes, he continues to belong even if he impoverishes himself, since that group is substantially defined by his occupation and his education. Nor should he be asked to undertake a sacrifice which will alienate his children, perhaps not now, but later, when, having grown up, they face a more burdensome life because of that sacrifice, and when they (as is entirely possible) happen not to believe in egalitarianism themselves. That is surely too much to expect of them.

The beauty of a state-imposed duty, or of a *general* ethos of giving, is that, when they obtain, each well-paid person can then give without departing from the norm, and therefore without having to accomplish an especially saintly response to peer group constraints. To expect a given rich person to be within a minority that give is to demand that he incur particular sorts of sacrifice that poor people need not face, such as (to stay with the example already invoked) the sacrifice, which a poor person is not called upon to make, of *deliberately denying* one's child what one has the power to give her and what comparably placed parents give theirs.[45] Accordingly, a person can, in full consistency, think it desirable for tax policy and/or a general ethos to favor the badly off, yet resist furthering their cause by extravagant personal initiative in an unequal society that lacks that policy or ethos.

A further point is in place here. We may assume that no one is obliged to sacrifice so much that she drops to a level *worse* than what she would be at in an egalitarian society. But an egalitarian society *ensures* that no one falls below a (decent) basic minimum, and that is not ensured for people of average income in an inegalitarian society, since they are subject to the buffetings of uncompensated bad luck. And once again, this applies with special force in the case of children. "My children," the rich egalitarian could say, "may, for all kinds of reasons, including unforeseeable ones, be in a much worse position than I am, as a result of which they might fare worse under our existing unjust institutions than they would in an egalitarian society, unless I take steps to insure them against our society's risks by an appropriate policy of saving and bequest. It is therefore justifiable for me to engage in such saving (though not to spend extravagantly), rather than to give away most of what I've got. It is for the same reason not unreasonable for me to spend a lot on helping to improve their prospective labor market position (e.g., through private schooling) to ensure that they will not be worse off than they would be under an egalitarian regime."

The relative-disadvantage problem might be thought to show that what goes for the public domain need not go for the private. One might say that for assurance reasons, equality is, necessarily, a *social* project.

13

The foregoing point, about disadvantage related to one's social milieu, including the disadvantage of imposing a special regime upon one's loved ones, seems to me to have some substance. And there is another substantial point. For although Fulvia Morgana is supposed to be, and on the whole is, a risible figure, she is definitely onto *something* when she claims that, unlike what holds for "Italian peasants" (see section 2, above), it is hard for those who are used to being rich to be poor with dignity. That something may be not exactly *dignity*, but, perhaps, the absence of a constant sense of deprivation. Unstarving, decently sheltered poor peasants are often better placed to enjoy a fulfilling life than self-expropriated wealthy people are. (And that is distinct from the relative-disadvantage point, since it has force against the demand that all rich people give up their wealth, and not just against one of them doing so when (most of) the others do not.)[46]

Deeply relevant to how much weight the deprivation justification has is the problematic question of the metric of equality. The deprivation justification of the ways of rich egalitarians is made within a welfarist metric; it fails utterly within a resourcist one. (Note that resource egalitarians should laugh harder at Fulvia's special pleading than should welfare egalitarians, since the latter take seriously the predicament of people whose tastes are expensive in the sense that they need more resources than others do to live a fulfilling life.) My own view is that *both* welfare *and* resources should count.[47] But I have not applied that view to the issues addressed here. I reserve the task of doing so for a future and more systematically structured study of the "rich-egalitarian" problem.

14

Before turning to one further justification that an egalitarian might adduce for not abandoning (much or most of) her wealth in an unequal society, let me restate, in capsule form, the justifications that have been examined thus far (the number indicates the section in which the stated justification appeared): (5) what's bad about inequality is that it divides people from one another, and my giving wouldn't help to reduce that division; (6) what's bad about inequality is that it produces bad lives, and my giving might not increase the number of good lives; (7) my giving would be a drop in the ocean; (8) the norm of equality is essentially a duty of the state, or of the collective it represents, rather than of the individual; (9) giving does not touch the fundamental injustice, which is inequality of power; (11) because of the burden it imposes on the will, giving (by contrast with being taxed) is oppressively costly; (12) giving sinks one below the level of one's peer group, and that carries special costs; (13) the sharp reduction in living standard that follows self-expropriation induces indignity and/or acute deprivation.

Now, within the general category of justifications[48] for not performing action X (here, X is yielding up one's riches), one can distinguish between those that make it wrong to do X and those that make X neither obligatory nor wrong. One can, moreover, distinguish, within the latter subcategory, between justifications that do, and those that do not, make

X supererogatory—that is, something *beyond* duty that it would be specially admirable to do.[49]

The resulting taxonomy may be depicted as follows:

JUSTIFICATIONS FOR NOT DOING *X*		
That make it wrong to do *X* (JW)	That make it neither obligatory nor wrong to do *X*	
	That make doing *X* supererogatory (JS)	That do not make doing *X* superogatory (J)

We may classify the eight justifications discussed above as follows: (5) through (9) are of type J,[50] and (11) through (13) are of type JS (in modified forms, the last three would be excuses rather than justifications, but that is not how they are to be understood here).[51]

Our ninth would-be justification contrasts with those that have already been examined, because it alone is of the JW type. This defense of the rich egalitarian says that it would be counterproductive—that is, not merely pointless, but destructive—for individuals to pursue the goal of improving the condition of the badly off through private munificence. The defense might be fleshed out in several ways.

First, it might be contended that, in the matter of promoting equality, isolated individual action produces not the good results that action engaged in by all or by many would produce, but, instead, bad results. Yet it is hard to see why that should be so. There are no coordination problems in this domain which would mean that individual acts of self-sacrifice might generate unproductive confusion.[52]

Second, it could be urged that community welfare programs and other voluntary assistance induce the persistence of a dependence that their beneficiaries might otherwise escape. But it is wholly implausible to insist that no such action can be significantly beneficial.[53]

Finally, and more persuasively, at least in certain contexts, there is the argument that retaining my resources enables me to do things in the interests of egalitarianism that I could not do if I gave them away. Since I'm rich, my position in society affords me access to influential people whose decisions affect the lot of the badly off. I could not bend the ear of the police commissioner if I never received invitations to the high-life social functions at which I am likely to meet him. I must retain lavish resources if I am to entertain, in appropriate fashion, important people who might help the cause. I could not, moreover, run for a position on the municipal authority if I lacked the connections that money brings. And because I am wealthy, I do not have to earn my living, and that enables me to do uncompensated egalitarian work that I would otherwise lack the time to do. (I should also mention what my money enables me to do in respect of my children. By buying them topnotch education and other privileges, while nevertheless instilling egalitarian values in them, I ensure that they will be among the most talented people in the labor market, and I thereby make it more likely that some who enjoy privileged positions will use them for egalitarian ends.)

The credibility of this rationale for remaining a *rich* egalitarian depends on the shape that politics takes in a given society. It is more credible the more remote a democratic movement for equality is, and I judge that it is more credible for the rather undemocratic politics of the United States than for the somewhat more democratic, less élite-determined (up until recently, anyway) politics of Britain. You may disagree with that assessment, but you will perhaps agree that it would be sheer dogmatism to say that the I-need-to-keep-my-money-precisely-in-order-to-promote-egalitarianism justification has no credibility under any circumstances.

I have acknowledged that a rich egalitarian may have good reasons for not giving extravagantly in an unequal society. But I have not tried to estimate how strong those reasons are, all things considered—how weighty they can plausibly be thought to be in one society or another. There is a great deal more to be said about the problem of the rich egalitarian, but the present exercise—whose ambition, you will recall (see section 2), was only to put forward considerations that bear on the problem—ends here.

Envoi

I said in the preface that Marxism set itself the task of liberating humanity from the oppression that the capitalist market visits upon it. In illustration of that oppression, I close this book by relating a true short story about my father, whose name was Morrie.

Morrie began his working life at the age of fourteen, in 1925. He worked in a factory as a dress cutter, and he retired fifty-five years later, in 1980, at the age of sixty-nine, at which point he was still working in a factory as a dress cutter. For a couple of years, toward the end of the 1940s, he tried, with one partner, to run a small dress factory of his own. That business failed, largely, I believe, because Morrie was unable to bring himself to make the workers in his little factory work fast enough so that the dresses the factory produced could be priced sufficiently low to match the competition. I am not ashamed that he was, for that reason, unable to prosper as a businessman.

I want to tell you how Morrie's factory career ended. One December day in 1979 the boss of the factory in which he was working called three dress cutters into his office: Morrie, and two younger ones. The boss told them that there was not enough work to keep them on, and that he would therefore have to let them go. So Morrie thought that his working life, which was also the matrix of his social life, had, instantly, come to an end.

But this turned out to be untrue, because, a few days later, on what was the following Sunday, the boss rang Morrie at home and told him that he had reassessed the position and that Morrie should return to work on Monday.

So Morrie came back to the factory. He noticed that the younger cutters who had been dismissed when he was dismissed were not there. Perhaps the boss had never intended to release Morrie permanently (Morrie was a particularly good cutter), but had found it difficult to fire the younger men while being seen to keep on an older man, with fewer family responsibilities, a man for whom suddenly being fired could be regarded as less awful. Perhaps, then, Morrie's original dismissal was just a smokescreen.

Soon after Morrie's return to the factory, the boss was doing the rounds, making sure that everybody was working hard enough. Morrie paused in his own work, and asked the boss: "Where do I stand now? I mean, am I back for good now? What's the position?" And the boss replied, "Don't worry about it, Morrie, don't worry about it, don't worry about it, Morrie." He did not say whether that meant that Morrie shouldn't worry about the question or that he shouldn't worry about its answer. Morrie sought clarification, but the boss stonewalled. He did not answer Morrie's question. And a few weeks later the boss came up to Morrie and said, "OK, Morrie, that's it." And that, indeed, was it. (Either the boss had originally miscalculated how much labor he needed, or commercial conditions had changed.)

The capitalist market does not, of course, require people to handle people roughly, but the boss's manner is not the main point of the story; its point is that the market does require people to *handle* people, to manage them, in a particular sense. The story would lose little of its force if the boss's manner had been more suave.

Morrie was dismissed because it no longer paid the boss to pay him. The dismissal of Willy Loman by his boss in Arthur Miller's *Death of a Salesman* was more brutal than Morrie's dismissal, and similarly instructive. Willy's boss says, "It's a business, kid, and everybody's gotta pull his own weight. . . . 'Cause you gotta admit, business is business." And Willy admits it. "Yes," he says, "business is definitely business."

Business is, among other things, people treating people according to a market norm—the norm that says they are to be dispensed with if they cannot produce at a rate which satisfies market demand. Of course that promotes "efficiency," but it also corrupts humanity. Business turns human producers into commodities. Nor does it spare their employers—"For what shall it profit a man, if he shall gain the whole world, and lose his own soul?" (Mark 8:36).

NOTES

Prospectus

1. Those brief descriptions of the three doctrines might be thought to exaggerate their differences, by ignoring similarities among them, but the descriptions suffice, here, to indicate the profound contrasts of focus and emphasis, the profound differences of feel, among these doctrines.

2. Given my Marxist provenance, it is ironic that the feature of Rawls's view to which I strongly object, its restriction of justice to the "basic structure" of society, has been plausibly presented as liberalism's belated catching-up with Marx: "If Rawls had achieved nothing else, he would be important for having taken seriously the idea that the subject of justice is what he calls 'the basic structure of society.' . . . When we talk about the basic structure of a society, we are concerned with the way in which institutions work systematically so as to advantage some and disadvantage others. Rawls's incorporation of this notion of a social structure into his theory represents the coming of age of liberal political philosophy. For the first time, a major figure in the broadly individualist tradition has taken account of the legacy of Marx and Weber." (Barry, *Justice as Impartiality*, p. 214; and cf. Pogge, *Realizing Rawls*, pp. 3, 11–12).

3. Quoted in Jaki, *Lord Gifford and His Lectures*, pp. 72–73.

4. This is how Lord Gifford named them; the quotation marks are his (see ibid., p. 73).

5. Ibid., pp. 73–74.

1. Paradoxes of Conviction

1. I specify that sense at p. 10 below.

2. I do not say always; see p. 10 below.

3. I have been asked whether this explanation of the difference between their beliefs explains it by causes or by reasons. The question is delicate, but its answer, I think, is: by causes, either mediately or immediately. It

is immediately by causes if nonrational aspects of upbringing—father's gruff, or kind, voice, for example—made the difference. It is mediately by causes if reasons presented to one of the parties were not presented to the other, as a causal result of who their parents were.

4. Note that the Principle is weaker than the following principle: *You lack good reason to believe p rather than q when your grounds for believing p are not better than another's grounds for believing q.* That principle is too strong, as a counterexample to it—devised by Michael Otsuka—shows:

Medical science points to the efficacy of a given minor surgical procedure as a necessary and sufficient means to save somebody's limb without risk to the patient's life. Nevertheless, some nefarious individual has rigged things so that, unbeknownst to the surgeon, an undetectable bomb will go off if and only if she performs this surgical procedure. The surgeon's belief that performing this surgery will save the person's limb rather than kill him is certainly justified. There is, nevertheless, somebody else (to wit, the nefarious individual) who has better grounds for believing otherwise. Yet the surgeon does not therefore lack good reasons for her belief.

5. Which means, here, no more than: without irrationality.

6. Some have suggested that this is too strong, that to believe that *p* is merely to lack the belief that one lacks good reason to believe that *p*. I am convinced that the stronger statement, above, is true, but none of my conclusions depend on that, as you will see from the Argument presented later in this section. (Is Tertullian's "credo quia absurdum" inconsistent with even the weaker one of the foregoing two claims? If so, who is confounded—Tertullian, or me?)

7.   Although I find myself in severe disagreement with Robert Nozick's approach to "rational belief" in the eponymous chapter of his *Nature of Rationality,* I need not reject the distinction he makes on p. 70 between "*p* is the rational thing to believe" and "believing *p* is the rational thing to do." My discussion concerns rationality with respect to the first half of that distinction, whether or not its second half has application. (Many would say that believing is too unlike doing for the second half of Nozick's distinction to apply.)

As Nozick says, the relevant goals with respect to rationality in the first case are purely cognitive; thus, it does not redeem the rationality in the relevant sense of a believer if she correctly claims that adherence to what she was taught to believe is less disruptive of her life, even if—what I do not concede—it is a rational thing for her to do to (contrive to) believe that. If you remain a Catholic after meeting your twin (meaning *not* that you simply choose to *express* your Christian belief—which need not differ from your twin's—through your wonted liturgy etc., but that you continue to *believe* what distinguishes your belief from Protestantism) because of that desire for continuity and nondisruption, then, in the terms of Nozick's distinction, even if that is a rational thing to do, what is rational here is believing a *p* which is not a rational thing to believe.

8. (a) To be more precise, the fact that I was brought up to believe it is not *in itself* a reason for believing it; it becomes one when conjoined with a belief that my own upbringing was sounder than hers, epistemically. But I am interested in the commonplace case where you know that you have no grounds for believing that your own upbringing was epistemically sounder.

(b) It could, of course, be the case that my upbringing *happened* to induce a true belief in me, other than by providing me with good grounds for believing it. But if (as I have insisted) I need to believe that I have good reason for believing what I do, then I cannot, without irrationality, believe of one of my beliefs that I lack grounds for it, and I therefore cannot rationally believe that it is true although I lack grounds for believing it.

9. In the statement of the Principle, "another" does not, of course, denote a particular person; the word functions here as an existentially quantified variable. Accordingly, a more precise rendering of (2) would be: "You lack good reason to believe *p* rather than *q* when you cannot justifiably disbelieve that there exists another whose grounds for believing *q* are at least as good as your grounds for believing *p*."

10. Note that it is irrelevant to the force of the Argument whether or not the people referred to in (3) can *identify* another or others whom they realize to be no less well placed epistemically than they themselves are. If you admit that there exists someone, you know not who, whose grounds for believing that *q* are as good as yours are for believing that *p*, then you can hardly say: Since I don't know who has grounds as good as mine are, I'm not bothered, but I would be if I knew who does have such grounds. Moreover, and as I have already urged, the extreme plausibility, in the present context, of the proposition that someone (merely) *could* have grounds for *q* as good as mine are for *p* should suffice to give me pause.

11. I try to deal with further challenges in an unpublished paper, which is available from me on request.

12. Maybe, that is, to put the point in Nozick's terms (see note 7 above), it is rational to believe propositions that structure our lives, even if they are not rational things to believe.

13. There was in the Oxford of that day an obsessional interest in the status of claims. The distinction between conceptual and empirical propositions

was also very important. I recall a discussion in 1962, in my room in New College at the top of Robinson Tower, with two close friends, who are still close friends (they are now Professor Stephen Scott of the Faculty of Law at McGill University, and Professor Marshall Berman of the Department of Political Science at the City University of New York) in which we were discussing some conceptual matter. Marshall made a large, interesting, and, to all appearances, nonconceptual claim. This enraged Stephen, who pounced on Marshall. "But that's just an *empirical* point!" he cried. Whereupon Marshall pleaded, "Can't we make empirical points *sometimes?*"

14. Note that round-earth believers will rightly deny that the crucial thing that made them into such was anything along those lines.

15. I do not say that I should be wary about my affirmation of the distinction merely because I would have rejected it had I gone to Harvard; what I said above about the flat earth / round earth case shows that I reject that inference. What I say, instead, is that I should suspect my reasons for affirming the distinction, since I know I would be much less impressed by them had I studied the issue in a place which I have every reason to believe sustained intellectual standards as high as those which prevailed at Oxford.

2. Politics and Religion in a Montreal Communist Jewish Childhood

1. Some of the material in sections 2 and 3 of this memoir appears in "The Future of a Disillusion," which is chapter 11 of my book *Self-Ownership*. The entire memoir appears in a Yiddish translation by Dovid Katz, in *Die Pen,* 22 (1996). Readers of Yiddish who would like a copy of that may have one on application to me.

2. I do not know what the family's condition was in the turbulent postrevolutionary period which preceded the adoption of the New Economic Policy in 1921.

3. They were gentile because discrimination against hiring Jewish teachers in the Quebec school system meant that there were few Jewish aspirants to the profession. And they were noncommunist not only because most people were, but also because the communist minority consisted mainly of French Canadians (the majority linguistic group), Jews, and Ukrainians. Most English-speaking Montreal schoolteachers at primary level were genteel Protestant women of British Isles extraction—not a category abounding in subversives.

4. A glossary of the Yiddish words used in this chapter will be found at the end of it.

5. Strong ideologies tend toward the Manichean: it's cowboys and Indians,

cops and robbers, good versus evil, progressives versus reactionaries. Nothing is a mixture of good and evil, and there is no variation, no shading, within either the good or the evil. In 1955, when I was fourteen, an American communist called William Mandel gave a talk at the Communist Party's Beaver Camp, the message of which was that, as a matter of intelligent tactics, we communists should distinguish among spokesmen of the ruling class between those who were completely reactionary and those who were more liberal. It says a lot about where my head was at then that I was surprised that such a distinction could be made. And it says a lot about Mandel's knowledge of the audience he was addressing that he thought it worthwhile to emphasize such a distinction, since it's a pretty self-evident one.

6. Camp Kinderland was the children's part of the camp where my parents courted. See section 1 above.

7. Entitled the *Act to Protect the Province against Communistic Propaganda,* 1 Geo. VI, S.Q. 1937, c. 11, it was enacted by the Legislature of Quebec on March 24, 1937, and was later consolidated as chapter 52 of the *Revised Statutes of Quebec,* 1941. On March 8, 1957, the Supreme Court of Canada struck it down in *Switzman v. Elbling* [1957] S.C.R. 285, as an intrusion into the exclusive legislative authority of the Parliament of Canada on the subject of "Criminal Law." (I thank Stephen Scott for this note.)

8. Foreign-party delegations were not permitted to attend Khrushchev's speech, but Tim Buck, the general secretary of the Canadian Party, got the details from the British Party leader, Harry Pollitt, who got them on the grapevine, and Buck transmitted them to the rest of the Canadian delegation. (I am grateful to Ruth Feigelson of Montreal, who provided this information, and who was then the wife of Gui Caron, the leader of the Quebec Communist Party at the time. Ruth recalls fierce exchanges between Caron and Buck when the latter was staying with the Carons, in the run-up to the resignations of the Quebec "Six.")

9. Those familiar with Montreal might like to know that these premises were on the north side of Mount Royal Avenue, opposite Fletcher's Field, just west of what was then the Young Men's Hebrew Association and what later became a Université de Montréal sports center, and above a delicatessen called, at different times, Shap's, Dunn's, Nu-Park, and Nu-Way.

10. The NFLY (pronounced "enfly," as in "fly") was, in all but name, the Young Communist League. The Communist Party had been outlawed when, because of the Molotov-Ribbentrop Pact, it refused to support the war against Germany. So it changed its name to the Labour Progressive Party, and the YCL became the NFLY. (The party reassumed its original name in 1959. In announcing the nomenclatural reclamation, the *Cana-*

dian Tribune (the party newspaper) explained that "Communist Party" was being restored because it was "scientifically more correct.")

11. The line of the softliners was not all that soft. Thus, for example, the Soviet action in Hungary in the autumn of October 1956 was regarded, at the time, by virtually everyone in the party, as an entirely justified suppression of a fascist rebellion. I myself so regarded it at least as late as 1968. I recall contrasting it, then, with the invasion of Czechoslovakia that year, which thoroughly rid me of my pro-Sovietism.

12. I emphasize that phrase to make it clear that I am not denying—or affirming—that there is an instrumental justification for the existence of a state that belongs to Jewish people. I do deny that every people, or indeed any people, has a right to a state just because it is a distinct people, which is to say for reasons that have nothing to do with its contingent geopolitical emplacement.

13. We also had contempt for the "Restricted Clientele" signs (see section 5 above), but they could nevertheless make you feel dirty.

   People who are themselves free of bigotry and racism, and who have never been at either end of the racist relationship, are aware of the injustice with respect to goods and opportunities that racism causes, because that effect is obvious; but, unless specially advised, they have no way of knowing how damaging racism is to the self-respect of its victims, and they sometimes (absurdly) take the responsive self-assertion of minorities—for example, that of black people who speak of black pride—at its (self-confident) face value. Stokely Carmichael would not have had to say that "black is beautiful" (with which magnificent utterance he launched an era of African-American spiritual rehabilitation) if his black audience had already thought so.

14. Hebrew for "a place and a name." Yad Vashem is the Holocaust memorial in Jerusalem.

15. For reasons not unconnected with those that motivated Hegel's critique of Judaism. See Lecture 5, section 7, below.

3. The Development of Socialism from Utopia to Science

1. Or, strictly, as it was then called, the Labour Progressive Party. See Lecture 2, note 10.

2. The obstetric conception generates what I call (in section 2 of chapter 4 of *History, Labour, and Freedom*) the "birth pangs solution" to the problem of how to reconcile an assertion of the historical inevitability of socialism with a call for revolutionary agency to bring it about. In that chapter I criticize the logic of the birth pangs solution to the stated problem and I

propose an alternative solution, which is fashioned without much reliance on inherited Marxist writings. The criticisms of the obstetric conception that are offered here go beyond (and do not reproduce) the criticisms of the logic of the birth pangs solution in *History, Labour, and Freedom*.

3. That nomenclatural fix was a misfortune, as I explain in section 4 of "Commitment without Reverence," which is to be reprinted in a forthcoming second edition of my book *Karl Marx's Theory of History*.

4. Engels, *Anti-Dühring*, Introduction, chapter 1; and part 3, chapters 1 and 2.

5. See section 6 of Lecture 4, below.

6. There is an arresting anticipation of Lenin in this passage from Marx's "Critical Marginal Notes on the Article 'The King of Prussia and Social Reform; By a Prussian,'" which he wrote in Paris on July 31, 1844, and which was published in *Vorwärts!* (August 7 and 10 of that year): "The German proletariat is the *theorist* of the European proletariat, just as the English proletariat is its *economist* and the French proletariat its *politician*. [Thus] Germany, though incapable of *political* revolution, has a *classical* summons to *social* revolution. As the impotence of the German bourgeoisie is the *political* impotence of Germany, the talent of the German proletariat—even apart from German theory—is the *social* talent of Germany. The disparity between philosophical and political development in Germany is no *abnormality*. It is a necessary disparity. Only in socialism can a philosophical people find its suitable practice; thus, only in the *proletariat* can it find the active element of its emancipation" (p. 353, emphases in original).

Etienne Balibar recounts further anticipations of Lenin: "The presentation of Marxism as a worldview long ago coalesced around the formula, the 'three sources of Marxism': *German philosophy, French socialism,* and *British political economy*. This derives from the way in which Engels divided up his exposition of historical materialism in *Anti-Dühring* (1878), and sketched the history of the antithetical relations between materialism and idealism, metaphysics and dialectics. This schema would be systematized by Kautsky in a lecture of 1907 entitled 'The Three Sources of Marxism: The Historic Work of Marx,' in which the 'science of society, starting out from the standpoint of the proletariat,' is characterized as 'the synthesis of German, French, and British thought.' The intention was not only to promote internationalism, but to present the theory of the proletariat as a totalization of European history, ushering in the reign of the universal. Lenin was to adopt the formulation in a lecture of 1913, 'The Three Sources and Three Component Parts of Marxism.' However, the symbolic model of a combination of the component parts of culture was, in reality, not new: it reflected the persistence of the great myth of the 'European triarchy,' expounded by Moses Hess (who had used the expression as the title of one of his books in 1841) and taken up by Marx in his early writings, in which the notion of the *proletariat* made its appearance." Balibar, *The Philosophy of Marx*, p. 7, citing Karl Kautsky, *Ethics and the Materialist Conception of History*, trans. John B. Askew (Chicago: Charles H. Kerr, 1906.)

See also David McLellan, *The Thought of Karl Marx*, p. 37: "Lassalle, the prominent German socialist leader of the 1869s, said of [*The Poverty of Philosophy*] that in the first half Marx showed himself to be a Ricardo turned socialist, and in the second part a Hegel turned economist."

7. I do not say that the dialectical idea was the only, or even the most important, idea that Marx retained from his philosophical formation, but it was, as we shall see, a central instrument that he used in creating from its different components the amalgam that came to be called "Marxism."

8. For elaboration of that theme in Hegel, see section 17 of Lecture 5.

9. One may, of course, question the analogy between acorns and cultures. For it is implausible that a culture's potentialities are there from its inception in the way an acorn's are. A culture has divergent potentialities; which one gets realized depends on accidents. Thus, Hellenism, one might say, was *one* potentiality, not *the* potentiality, of Athens. The potentiality thereby attributed to Athens is what I defined on page 14 of *Karl Marx's Theory of History* as potentiality of the "second grade": a culture is potentially *f* in the sense that under *some* normal conditions it will become *f*. Contrast the acorn, whose potential to become an oak is of the "first grade": it becomes one under *all* normal conditions. (I thank Amélie Rorty for remarks that led to this footnote.)

10. In, that is, its native and flourishing form; see McLellan, *Marx before Marxism*, p. 156. Marx did have some acquaintance with it while still a young man in Germany: "The Fourierist Ludwig Gall lived in [Marx's native] Trier during Marx's period at high school (1830–5) . . . [and Marx's father-in-law-to-be] Baron von Westphalen . . . was certainly abreast of the latest social and political ideas and communicated his enthusiasm to Karl" (Michael Evans, *Karl Marx*, p. 15). See further Rubel and Manale, *Marx without Myth*, p. 24; and McLellan, ibid., pp. 13–14, 25–26, 39, 50–51, 65.

11. That was the first of his three exiles. He left Germany for Paris in October 1843, Paris for Brussels in January 1845, and Brussels for London in August 1849.

12. Marx had already begun to read the classical economists in his Paris days,

but his study of them was immeasurably extended in the British Museum.

13. "Socialism" here denotes the immediately postcapitalist social form, called (by implication) "the lower phase of communism" in Marx's *Critique of the Gotha Programme* (p. 24), as opposed to the higher phase of communism, in which, among other things, the market disappears, and which is hardly just capitalism minus the capitalist.

14. For an illustration of the concealment/defense distinction, see Cohen, *Karl Marx's Theory of History,* pp. 332–335.

15. Lenin, "The Three Sources and Component Parts of Marxism," p. 452. (Since Scotland is not part of England, Lenin should have written "*British* political economy.")

16. See Engels, *Socialism: Utopian and Scientific,* pp. 10–12.

17. Marx, *The Poverty of Philosophy,* pp. 140–141.

18. Marx to Friedrich Sorge, 19 October 1877, in *Letters to Americans,* p. 117.

19. For how strongly this is meant, see Lecture 4, note 29, and the text to note 19.

20. See Engels, *Socialism: Utopian and Scientific,* p. 27.

21. The most extravagant development of this theme in Marxism appears in Georg Lukács, *History and Class Consciousness* (1923). See especially the long chapter "Reification and the Consciousness of the Proletariat."

22. There is nothing obvious about this inference, which is not mine but Engels'. I examine inferences related to it in section 13, below.

23. See Engels, *Socialism: Utopian and Scientific,* p. 75. And see the quotation from ibid., pp. 45–46, given two paragraphs below.

24. Ibid., pp. 45–6. See also ibid., pp. 10–11, 42.

25. If *q* is true, how was *utopian* socialism possible? Only if it failed the "broad-scale" requirement *and/or* because it was possible, then (prospectively, as it were), to overturn capitalism.

26. See Cohen, *History, Labour, and Freedom,* chapter 6 ("Fettering"), especially section 1.

27. Marx, preface to *A Contribution to the Critique of Political Economy,* pp. 12–13.

4. Hegel in Marx

1. See Hegel, *Hegel's Logic,* p. 147.

2. In Walter Kaufmann's translation of it, which is vastly superior to Baillie's or Miller's, and which appears in his *Hegel.* The exposition of Hegel and Schopenhauer that follows is heavily indebted to Kaufmann's book.

3. Kaufmann explains: "Quantitative differences, as opposed to qualitative

ones, do not concern the essence of a thing: as soon as they do, we say that the difference is not merely quantitative." Kaufmann, *Hegel*, p. 423.

4. Ibid., p. 420.

5. Ibid., pp. 421, 423.

6. Engels, *Socialism: Utopian and Scientific*, p. 87.

7. Marx, Letter to his father, 10 November 1837, in *Karl Marx: Selected Writings*, p. 8.

8. Marx ends his letter as follows: "Please give my love to dear, wonderful Jenny. I have already read her letter twelve times and I still find new delights. It is in every particular, including that of style, the most beautiful letter that I can imagine written by a woman." Ibid., p. 9.

9. Ibid., p. 6.

10. Ibid., pp. 6–7.

11. Ibid., p. 7.

12. Ibid., p. 8. The reader may be puzzled that Hegel's outlook is here counterposed to an idealist one. But the "idealism" of Kant and Fichte is, here, the independence and superior authority of the ideal over the real, which contradicts the Hegelian idealism that recognizes no reality independent of the idea, and therefore, unlike Kant and Fichte, no is/ought opposition.

13. I cannot be sure, but I believe that this clause represents not a belated exoneration of mathematics but an invocation of a heterodox "Schopenhauerian" mathematics.

14. Marx, "The Centralization Question," in *Writings of the Young Marx on Philosophy and Society*, pp. 106–107. Note how swift in the latter part of this text is the movement from the theoretical to the historico-political construal of the doctrine about problems set out in section 3 above.

15. Marx, Letter to Arnold Ruge, May 1843, in *Karl Marx: Selected Writings*, p. 36.

16. The completion of this paragraph reads: "as is also the case in Feuerbach's critique of religion." The structural parallel between the message of the present paragraph of this letter to Ruge (together with that of the one that follows) and Marx's spin on Feuerbach is laid out in Lecture 5, section 1, below.

17. Marx, Letter to Ruge, September 1843, pp. 37–38.

18. Compare this flourish from Marx's "On the Jewish Question," which was written in the autumn of 1843: "The formulation of a question is its solution. The criticism of the Jewish question is the answer to the Jewish question." In *Writings of the Young Marx on Philosophy and Society*, p. 218, translation amended.

19. Marx and Engels, *The German Ideology*, p. 47. *The German Ideology* also

foreshadows the sentence in the 1859 Preface which I have placed beside Engels' obstetricism as we find it in *Socialism: Utopian and Scientific* (see Lecture 3, sections 13 and 14) and which I shall shortly have occasion to quote at greater length. For Marx says that if consciousness "comes into contradiction with the existing relations, this can only occur because existing social relations have come into contradiction with existing forces of production" (p. 43).

20. See the second paragraph of the present section.

21. The German original of the text on exhibit reads as follows: "Der Kommunismus ist für uns nicht ein Zustand, der hergestellt werden soll, ein Ideal, wonach die Wirklichkeit sich zu richten haben wird. Wir nennen Kommunismus die wirkliche Bewegung, welche den jetzigen Zustand aufhebt" (*Die deutsche Ideologie*, p. 35).

22. See, further, section 5 below.

23. Marx, Preface to *A Contribution to the Critique of Political Economy*, pp. 12–13, emphasis added, translation amended. Compare the Introduction to *A Contribution to the a Critique of Hegel's Philosophy of Right*: "The needs of nations are . . . the ultimate reason for their satisfaction" (p. 45, translation amended).

24. As is shown in Cohen, *Karl Marx's Theory of History*, pp. 172–174.

25. Marx, *Capital*, vol. 1, p. 182. The context and content of the phrase are entirely different from those of the comparable passage in the 1859 Preface, but the thought structure is similar. And the thought content of the 1859 Preface statement is echoed elsewhere in Volume 1 of *Capital* (p. 619), when Marx says that "the development of the contradictions of a given historical form of production is the only historical way in which it can be dissolved and then reconstructed on a new basis."

26. Compare the *Grundrisse*, according to which the solution will be found in capitalist reality, and, were it not discernible there, would never be found: "Capitalism displays a mass of the antithetical forms of the social unity, whose antithetical character can never be abolished through quiet metamorphosis. On the other hand, if we did not find concealed in society as it is the material conditions of production and the corresponding relations of exchange prerequisite for a classless society, then all attempts to explode it would be quixotic" (p. 159).

27. Engels, *Socialism: Utopian and Scientific*, pp. 46, 48. The first part of this excerpt was quoted in Lecture 3, section 13, above.

28. Marx, "Report to the Brussels Congress" (1868), in *The First International and After*, p. 99.

29. Marx, *The Civil War in France*, p. 545. In saying that "the working class have no ideals to realize," Marx did not, of course, mean, absurdly, that

they had no aims or ends, but merely that those *aims* or *ends* were not inspired by a supra- or transhistorically valid *ideal*. Having quoted the passage from *The Civil War in France* which ends with the flourish reproduced above, Steven Lukes perceptively reports as follows:

"Interestingly, in a draft of the very same work, *The Civil War in France,* Marx observed that the Utopian Socialists were 'clearly describing the goal of the social movement, the supersession of the wage system with all its economical conditions of class rule'; but they 'tried to compensate for the historical conditions of the movement by phantastic pictures and plans of a new society in whose propaganda they saw the true means of salvation. From the moment the workingmen class movement became real, the phantastic utopias evanesced, not because the working class had given up the end aimed at by these Utopists, but because they had found the real means to realise them, but in their place came a real insight into the historic conditions of the movement and a more and more gathering force of the military organisation of the working class. But the last two ends of the movement proclaimed by the Utopians are the last ends proclaimed by the Paris Revolution and by the International. Only the means are different and the real conditions of the movement are no longer clouded in utopian fables.'" Lukes, *Marxism and Morality,* p. 8; quoting Marx, First Draft of *The Civil War in France,* in *Marx-Engels: Gesamtausgabe* (Berlin: Dietz, 1978), vol. 1, p. 22.

30. Engels, *On the History of the Communist League,* p. 345. Compare Engels to Paul Lafargue, 11 August 1884: "Marx would protest against the economic 'political and social ideal' which you attribute to him. When one is a 'man of science,' one does not have an ideal; one works out scientific results, and when one is a party man to boot, one fights to put them into practice. But when one has an ideal, one cannot be a man of science, for one starts out with preconceptions [*on a un parti pris d'avance*]" (p. 235). I am indebted for this reference to Daniel Goldstick's unpublished essay "Objectivity and Moral Commitment in the World-View of Marx and Engels."

31. Luxemburg, "The Russian Revolution," in *"The Russian Revolution" and "Leninism or Marxism?"* p. 70. For further discussion of this text, see section 8 below.

32. The present section is (I think) rather better than it would have been had I not had to struggle with excellent criticism of an earlier version of it from Elizabeth Kiss.

33. Marx, *The Poverty of Philosophy,* p. 193.

34. Engels, *The Condition of the Working-Class in England in 1844,* pp. 236–237.

35. Marx, "Wages, Price, and Profit," in *Marx and Engels: Selected Works in Two Volumes*, p. 446.
36. See Marx, "Inaugural Address of the Working Men's International Association," in *Marx and Engels: Selected Works in Two Volumes*, p. 383.
37. "Wages, Price, and Profit," p. 447, my emphasis.
38. See Lecture 3, sections 10 and 11.
39. This second point is, I grant, more freely interpretive than the first, because one could also interpret the realization of "being precedes consciousness," in this context, not in scientific socialism's having a utopian precursor, but in its having as precursor a movement—rather than a doctrine—that was unconscious of its own (implicitly) socialist character.

    For all that, it does seem that Marx thought that scientific socialism is utopian socialism risen to consciousness of itself, whether or not he thought that it needed to be. This we can infer from the phrase *"in nuce"* in the letter by Marx to Friedrich Sorge, which is quoted in Lecture 3, section 11, above.
40. Marx, "1844 Manuscripts," in *Karl Marx: Early Writings*, p. 155.
41. Elster, *Logic and Society*, p. 92, n. 21.
42. For an excellent succinct exposition of this motif, see Kolakowski, *Main Currents of Marxism*, vol. 1, p. 154.
43. See Marx and Engels, *The German Ideology*, pp. 63–64. And compare Engels to Franz Mehring, 14 July 1893: "Ideology is a process which is indeed accomplished consciously by the so-called thinker, but it is the wrong kind of consciousness. The real motive forces impelling him remain unknown to the thinker; otherwise it simply would not be an ideological process. Hence, he imagines false or illusory motive forces. Because it is a rational process, he derives its form as well as its content from pure reasoning, either his own or that of his predecessors. He works exclusively with thought material, which he accepts without examination as something produced by reasoning, and does not investigate further for a more remote source independent of reason; indeed this is a matter of course to him, because, as all action is mediated by thought, it appears to him to be ultimately based upon thought." Engels, in *Karl Marx and Frederick Engels: Selected Correspondence*, p. 434; and compare Engels to Conrad Schmidt, 27 October 1890, ibid., p. 400.
44. See Cohen, "The Workers and the Word: Why Marx Had the Right to Think He Was Right," especially pp. 381–387, where further Marx-attributable arguments for the conclusion that the proletariat lacks illusions are developed.
45. In a communication of 12 June 1920, Lenin criticized the Hungarian communist leader Bela Kun for "absolutely evad[ing] what is most im-

portant, that which constitutes the very gist, the living soul, of Marxism—a concrete analysis of a concrete situation." Lenin, *Collected Works,* vol. 31, p. 166.

46. Marx, *Capital,* vol. 1, p. 92. Compare ibid., p. 916: "Force is the midwife of every old society which is pregnant with a new one."

47. "The tacit assumption underlying the Lenin-Trotsky theory of the dictatorship is this: that the socialist transformation is something for which a ready-made formula lies completed in the pocket of the revolutionary party, which needs only to be carried out energetically in practice. This is, unfortunately—or perhaps fortunately—not the case. Far from being a sum of ready-made prescriptions which have only to be applied, the practical realization of socialism as an economic, social, and juridical system is something which lies completely hidden in the mists of the future. What we possess in our program is nothing but a few main signposts which indicate the general direction in which to look for the necessary measures, and the indications are mainly negative in character at that. Thus, we know more or less what we must eliminate at the outset in order to free the road for a socialist economy. But when it comes to the nature of the thousand concrete, practical measures, large and small, necessary to introduce socialist principles into economy, law, and all social relationships, there is no key in any socialist party program or textbook. That is not a shortcoming but rather the very thing that makes scientific socialism superior to the utopian varieties." Luxemburg, "The Russian Revolution," in *"The Russian Revolution" and "Leninism or Marxism?"* p. 70.

48. I allude, here, to Marx's disparaging attitude to "writing recipes . . . for the cook-shops of the future." *Capital,* vol. 1, p. 99.

49. Hence the great political importance of works such as John Roemer's *A Future for Socialism.*

5. The Opium of the People

1. Karl Marx, "Introduction to *A Contribution to the Critique of Hegel's Philosophy of Right,*" p. 42.

2. See Lecture 4, section 4, above.

3. The Introduction (see note 1) was written at the end of 1843 and the beginning of 1844, and published in 1844 in the *Deutsch-Französische Jahrbücher.*

4. Marx, "Introduction to *A Contribution to the Critique of Hegel's Philosophy of Right,*" p. 50.

5. Since that discussion was largely musical in form, it cannot be reproduced in this book.

6. The present question is closely related to the question posed in the first sentence of *What Is Metaphysics?* by Martin Heidegger, who was probably the most distinguished philosopher ever to display Nazi sympathies. Heidegger asks, "Why is there something rather than nothing at all?" And the great Columbia philosopher Sidney Morgenbesser has imagined himself answering Heidegger as follows: "So if there was nothing, you would still complain!"

7. Hegel, *Hegel's Philosophy of Nature*, p. 205, translation slightly amended.

8. Hegel, *Lectures on the Philosophy of Religion*, vol. 1, p. 200.

9. For an interesting disquisition on this Hegelian theme, with special reference to Hindu religious belief, see Robert Nozick, *Philosophical Explanations*, pp. 607-608.

10. In the present paragraph I am heavily indebted to Michael Rosen.

11. See "Prospectus," above. Lord Gifford provided an interesting commentary on that thought. His brother John reported as follows: "He studied and admired Spinoza, yet always denied that he himself was a Pantheist, marking the distinction thus: 'Spinoza holds that everything is God. I hold that God is everything; if I were to assume a name descriptive of my belief, I should be called a Theopanist.'" Jaki, *Lord Gifford and His Lectures*, p. 98.

12. Hegel, *Hegel's Logic*, p. 164.

13. The absolute necessity of the incarnation is an aspect of the general truth that "the only means by which the Essence and the inner self can be verified [or made true] is their appearance in outward reality" (ibid., p. 164), which is the Wittgensteinian principle honored in Hegel's doctrine of God.

14. Hegel, *The Philosophy of History*, Introduction, p. 17.

15. Hegel, *Hegel's Logic*, p. 39.

16. Ibid., p. 64.

17. Hegel, *The Phenomenology of Mind*, p. 780. The motif pervades Hegel's thought. Some further illustrations:

"The substance of mind is freedom—i.e., the absence of dependence on an Other, the relating of self to self." (*Hegel's Philosophy of Mind*, p. 15.)

"In thinking, I am free, because I am not in an other, but remain simply and solely in touch with myself; and the object, which for me is my essential reality, is in undivided unity my being-for-myself." (*Phenomenology of Mind*, p. 243, translation slightly amended.)

"In the formula I = I is enunciated the principle of Reason and Freedom. Freedom and Reason consist in this: that I raise myself to the form of I = I, that I know everything as mine, as 'I,' that I grasp every object as a member of the system of what I myself am—in short, that I have in one and the same consciousness myself and the world, that in the world I find myself again, and, conversely, in my consciousness have what is, what possesses objectivity." (*Hegel's Philosophy of Mind,* p. 165.)

"When I think of an object [*Gegenstand*], I make it into a thought and deprive it of its sensuous quality; I make it into something which is essentially and immediately mine. For it is only when I think that I am with myself [*bei mir*], and it is only by comprehending it that I can penetrate an object; it then no longer stands opposed to me, and I have deprived it of that quality of its own which it had for itself in opposition to me. Just as Adam says to Eve, 'You are flesh of my flesh and bone of my bone,' so does spirit say, 'This is spirit of my spirit, and its alien character has disappeared.'" (*Elements of the Philosophy of Right,* p. 35.)

18. The materialism which Marx and Engels ascribe to themselves in *The German Ideology* is pretty well identical with empiricism: "The premises from which we begin . . . can . . . be verified in a purely empirical way" (p. 31.)
19. Hegel, *Hegel's Logic,* p. 64.
20. Ibid., p. 222.
21. I do not think that Hegel was himself a totalitarian. For remarks pertinent to that issue, see Wood, *Hegel's Ethical Thought,* p. 238.
22. Hegel, *The Phenomenology of Mind,* p. 422.
23. Hegel, *The Philosophy of History,* p. 76. Compare: "The business of spirit is to produce itself, to make itself its own object, and to gain knowledge of itself; in this way, it exists for itself. Natural objects do not exist for themselves; for this reason, they are not free." (*Lectures on the Philosophy of World History: Introduction,* p. 48.)
24. Hegel, *The Philosophy of History,* ibid., p. 64.
25. Ibid., p. 74; see also p. 53.
26. Hegel, *Hegel's Philosophy of Mind,* para. 564, p. 298. Note that, since God is not God insofar as He does not know himself, the human vehicles of His self-consciousness are not to be understood as mere instruments that He uses, for He does not exist in His plenitude without them. Compare section 7 above. (I am indebted to Piero Pinzauti for insisting that I honor this point.)
27. Hegel, *The Philosophy of History,* pp. 17–18.
28. John Maguire provides a lucid statement of the relevant mechanism: Feuerbach "argues that man has an infinite consciousness, unlike any

other creature, and is thus able to conceive of himself not as an isolated unit, but rather as a being whose essence is his species-essence (*Gattungs-wesen*). Each individual is but a limited, finite member of this species; nevertheless he possesses human attributes such as goodness, wisdom, strength, creativity and so on. Realising that these attributes are in principle infinite, the individual is caught in a contradiction between his own finitude and the inherent infinity of the attributes which he finitely possesses. This he resolves by conferring these attributes on a superhuman being, whom he calls God." (Maguire, *Marx's Paris Writings*, p. 123.)

29. Feuerbach, *The Essence of Christianity*, p. 14.
30. Ibid., p. 13.
31. Ibid., p. 21.
32. Engels, *Ludwig Feuerbach and the End of Classical German Philosophy*, p. 368.
33. Marx, *Theses on Feuerbach*, p. 7. The *Theses* were discovered by Engels after Marx's death and published by him, in edited form, in 1888, as an appendix to his *Ludwig Feuerbach*. I give here Engels' historically influential version.
34. For a more extended discussion of this metaphor, see Cohen, *Karl Marx's Theory of History*, app. 1.
35. Feuerbach, "*The Essence of Christianity* in Relation to *The Ego and Its Own*," p. 82.
36. Compare Marx and Engels, *The German Ideology*, p. 51: "While the French and the English at least hold by the political illusion, which is moderately close to reality, the Germans move in the realm of the 'pure spirit,' and make religious illusion the driving force of history."
37. Plato, *The Republic*, p. 235 (bk. 6, Stephanus no. 499).
38. "Abolish" = "aufheben," which literally means to raise up, and also suggests transcend, supersede, transform, and preserve at a higher level. It is the main word for dialectical change. See Lecture 3, section 4, above.
39. Marx, "Introduction to *A Contribution to the Critique of Hegel's Philosophy of Right*," p. 58.
40. Engels, *Ludwig Feuerbach and the End of Classical German Philosophy*, p. 402.
41. Marx, "Introduction to *A Contribution to the Critique of Hegel's Philosophy of Right*," p. 42.

6. Equality

1. The rest of this lecture is a revised version of part of the Introduction to Cohen, *Self-Ownership, Freedom, and Equality*.

2. "Communism is not a doctrine but a *movement*; it proceeds not from principles but from *facts*." Engels, "The Communists and Karl Heinzen," p. 303.

3. See Lecture 3, section 2, above.

4. Marx, *The Critique of the Gotha Programme*, p. 24.

5. Marx and Engels, "The Communist Manifesto," p. 495.

6. I do not mean that the proletariat as a whole was on the march for equality, but just that such struggle for equality as there was—and there was plenty—was in major part proletarian.

7. Words by Ralph Chaplin, and sung to the tune of "John Brown's Body." See Hille, ed., *The People's Song Book*, p. 68.

8. Words by E. Y. ("Yip") Harburg, music by Jay Gorney. In their biography of the former, Harold Meyerson and Ernie Harburg report, most revealingly for my purposes here, as follows:

"'In the song,' Yip told Studs Terkel, the man is really saying: I made an investment in this country. Where the hell are my dividends? . . . It's more than just a bit of pathos. It doesn't reduce him to a beggar. It makes him a dignified human being, asking questions—and a bit outraged, too, as he should be.' The outrage—Yip and Jay's outrage—is grounded in a particular Marxian precept: that labor is denied the full reward for its work. '[I was] well aware at that time,' Yip said, 'of what was wrong with our whole economic system: that the man who builds, the man who creates, is not always the man who gets the profit. He's always working for the man who sells him. So that bewildered person in the street is now saying: I built the railroad, I built the tower, I went to war for this country. Why are my hands empty? And I think what made that song popular and great, and why it's lasting now, is that it's still asking the universal question of why does the man who produces not share in the wealth?'"

(*Who Put the Rainbow in "The Wizard of Oz"?* p. 50. The answer to the question that forms the book's title is: E. Y. "Yip" Harburg, who wrote the lyrics for that film.)

9. To illustrate the depth of the implantation of the first, essentially bourgeois, principle in supposedly radical socialist thought, I offer these quotations from Edward and Eleanor Avelings' *Shelley's Socialism*, which was privately printed in 1888.

The Avelings look forward to a dispensation in which "the two classes at present existing will be replaced by a single class consisting of the whole of the healthy and sane members of the community, possessing all the means of production and distribution in common, and working in common for the production and distribution of commodities" (p. 15).

They do not say what happens to unhealthy or insane people in this dispensation.

They are also explicit in their endorsement of Shelley's de facto exclusion of all nonproducers from the fruits of production: "The opinion of Shelley as to what could be rightly enjoyed as a person's own property and what could only be enjoyed wrongly, will be in part gathered from the following quotation: 'Labour, industry, economy, skill, genius, or any similar powers honourably or innocently exerted, are the foundations of one description of property. All true political institutions ought to defend every man in the exercise of his discretion with respect to property so acquired. . . .' We do not think the meaning of this quotation is strained if it is paraphrased in the more precise language of scientific socialism, thus: "'A man has a right to anything his own labour has produced, and that he does not intend to employ for the purpose of injuring his fellows. . . .'" (p. 36).

Shelley's "Song to the Men of England" continues the theme, in its fifth stanza:

> The seed ye sow, another reaps;
> The wealth ye find, another keeps;
> The robes ye weave, another wears;
> The arms ye forge, another bears. (p. 48)

As does the beginning of his "What Men Gain Fairly":

> What men gain fairly—that they should possess,
> And children may inherit idleness,
> From him who earns it—This is understood;
> Private injustice may be general good. (p. 59)

10. What makes it unclear that it is a fact is the effective option, for many, of unemployment, and the possibility available to some well-salaried people of saving their way out of (truly) being forced to sell their labor power *throughout* their active lives.

11. I do not say that nobody so much as noticed the problem in the past. Anton Menger formulated it clearly a century ago: "Any attempt to carry to a logical conclusion the idea of the labourer's right to the whole produce of his labour is immediately confronted with the numerous persons who are incapable of work (children, the aged and invalids, etc.), and who must depend for the satisfaction of their wants on unearned income." (*The Right to the Whole Produce of Labour,* p. 5; and cf. ibid., pp. 28, 109).

12. This posture is struck in the song "Solidarity Forever," (see section 2 above), which brings all of the features together, and whose verses run, in full, as follows:

> When the union's inspiration through the workers' blood shall run,
> There can be no power greater anywhere beneath the sun;
> Yet what force on earth is weaker than the feeble strength of one,
> For the union makes us strong.
>
> It is we who ploughed the prairies, built the cities where they trade,
> Dug the mines and built the workshops, endless miles of railroad laid;
> Now we stand outcast and starving, 'mid the wonders we have made,
> But the union makes us strong.
>
> They have taken untold millions that they never toiled to earn,
> But without our brain and muscle not a single wheel can turn;
> We can break their haughty power, gain our freedom when we learn
> That the union makes us strong.
>
> In our hands is placed a power greater than their hoarded gold,
> Greater than the might of atoms magnified a thousandfold;
> We can bring to birth a new world from the ashes of the old,
> For the union makes us strong.

Feature 1, that the workers constitute the majority of society, is not explicitly affirmed, but it is surely implied as part of the explanation of the immense potential power of the working class, which is asserted in the first, third, and fourth stanzas. The other part of the explanation of that power is that the workers are the producers, as the second stanza, and the all-important second line of the third, assure us. The feature of exploitation is apparent in the first line of the third stanza, and the third line of the second indicates how utterly deprived the workers are, no doubt on such a scale that the fifth feature (nothing to lose) obtains. As for the revolution feature, the third lines of each of the last two verses, and the second of the first, imply that the workers can transform society, and it is clearly part of the message of the whole song that they will.

13. Marx and Engels, "The Communist Manifesto," p. 519.

14. And they never will, because, if and as their societies undergo further industrialization, then the dissociation of the characteristics which has characterized Western class structure will also occur in the East and South: the majority of producers will no longer be both exploited and in severe need.

15. "The Banks of Marble," words and music by Les Rice, in Silber, ed., *Lift Every Voice!* pp. 92–93.

16. By which I emphatically do not mean that it really was unnecessary, or absent.

17. See Marx and Engels, "The Communist Manifesto," p. 496.

18. This means that I believe (among other things) that if a "nuclear fusion gun" is coming, then, relative to how parlous our situation already is, it is not coming soon enough to vitiate the remarks that follow. (It cannot be excluded that Marx's abundance prediction will be vindicated in some distant future. The present remarks perforce reflect my own assessment of likely constraints for a portion of future time that is sufficiently extended to justify extreme concern, whether or not the classical abundance prediction will one day be fulfilled.)

19. Marx, "Critique of the Gotha Programme," p. 24.

20. Marx and Engels, *The German Ideology*, p. 46. Marx also thought that the socialist transformation would be socially possible only when it was materially necessary—necessary, that is, for continued development of the productive forces:

     "If therefore the proletariat overthrows the political rule of the bourgeoisie, its victory will be only temporary, only an element in the service of the *bourgeois revolution* itself, as in the year 1794 [that is, as in the French Revolution], as long as in the course of history, in its "movement," the material conditions have not yet been created which make necessary the abolition of the bourgeois mode of production and therefore also the definitive overthrow of the political rule of the bourgeoisie." (Marx, "Moralising Criticism and Critical Morality," p. 319.)

     See, further, Cohen, *Self-Ownership, Freedom, and Equality*, ch. 5, sect. 6.

21. It does not follow that his optimism on that score was entirely irrational—driven, that is, by nothing but an aversion to inequality. Whether Marx also had good reasons for believing in a future abundance cannot be judged without a closer study than I have conducted of his critique of classical political economy's pessimistic forecasts.

22. See Lecture 3, section 1.

23. What Marx called "the lower stage of communism" (which, following later Marxist discourse, I shall here call "socialism") provides an objection to that statement, but not a devastating one. The objection is that socialism enforces a rule of distribution ("to each according to his contribution") which can be represented as an answer that Marxists give to the question of what is the right way to distribute. But this objection to the statement in the text is not devastating, for two reasons. First, socialism is seen as a merely transitional form, and the rule governing it is justified as appropriate to socialism's task of preparing the way for full commu-

nism, rather than as required by abstract justice. Second, Marxism considers the socialist rule to be more or less inescapable, at the given historical stage; it does not regard that rule as a choice requiring normative justification from a substantial menu of policy options. (For further discussion of the two stages of communism, see Cohen, *Self-Ownership, Freedom, and Equality,* ch. 5, sect. 3.)

8. Justice, Incentives, and Selfishness

1. See sections 3 and 7 of Lecture 6.
2. See Lecture 2, above.
3. See Cohen, *Karl Marx's Theory of History,* p. 151.
4. Although I do not want to enter into the controversy about sociobiology any more than this footnote does, I should say, to prevent misunderstanding, that I do not regard the propositions in the foregoing paragraph as inconsistent with sociobiology, if that is the doctrine laid out in Richard Dawkins' book *The Selfish Gene*—a doctrine which, I should add, I find utterly compelling. (I know that it is unusual for a leftist to have, and perhaps more unusual still for a leftist to voice, such an opinion. As John Maynard Smith has remarked, "There is a connection between a dislike of molecular genetics and a taste for radical politics." "An Eye on Life," p. 3.)
5. My rejection of the sociological premise embodied an optimism about social possibility that Marx, in effect, eschewed. For it was his view that only material abundance could neutralize the tendency to inequality in human society, and, therefore, that no kind of social structure, as such, could do it. See Lecture 6, sections 6 and 7.
6. Unless, perhaps, through the application of coercion on so massive a scale that it would be virtually impossible to mount it and certainly impossible to endorse it. (If it is possible to mount the required massive coercion, but one nevertheless rejects equality because it is impossible to endorse massive coercion, then the defense of inequality becomes neither purely factual nor (as I understand this label here—see p. 118 above) purely normative. It would now stand defended as required to avoid violating overriding values, *even if it is unjust.* In Albert Hirschman's terms, such a defense says not that the project of eliminating equality is *futile,* but rather that it puts more important (on the relevant scale) values in *jeopardy.* See Hirschman, *The Rhetoric of Reaction,* passim.

   Of course, the massive coercion anyway produces, contingently, a massive inequality of power, because (not as a matter of logic) such coercion can't be applied democratically. So the factuality of the defense is, in the end, pretty "pure."

7. Note that this is not the trivial claim that, if people are irreversibly selfish, then structure cannot reverse that selfishness. It is the nontrivial claim that structure cannot, as I once thought it could, deliver equality *despite* that (irreversible) selfishness.

8. Actually, Rawls holds, quite independently of the project of bettering the condition of the badly off, that "deep inequalities [in] . . . initial chances in life . . . [are] inevitable in the basic structure of *any* society" (*A Theory of Justice,* p. 7, emphasis added). The incentive argument contributes to showing which such deep inequalities would be justifiable.

9. That would put his defense of inequality in the *jeopardy* rather than the *futility* category (see note 6 above), but only conditionally on equality's being possible, a condition which (see note 8) he thinks to be unfulfilled.

10. Rawls, "Justice as Fairness," p. 140 (emphasis added).

11. See Cohen, "Incentives," pp. 324–325.

12. Rawls, *Theory of Justice,* p. 151 (emphasis added).

13. I by no means agree that they are indeed necessary. I believe this selfishness, and our equanimity about it, to be precipitates of centuries of capitalist civilization.

14. I do not know why Rawls made this big change. But I think it might be thought justified by the constructivism that he self-consciously embraced in *A Theory of Justice,* and which is not so apparent in "Justice as Fairness." According to constructivism, justice consists of the rules we would agree on in a privileged choosing situation, in the light, inter alia, of (what are taken to be given) facts of human nature. Since justice is constructed with facts of human nature as assumptions that the search for justice presupposes, it seems impossible for constructivism to regard any such facts as manifesting a "vice" of *injustice* in human nature. (This is not to say that Rawls thinks it impossible that human beings are by nature unjust: they are by nature unjust if they are unable to comply with any principles that would emerge from an appropriate constructive procedure. And Rawls thinks that they might indeed be unable to do so: see *Political Liberalism,* p. lxii. But that is a quite different reason for saying that people might by nature be unjust from the one that Rawls came close to accepting in 1957.)

I believe that constructivism is mistaken, partly, indeed, because the principles it constructs depend on facts of human nature. I shall argue against that aspect of its procedure, and against constructivism as such, elsewhere.

15. *Private Vices, Publick Benefits* is the subtitle of Mandeville's *Fable of the Bees.*
16. See the epigraph to this chapter.
17. But it was, apparently, used by Christian liberation theologians before it was used by feminists. See Denys Turner, "Religion: Illusions and Liberation," p. 334.
18. Or, more precisely, that which *distinguishes* its form. (Insofar as the feminist critique targets government legislation and policy, there is nothing distinctive about its form.)
19. Okin is singularly alive to Rawls's ambivalence about admitting or excluding the family from the basic structure (see, e.g., Okin, "Political Liberalism, Justice, and Gender," pp. 23–24; and, more generally, Okin, *Justice, Gender, and the Family*). But, so far as I can tell, she is unaware of the wider consequences, for Rawls's view of justice in general, of the set of ambiguities of which this one is an instance.
20. See Cohen, "Incentives, Inequality, and Community"; and idem, "The Pareto Argument for Inequality." These articles are henceforth here referred to as "Incentives" and "Pareto," respectively.
21. See Cohen, "Incentives," p. 266, note 6, for four possible formulations of the difference principle, all of which, arguably, find support in Rawls' *A Theory of Justice.* The argument of Lectures 8 and 9 is, I believe, robust across those variant formulations of the principle.
22. I do have some reservations about the principle, but they are irrelevant to the present argument. I agree, for example, with Ronald Dworkin's criticism of the "ambition-insensitivity" of the difference principle; see Dworkin, "Equality of Resources," p. 343.
23. "Proposes to conceive it": I use this somewhat precious phrase because part of the present criticism of Rawls is that he does not succeed in so conceiving it. He does not, that is, recognize the implications of so conceiving it.
24. The qualification is that, so I believe, each person has a right to pursue her own self-interest to some reasonable extent. But that is a quite different justification of inequality from the incentives justification; see Cohen, "Incentives," pp. 302–303, 314–315.
25. Rawls, *A Theory of Justice*, p. 7.
26. This is just the crudest causal story connecting superior payment to the better off with benefit to the worst off. I adopt it here for simplicity of exposition.
27. They do not, more precisely, share *justificatory community* with the rest, in the sense of the italicized phrase that I specified in "Incentives," p. 282.

28. "Citizens in everyday life affirm and act from the first principles of justice." They act "from these principles as their sense of justice dictates" and thereby "their nature as moral persons is most fully realized." (Quotations drawn from, respectively, Rawls, "Kantian Constructivism in Moral Theory," pp. 521, 528; and idem, *A Theory of Justice*, p. 528.)

29. This way of achieving equality preserves the information function of the market while extinguishing its motivational function. See Joseph Carens, *Equality, Moral Incentives, and the Market*, passim.

30. See Cohen, "Incentives," p. 298 et circa, for precisely what I mean by "the standard case."

31. Rawls allows the talented to say that their high rewards are justified because they are needed to make the low rewards of the badly off no worse than they already are. But, as I pointed out in Part 2 of "Incentives," that may serve as a justification of their high rewards when the talented are referred to in the third person, but, crucially, not when they are themselves offering it to the poor. Analogously, I do have good reason to pay a kidnapper who has taken my child, but he cannot, on that basis, justify his demand for payment from me: he cannot say that he is justified in demanding it because only if I meet that demand will I get my kid back. The talented rich are not, of course (at any rate as such), as bad as kidnappers, but the justification they give for demanding incentives collapses as much as his does when it is cast in "I—thou" terms. As I said above, the justification of incentives to them works only if they are conceived as alien to the society in question.

32. A major reason why no such "public" rules could be designed is that it is not always possible to tell, even for the person in question, whether or not her demand for more money as a condition of moving to a socially more desirable job is justified as compensation for "special burden," and is therefore permissible within the frame of equality, all things considered. For more on publicity, see the final paragraph of the final note in Lecture 9.

33. See Cohen, "Incentives," p. 316.

34. It should be noted that the foregoing critique of the incentives argument for inequality is not trained against "everything that could be called an incentive, but only of incentives that produce inequality and which are said to be justified because they make badly off people better off. I raise no objection against incentives designed to eliminate a poverty trap, or to induce people to undertake particularly unpleasant jobs. It is not constitutive of those incentives that they produce inequality. My target is incentives conferring high rewards on people of talent who would otherwise not perform as those rewards induce them to do" (Cohen, "Incentives,"

p. 272). The incentives countenanced here justify inequality of earnings, but they do not justify inequality as such. They are, on the contrary, required to promote equality, all things considered.

35. For a typical statement of this restriction, see Rawls, *Political Liberalism,* pp. 282–283.

36. See the first sentence of section 2 of Rawls, *A Theory of Justice* ("The Subject of Justice"): "Many different kinds of things are said to be just and unjust: not only laws, institutions, and social systems, but also particular actions of many kinds, including decisions, judgments, and imputations" (ibid., p. 7). But Rawls excludes examples such as the one given in the text above from his purview, because "our topic . . . is that of social justice. For us the primary subject of justice is the basic structure of society" (ibid.).

37. Ibid., p. 303.

38. Ibid., pp. 274–275: "The principles of justice apply to the basic structure. . . . The social system is to be designed so that the resulting distribution is just however things turn out." Compare ibid., p. 545: "The distribution of material means is left to take care of itself in accordance with the idea of pure procedural justice."

39. This is a different point from the one made at the beginning of the present section, to wit, that there is scope within a just structure for justice and injustice in choice in a "nonprimary" sense of "justice."

40. Dworkin made this point at an Oxford seminar in Hilary Term of 1994.

41. It might, moreover, be true of the society in question that, because of its traditions, which control its citizens' motivational structures, attempts to make its ethos just, as opposed to Protestant, would be unavailing, and, to the limited extent that they were successful, induce less justice in distribution than the Protestantism figured above does.

42. See Parfit, *Reasons and Persons,* ch. 4.

43. If, that is, my argument survives the basic structure objection, to which I reply in sections 1 and 2 of Lecture 9.

9. Where the Action Is

1. Because of these tensions in Rawls, people have resisted my incentives critique of him in two opposite ways. Those convinced that his primary concern is the basic structure object in the fashion set out in section 6 of Lecture 8. But others do not realize how important that concern is to him: they accept my (as I see it, anti-Rawlsian) view that the difference principle should condemn incentives, but they believe that Rawls would also accept it, since they think his commitment to the principle is relevantly

uncompromising. They therefore do not regard what I say about incentives as *a criticism* of Rawls.

Those who respond in that second fashion seem not to realize that Rawls's liberalism is jeopardized if he takes the route that they think open to him. He then becomes a radical egalitarian socialist, whose outlook is very different from that of a liberal who holds that "deep inequalities" are "inevitable in the basic structure of any society" (*A Theory of Justice*, p. 7).

2. Rawls, *A Theory of Justice*, p. 105.

3. See, further, Cohen, "Incentives, Inequality, and Community," pp. 321–322; and idem, "The Pareto Argument for Inequality," pp. 178–179. Note that I do not here deny that there is *more* fraternity when high earners willingly submit to taxation shaped by the difference principle than when they insist on laissez-faire.

4. See, further, Cohen, "Incentives," pp. 320–321.

5. Rawls, *A Theory of Justice*, p. 528, my emphasis. See, further, note 28 of Lecture 8; and Cohen, "Incentives," pp. 316–320.

6. Rawls, "Justice as Fairness: A Briefer Restatement," p. 154.

7. Rawls made this point in reply to a lecture that I gave at Harvard in March 1993.

8. That is, as (part of) a complete moral theory, as opposed to a purely political one. See, for explication of that distinction, Rawls, *Political Liberalism*, passim, in particular pp. xv–xvii, xliii–xlvii.

9. See Cohen, "Incentives," p. 322.

10. Though not necessarily an ethos embodying the very principles that the rules formulate; see the last four paragraphs of Lecture 8. Justice will be shown to require an ethos, and the basic structure objection will thereby be refuted, but it will be a contingent question whether the ethos required by justice can be discerned in the content of the just principles themselves. Still, as I suggested in Lecture 8, section 6, the answer to this question is almost certainly yes.

11. That is, the subject matter that principles of justice judge. I follow Rawls's usage here—e.g., in the title of Lecture 7 of *Political Liberalism* ("The Basic Structure as Subject"). See also note 36 of Lecture 8, above.

12. Throughout the rest of this lecture, I shall use "coercive," "coercion," etc. to mean "legally coercive," "legal coercion," etc.

13. Thus, the difference principle, though pursued through (coercively sustained) state policy, cannot, so Rawls thinks, be aptly inscribed in a society's constitution. See Rawls, *Political Liberalism*, pp. 227–230.

14. Consider, for example, the passage from *A Theory of Justice* (pp. 7–8) in which the concept of the basic structure is introduced:

"Our topic . . . is that of social justice. For us the primary subject of justice is the basic structure of society, or more exactly, the way in which the major social institutions distribute fundamental rights and duties and determine the division of advantages from social cooperation. By major institutions I understand the political constitution and the principal economic and social arrangements. Thus the legal protection of freedom of thought and liberty of conscience, competitive markets, private property in the means of production, and the monogamous family are examples of major social institutions. . . . I shall not consider the justice of institutions and social practices generally. . . . [The two principles of justice] may not work for the rules and practices of private associations or for those of less comprehensive social groups. They may be irrelevant for the various informal conventions and customs of everyday life; they may not elucidate the justice or, perhaps better, the fairness of voluntary cooperative arrangements or procedures for making contractual agreements."

I cannot tell from those statements what is to be included in, and what excluded from, the basic structure, nor, more particularly, whether coercion is the touchstone of inclusion. Take, for example, the case of the monogamous family. Is it simply its "legal protection" that is a major social institution, in line with a coercive definition of the basic structure (if not, perhaps, with the syntax of the relevant sentence)? Or is the monogamous family itself part of that structure? And, in that case, are its typical usages part of it? They certainly constitute a "principal social arrangement," yet they may also count as "practices of private associations or . . . of less comprehensive social groups," and they are heavily informed by the "conventions and customs of everyday life." (Section 5 of Rawls's essay "The Idea of Public Reason Revisited" offers an exceedingly interesting account of the family as a component of the basic structure. It does not, however, expressly address the question whether it is only in virtue of the coercive rules that govern it that the family belongs to that structure. But I think it tends, on the whole, to answer that question in the negative.)

Puzzlement with respect to the bounds of the basic structure is not relieved by examination of the relevant pages of *Political Liberalism*—to wit, 11, 68, 201–202, 229, 258, 268, 271–272, 282–283, and 301. Some formulations on those pages lean toward a coercive specification of the basic structure. Others do not.

15. See the final paragraph of Lecture 8, section 4.
16. I severely qualify this acceptance in section 4 below, and I thereby strengthen the present reply to the basic-structure objection.
17. In section 4 below, I entertain a doubt about the strength of the distinction drawn here, but, as I indicate, if that doubt is sound, then my case against Rawls is strengthened.

18. Rawls, *A Theory of Justice,* p. 7. "Present from the start" means, here, "present from birth"; see ibid., p. 96. But what matters, surely, is the asserted profundity of effect, whether or not it is "present from birth."

19. Or consider access to that primary good which Rawls calls "the social basis of self-respect." While the law may play a large role in securing that good to people vulnerable to racism, legally unregulable racist attitudes also have an enormous negative impact on how much of that primary good they get.

20. Rawls, *Political Liberalism,* p. 139.

21. Note that one can condemn the said practice without condemning those who engage in it. For there might be a collective action problem here, which weighs heavily on poor families in particular. If, in addition to discrimination in education, there is discrimination in employment, then a poor family might sacrifice a great deal through choosing evenhandedly across the sexes with whatever resources it can devote to its children's education. This illustrates the important distinction between condemning injustice and condemning the people whose actions perpetuate it. See, further, section 3 below.

22. See the text to note 18 above.

23. Hugo Adam Bedau noticed that the family falls outside the basic structure, under the coercive specification of it often favored by Rawls, but he did not notice the connection between noncoercive structure and choice that I emphasize in the above sentence. See Bedau, "Social Justice and Social Institutions," p. 171.

24. That is, legislation which maximizes the size of the primary-goods bundle held by the worst off people, given whatever is correctly expected to be the pattern in the choices made by economic agents.

25. As Liam Murphy points out, Rawls's focus on just institutional structure is utterly implausible for the case where institutions are unjust. On Rawls's intrinsically institutional approach, the only duty of justice that then falls on individuals is to *promote* just institutions (rather than to *comply* with them, since they do not obtain). But the worst off might be better served in an unjust society through direct assistance, rather than through a possibly fruitless, or less productive, attempt to improve the justice of institutions. (Private communication, 19 January 1997. And see Murphy, "Institutions and the Demands of Justice.")

26. See the parenthesized remarks at the end of section 5 of Lecture 8.

27. We can here set aside the fact that women often subscribe to, and inculcate, male-dominative practices.

28. We can distinguish between how unjust past practices (e.g., slavery) were and how unjust those who protected and benefited from those unjust practices were. Most of us (rightly) do not condemn Lincoln for his (con-

ditional) willingness to tolerate slavery as strongly as we would a states-
man who did the same in 1999, but the slavery institution itself was as
unjust in Lincoln's time as it would be today.

What made slavery unjust in, say, Greece, is exactly what would make
slavery (with, of course, the very same rules of subordination) unjust today—to wit, the content of its rules. But sound judgments about the justice and injustice of people are much more contextual; they must take
into account the institutions under which people live, the prevailing level
of intellectual and moral development, collective action problems such as
the one delineated in note 21 above, and so forth. The morally best slave-
holder might deserve admiration. The morally best form of slavery would
not. (Of some relevance here is the brilliant discussion of "how far our rejection of [ancient slavery] . . . depends on modern conceptions that were
not available in the ancient world" (p. 106) in Bernard Williams, *Shame
and Necessity,* chapter 5.)

29. See note 28.

30. See Mishel and Frankel, *The State of Working America,* p. 122.

31. That ethos need not have been a (relatively) egalitarian one. For present
purposes, it could have been an ethos which disendorsed acquisitiveness
as such (see note 10 above, and the digression at the end of Lecture 8),
other than on *behalf* of the worst off. (I have here supposed that the stated
difference in salary ratios was not due, or not wholly due, to social legislation that raised the wages of German workers, and/or other features of
Germany's basic structure. If that supposition is false, the example can be
treated as invented. It would still make the required point.)

32. And note how implausible it would be to say that Germany's (relatively
speaking) equality-friendly ethos reduced the *liberty* of the German
better off. I make this point in anticipation of the objection that my extension of the difference principle to everyday life violates the first principle of Rawlsian justice.

33. The distinction given above corresponds to that between the difficulty
and the cost of actions, which is elaborated in Lecture 10, section 11, below.

34. See the last sentence of the fourth paragraph of section 2.

35. It does not follow that they are not *laws* unless they enjoy such compliance. Perhaps they are nevertheless laws, if they "satisfy a test set out in a
Hartian rule of recognition, even if they are themselves neither complied
with nor accepted" (Joshua Cohen, in comment on a draft of this lecture). But such laws (or "laws") are not plausibly represented as part
of the basic structure of society, so the statement in the text can stand as
it is.

36. My 1997 article "Where the Action Is" forms the basis of most of Lectures

8 and 9. It has attracted a number of published and as yet unpublished responses. Among those that have been published of which I am aware, I should like to mention two very considerable ones.

The first is David Estlund's "Liberalism, Equality and Fraternity in Cohen's Critique of Rawls." Estlund exploits (in the best sense of the word) my friendliness to a Scheffler-like personal prerogative (see Lecture 8, note 24) to argue, very powerfully, that "inequality-producing incentives will still be required by many conscientious citizens exercising" not only that prerogative but three other "prerogatives that Cohen must allow" (p. 101). I believe that I would accede to some, but not all, of Estlund's criticism. I have to express myself in that guarded way because I have not had the time fully to take the measure of Estlund's critique. I am, however, fairly confident that the interesting position he develops is not, as he thinks it is, entirely consistent with Rawls's view, but a substantial revision of it, a kind of halfway house between Rawls's view and my own.

The other very considerable critique of "Where the Action Is" that I must mention is Andrew Williams' "Incentives, Inequality, and Publicity." In the course of a beautifully organized argument, Williams claims that my view that the difference principle must apply to economic choice fails the publicity requirement that Rawls says principles must satisfy to qualify as principles of justice, a requirement that Williams defends. I believe, however, that publicity, as Williams (following Rawls) explicates that notion, is demonstrably not a requirement of justice, and that the difference-principle-sensitive ethos that I require for justice meets every *defensible* publicity requirement on justice. These claims need, of course, to be argued, but I cannot provide the arguments for them here.

10. Political Philosophy and Personal Behavior

1. The last question is related to the question about the demands of justice on individuals in an unjust society, but is not identical with it, since there exist nonegalitarian conceptions of justice (which will not be discussed here) and nonjustice justifications of equality (two of which are noted in sections 5 and 6 below). (The questions are also different in that mine asks what a belief—egalitarianism—commits its holder to, while the question about the demands of justice in an unjust society does not take that form.)

2. I do not mean that there is nothing which her egalitarianism should prompt her to do. Perhaps she should work politically for more equality. This suggestion will not be investigated here, but the third sentence of section 7 below introduces a distinction that bears on it.

3. I do not myself think that. See section 3 below.

4. I here set aside "egalitarians" (if there can be such) who get their money through violence, fraud, and so forth.

5. Someone might ask me: "If you're the egalitarian who wrote *If You're an Egalitarian, How Come You're So Rich?* how come you're so rich?"

6. I very much regret that I became aware of Saul Smilansky's excellent article "On Practicing What We Preach" only when this book was in press, and, therefore, too late to include a consideration of it here.

7. A rejection of Kagan's position follows from the remarks on consequentialism in the final paragraph of section 6 below.

8. In recent years, British Conservative propagandists have had a field day deriding Labour leaders who have appeared not to practice the (massively watered-down but still somewhat) egalitarian principles that they preach. In April 1996 the Tories went so far as to put out a board game called *Hypocrisy!* (price £19.99), in which, for example, you gain three hypocrisy points for sending your child to a grammar (that is, selection-by-merit) school. See *The Guardian,* 30 April 1996, p. 3.

Labour politicians are made of the same human clay as socialist professors. Unfortunately—politics being what it is—they are less well placed than professors are to acknowledge the possibility of a gap between their principles and their practice. This is no doubt one reason they have recently striven to deform those principles. See Cohen, "Back to Socialist Basics," for a discussion of that process.

9. I don't say that I can imagine no answer to the caller's question. Maybe this would have been a good answer to it: "The people's party should be funded by the people, not by millionaires (even if it is quite proper for millionaires to serve in the people's party's cabinet)."

10. Lodge, *Small World,* pp. 127–129.

11. See Austin, "A Plea for Excuses," p. 146.

12. See Hare, *Freedom and Reason,* ch. 3.

13. It may be that only a minority of rich egalitarians would profess this belief. What fascinates me is that many intelligent and reflective ones do profess it.

14. Strictly, then, my question is: "*Since* you're an egalitarian, how come you think it's OK for you to be so rich?" (What chiefly exercises me is the apparent inconsistency of the *beliefs* held by rich people who *really* do believe in egalitarianism.) To give that question an especially sharp edge, imagine a poor person posing it. See Cohen, "Incentives, Inequality, and Community," sections 3 through 11, esp. p. 274.

15. That question might be a good response to a question which is not ours, to wit: If you're so rich, how come you're an egalitarian?

16. For an excellent treatment of the difference between justice-based and

non-justice-based justifications of equality, see David Miller, "Equality and Justice."

17. You *might* regard a society where ninety-nine people each have 1.09 of whatever ultimately matters and one person has 10 such units as *more* divided than one in which ninety-eight people have 1 each and two have 10 each, because no one is so isolated in the second society as the sole rich person is in the first. A self-sacrificing rich donor might make his society more like that first one, and he might, therefore, make it more divided than it was.

18. What is perhaps a variant of the division defense was suggested to me (in jest) by Nicholas McBride: "I hate inequality because I hate the attitudes it engenders, and, in particular, an attitude of contempt for the poor on the part of the rich. Since I, *ex hypothesi*, lack, and hate, that contempt, there is no call for *me* to give my money away."

19. (1) In an extreme variant of this justification for personal inaction, the rich egalitarian says—I have often heard this said—"But I want *everybody* to have the sort of life I have." This variant need not detain us. For *either* its proponent accepts that her view implies that equality is impossible, in which case the view falls outside our brief (which is to see whether those who believe that an egalitarian society is desirable and feasible have good reason not to engage in some do-it-yourself self-expropriation), *or* she projects future resource levels that belong to the realm of fantasy.

    (2) Some egalitarians, and rich ones among them, might say that nobody's life can be *really* good as long as there is inequality, or as long as inequality means that many people have lives that are distinctly *ungood*. But such a consideration would be merely diversionary here, since no one could deny that a life at or above a decent material standard is typically better than one below it, even when neither life is, for one or both of the stated reasons, *really* good.

20. Note that this justification for greater equality is, in certain circumstances, a justification for (greater) inequality—when, for example, it is not possible for everyone to have a good life. This shows that it is not a justice justification of inequality, since no one could claim that the regressive procedures (such as making the quite miserable a little more miserable so that the nearly unmiserable can be made unmiserable) required to promote its aim in the contemplated circumstances serve *justice*.

21. Speaking more generally, that is, not about this defense of the rich egalitarian in particular, it amazes me how often some (sufficiently) rich person protests that, while he would be very happy to give a lot of money away, he is unclear what the *best* way to do it is, because he cannot tell, for example, which charity has the lowest administrative costs. The premise of his resistance is sound, but his inference—that he therefore

cannot reasonably act on his philanthropic wish—is absurd. Who would say: I'd love to go out to eat, but, since I can't tell which is the best restaurant, I'll stay at home? It is rational to go to any restaurant which you do not judge to be excelled by another, after a reasonable amount of reflection. When self-sacrifice is in the offing, people reject manifestly rational procedures that they do not hesitate to use when the satisfaction of self-interest is at stake.

22. A complication should be noted here. While rich egalitarians do not believe that they enjoy unblemished moral entitlement to their large holdings, few of them think themselves *as* unentitled to their holdings as plain ordinary thieves and embezzlers are to theirs (in a just—or even in an *unjust*—society). If you acquire according to an unjust property law, it does not plainly follow that you acquire unjustly, and the question whether you unjustly hold what you have acquired therefore lacks a straightforward answer. It matters to the egalitarian rich that they got what they have without violating the rules of the game they perforce face, but it also matters that they condemn those rules. ("Perforce": recall the wonderful sentence that opens Karl Marx's summary statement of his theory of history: "In the social production of their life, men enter into relations that are indispensable and independent of their will." Marx, Preface to *A Contribution to the Critique of Political Economy*, p. 11.) They cannot offer a plain yes or a plain no in answer to the question: Do you have a right to your wealth? This complexity affects how they think about their behavior, in subtle ways that need more consideration than I have as yet been able to devote to this aspect of our topic.

23. (1) Some might think that one should abstain from benefiting from injustice even when that self-denial would benefit no one, but I am not here addressing the breast-beating position according to which it is wrong to be rich when others are poor, even if the only way to rectify the situation is to burn one's money. Our rich egalitarians are not being asked to engage in counter-Paretian behavior.

(2) The question posed above—to wit, why believers in egalitarian justice do not forgo the benefits they unjustly (in their view, and prescinding here from the complication noticed in note 22) enjoy, when they can forgo them in a manner that benefits sufferers of that injustice—is double-barreled, and it should be observed that its two barrels can come apart. A wealthy egalitarian might want to benefit a confined number of people very greatly, by, for example, endowing handsome scholarships for very poor children. He might prefer that to acting in a way which is strictly egalitarian (whether relational or prioritarian; see p. 162 below). He might add that he is not reluctant to give, but that he is reluctant to give inconsequentially, with the fruit of his gift so dispersed that he

cannot see the upshot of it. In an egalitarian society, consequentiality is assured by the fact that redistribution is general; he would then be part of a cause that has an enormous effect.

Such a person does not retain the fruits of his unjust enrichment, but he does not promote equality per se; the two barrels in the stated question are thereby uncoupled. Another rich egalitarian might give up those fruits by donating massively to the arts, under the plea that equality is not the only value that he can reasonably promote with his misbegotten gains. No equivalent issues arise in a structurally equal society.

I shall not pursue this complication here.

24. The excuse/justification distinction is explained at the end of section 3 above.

25. Specification of a principle of equality is not the same as a statement of the reason for affirming it, which is an issue that I did raise, in section 4 above.

26. The qualification is necessary because one might believe that, in some areas, including this one, the moral truth is itself imprecise (even if it is not as imprecise as nonphilosophical statements about these matters typically are).

27. For a masterly treatment of the contrasts and connections between these egalitarianisms, see Derek Parfit, "Equality or Priority?"

28. Their position is the one that I sketch in "Incentives, Inequality, and Community," pp. 266–270.

29. I here report Dworkin's response to a query that I pressed.

30. See Dworkin, "Equality of Resources," p. 285.

31. On the distinction between causal and normative fundamentality, see Cohen, *Self-Ownership, Freedom, and Equality*, ch. 8, sect. 2.

32. Compare the case for equality presented in the first sentence of Oscar Wilde, *The Soul of Man under Socialism:* "The chief advantage that would result from the establishment of Socialism is, undoubtedly, the fact that Socialism would relieve us from that sordid necessity of living for others which, in the present condition of things, presses so hardly upon almost everybody."

33. See Nozick, *Anarchy, State, and Utopia*, pp. 265–268. Many people, including, notably, John Rawls, would deny that a society which functions under egalitarian state legislation is one in which people are forced to give (unilaterally), rather than forced to share a collective product in an equalizing way. But I stand with Nozick and against Rawls on this matter (see Cohen, *Self-Ownership*, ch. 9, sect. 5), and Nagel does not disagree with Nozick on this particular score.

34. The redistribution defended by Nagel falls short of the full egalitarian prescription, on any interpretation thereof, but what matters in our dis-

cussion of Nagel is the contrast between state-imposed and voluntary re-distribution, on whatever scale may be regarded as appropriate.

35. Nagel, "Libertarianism without Foundations," pp. 199–200, my emphases.

36. Recall the distinction invoked in section 3 above between moral weakness and weakness of will.

37. For elaboration of this point, see Jan Narveson, *The Libertarian Idea,* pp. 249–250. I do not agree with everything Narveson says there, and certainly not with his preposterous charge that Nagel's "moral imagination [has] been reduced to pudding" (p. 249).

38. "Costly" and "difficult" overlap in ordinary language. The distinction that I draw here is a quasi-technical one, got by focusing on those uses of the relevant words in which they are not semantically interchangeable with each other. See Cohen, *Karl Marx's Theory of History,* pp. 238–239.

39. The evident truth that a desirable job for a given person must be neither too difficult nor too easy for him proves that difficulty and cost (which is by definition (in itself) undesirable) are entirely distinct, conceptually. If difficulty were, as such, a form of cost, then, other things equal, one would always want the job that is least difficult. But of two jobs whose other costs are indeed equal, one wants one of optimal difficulty, that is, of a difficulty neither too great nor too small, rather than one of the least difficulty.

40. At any rate if we prescind from the complication noted five paragraphs ahead ("Difficulty and cost, though distinct . . .").

41. For people, that is, who can reasonably deny that, in declaring that it is this costly for them, they are confessing to a contemptible, and therefore unjustifiable, degree of selfishness. Recall that we must avoid the (first) misinterpretation of Nagel that I tried to deflect above.

42. I mean that the *concepts* I have isolated are frequently confused. This point is independent of the one made in note 38, which was that the *words* "difficulty" and "cost" are often used interchangeably.

43. Schematically: the prospective money cost CAUSES difficulty in decision, which CAUSES an extra cost (in the process of decision itself).

44. I mean, here, the consequences that go beyond the mere fact that I am shouldering a burden which others are avoiding. Nagel may also have that mere fact in mind, but it is a distinct consideration, which is explored at length in the work of Liam Murphy (see his "Demands of Beneficence"). I have addressed Murphy's claims, and their relationship to the theme of this lecture, in an unpublished piece that I will supply on request to the reader.

45. One might consider, in this connection, what the attitude of a rich egalitarian should be to the taxation of some rich people (including him) ac-

cording to an arbitrary selection, while others are not taxed, and what bearing that might have on the special disadvantage question. (He would *not* then be deliberately denying something to his child.)

Note, further, that neither Nagel's "mental-burden" consideration nor this "deliberate-denial" one is a reason to condemn (they are, on the contrary, reasons to welcome) local redistribution induced by a Robin Hood (or, more modernly, by an egalitarian robbin' hood). There is, of course, *a* (not necessarily conclusive) reason for disapproving of that—to wit, the terror that Hood-(and hood-)type encounters engender. But such fear does not supervene when Robin Hood trades his crossbow (or, if he's just a hood, his gat) for a computer hacking manual. (You won't, of course, relish him targeting you, but the same goes with respect to your attitude to the "selective taxman." You don't have to enjoy the implementation of policy that you regard as just.)

Might it be said that a rich egalitarian also acts in deliberate denial of his child's interests when he votes for a redistributing government? Even if that is true, the consequence to which he then signs up do not disadvantage his child in particular, since the redistribution would apply across the whole of his class. The "deliberate denial" defense developed above is therefore not inconsistent with support for state-imposed egalitarianism.

46. What should Fulvia's position be with respect to a hood or a hacker (see note 45 above)? Should she not, in the light of what she says about peasants and wealthy folk, disapprove of the deprivation they would impose on her? But how, as a revolutionary, could she disapprove, if their activity amounted to a total social revolution?

The question might be thought to induce a dilemma for Fulvia: if she welcomes such a revolution, she is abandoning the deprivation consideration; if she condemns it, she loses her revolutionary credentials. Her best response might be to welcome revolution and to say that the deprivation doesn't bite so much if it's general to her class, and/or that it would be sufficiently counterbalanced by the excitement, and the promise, of the revolution. (To be sure, to the extent that she relies on the former of those considerations, she is moving toward the assurance point from which hers was distinguished in the text above. But she might put this finish on her position: contrary to what was suggested in the first paragraph of this note, the deprivation is an indignity only when it isn't general to the rich class—when, that is, class division continues.)

47. See Cohen, "On the Currency of Egalitarian Justice."

48. See the end of section 3 for a statement of what justifications are, in general, and of how they differ from excuses.

49. Note that yielding up one's riches might be specially admirable from a

point of view other than that of the promotion of equality. One might, for example, admire a once-rich person who, having settled accounts with what equality demands, gives up what he need not give up for the sake of equality in order to help finance the expensive career requirements of a (not particularly poor) young musician. Let us here set aside such non-equality-related grounds for admirability. (See, further, part (2) of note 23 above.)

50. Under the restriction imposed by note 49, they render extravagant giving not supererogatory but pointless.
51. See the last two paragraphs of section 3 above, and the comment on Nagel's intentions in section 11 above.
52. Cf. Nozick, *Anarchy, State, and Utopia,* pp. 266–267.
53. See, further, the last paragraph of section 9 above.

BIBLIOGRAPHY

Austin, J. L. "A Plea for Excuses." In Austin, *Philosophical Papers*. Oxford: Clarendon, 1961.

Aveling, Edward, and Eleanor Marx Aveling. *Shelley's Socialism*. London: Journeyman, 1975.

Balibar, Etienne. *The Philosophy of Marx*. Trans. Chris Turner. London: Verso, 1995.

Barry, Brian. *Justice as Impartiality*. Oxford: Clarendon, 1995.

Bedau, Hugo Adam. "Social Justice and Social Institutions." *Midwest Studies in Philosophy*, 3 (1978): 159–175.

Carens, Joseph. *Equality, Moral Incentives, and the Market*. Chicago: University of Chicago Press, 1981.

Cohen, G. A. "The Workers and the Word: Why Marx Had the Right to Think He Was Right." *Praxis*, 3 (1968): 376–390.

———— *Karl Marx's Theory of History: A Defence*. Oxford: Clarendon, 1978.

———— *History, Labour, and Freedom*. Oxford: Clarendon, 1988.

———— "On the Currency of Egalitarian Justice." *Ethics*, 99 (1989): 906–944.

———— "Incentives, Inequality, and Community." In Grethe B. Peterson, ed., *The Tanner Lectures on Human Values*, vol. 13. Salt Lake City: University of Utah Press, 1992.

———— *Self-Ownership, Freedom, and Equality*. Cambridge: Cambridge University Press, 1995.

———— "Back to Socialist Basics." *New Left Review*, 207 (1994): 3–16. Also in Jane Franklin, ed., *Equality*. London: Institute for Public Policy Research, 1997.

———— "The Pareto Argument for Inequality." *Social Philosophy and Policy*, 12 (1995): 160–185.

———— "Commitment without Reverence: Reflections on Analytical Marxism." *Imprints*, 1 (1997): 23–36.

———— "Where the Action Is: On the Site of Distributive Justice." *Philosophy and Public Affairs*, 26 (1997): 3–30.

Dawkins, Richard. *The Selfish Gene*. New York: Oxford University Press, 1989.

Dworkin, Ronald. "Equality of Resources." *Philosophy and Public Affairs*, 10 (1981): 283–345.

Eliot, George. *Middlemarch*. London: Everyman's Library, 1991.

——— *Adam Bede*. London: Everyman's Library, 1992.

——— *Scenes of Clerical Life*. Harmondsworth: Penguin, 1985.

Elster, Jon. *Logic and Society*. New York: Wiley, 1978.

Engels, Friedrich. *The Condition of the Working-Class in England in 1844* (1845). Trans. Florence Kelley Wischnewetzky. London: Allen and Unwin, 1892.

——— "The Communists and Karl Heinzen" (1847). In *Marx and Engels: Collected Works*, vol. 6. London: Lawrence and Wishart, 1976.

——— *Anti-Dühring* (1878). Moscow: Foreign Languages Publishing House, 1954.

——— *Socialism: Utopian and Scientific* (1880). London: Allen and Unwin, 1892.

——— Letter to Paul Lafargue, 11 August 1884. In *Frederick Engels / Paul and Laura Lafargue Correspondence*, vol. 1. Moscow: Foreign Languages Publishing House, 1959.

——— *On the History of the Communist League* (1885). In *Marx and Engels: Selected Works in Two Volumes*, vol. 2. Moscow: Foreign Languages Publishing House, 1958.

——— *Ludwig Feuerbach and the End of Classical German Philosophy.* (1886). In *Marx and Engels: Selected Works in Two Volumes*, vol. 2. Moscow: Foreign Languages Publishing House, 1958.

——— Letter to Conrad Schmidt, 27 October 1890. In S. W. Ryazanskaya, ed., *Karl Marx and Frederick Engels: Selected Correspondence*. Moscow: Progress Publishers, 1975.

——— Letter to Franz Mehring, 14 July 1893. In S. W. Ryazanskaya, ed., *Karl Marx and Frederick Engels: Selected Correspondence*. Moscow: Progress Publishers, 1975.

Estlund, David. "Liberalism, Equality and Fraternity in Cohen's Critique of Rawls." *Journal of Political Philosophy*, 6 (1998): 99–112.

Evans, Michael. *Karl Marx*. London: Allen and Unwin, 1975.

Feuerbach, Ludwig. *The Essence of Christianity.* Trans. George Eliot. New York: Harper, 1957.

——— "*The Essence of Christianity* in Relation to *The Ego and Its Own*." Trans. Frederick M. Gordon. *The Philosophical Forum*, 8 (1978): 81–91.

Fitzgerald, F. Scott. *The Great Gatsby*. Harmondsworth: Penguin, 1950.

Hare, R. M. *Freedom and Reason*. Oxford: Clarendon, 1963.

Hegel, G. W. F. *Lectures on the Philosophy of Religion*, vol. 1. Trans. E. B. Speirs and J. Burdon Sanderson. London: Routledge and Kegan Paul, 1892.

——— *The Philosophy of History*. Trans. J. Sibree. London: Colonial, 1900.

——— *The Phenomenology of Mind.* Trans. J. B. Baillie. London: Allen and Unwin, 1949.

——— *Hegel's Philosophy of Mind.* Trans. A. V. Miller. Oxford: Clarendon, 1971.

——— *Hegel's Philosophy of Nature.* Trans. M. J. Petry. London: Allen and Unwin, 1971.

——— *Hegel's Logic: Being Part I of the Encyclopoedia of the Philosophical Sciences.* Trans. William Wallace. Oxford: Clarendon, 1975.

——— *Lectures on the Philosophy of World History: Introduction.* Trans. H. B. Nisbet. Cambridge: Cambridge University Press, 1975. (This translation is based on a more complete text of the *Introduction* than that from which Sibree, whose translation I generally use, worked).

——— *Elements of the Philosophy of Right.* Trans. H. B. Nisbet. Cambridge: Cambridge University Press, 1991.

Hille, Waldemar, ed. *The People's Song Book.* New York: Boni and Gaer, 1948.

Hirschman, Albert. *The Rhetoric of Reaction.* Cambridge, Mass.: Harvard University Press, 1991.

Jaki, Stanley L. *Lord Gifford and His Lectures: A Centenary Retrospect.* Edinburgh: Scottish Academic Press, 1986.

Kagan, Shelly. *The Limits of Morality.* Oxford: Clarendon, 1989.

Kaufmann, Walter. *Hegel.* New York: Doubleday, 1965.

Kolakowski, Leszek. *Main Currents of Marxism,* vol. 1. New York: Oxford University Press, 1978.

Lenin, V. I. "The Three Sources and Component Parts of Marxism" (1913). In *Marx, Engels, Lenin on Historical Materialism.* Moscow: Progress Publishers, 1972.

——— Communication of 12 June 1920. In V. I. Lenin, *Collected Works,* vol. 31. Moscow: Progress Publishers, 1966.

Let's Sing the Songs of the People. Cultural Committee of the United Jewish People's Order. Toronto: UJPO, n.d. [ca. 1950].

Lodge, David. *Small World.* Harmondsworth: Penguin, 1984.

Lukács, Georg. *History and Class Consciousness* (1923). Trans. Rodney Livingstone. London: Merlin, 1971.

Lukes, Steven. *Marxism and Morality.* Oxford: Clarendon, 1985.

Luxemburg, Rosa. "The Russian Revolution." In Luxemburg, *"The Russian Revolution" and "Leninism or Marxism?"* Ann Arbor: University of Michigan Press, 1970.

Maguire, John. *Marx's Paris Writings.* Dublin: Gill and Macmillan, 1972.

Mandeville, Bernard. *The Fable of the Bees: Private Vices, Publick Benefits.* Oxford: Oxford University Press, 1924.

Marx, Karl. Letter to his father, 10 November 1837. In *Karl Marx: Selected Writings,* ed. David McLellan. Oxford: Oxford University Press, 1977.

———— "The Centralization Question" (1842). In *Writings of the Young Marx on Philosophy and Society,* ed. Loyd D. Easton and Kurt H. Guddat. Garden City, N.Y.: Doubleday, 1967.

———— "On the Jewish Question" (1843). In *Writings of the Young Marx on Philosophy and Society,* ed. Loyd D. Easton and Kurt H. Guddat. Garden City, N.Y.: Doubleday, 1967.

———— Letters to Arnold Ruge, May and September 1843. In *Karl Marx: Selected Writings,* ed. David McLellan. Oxford: Oxford University Press, 1977.

———— "Introduction to *A Contribution to the Critique of Hegel's Philosophy of Right*" (1844). In *Marx and Engels on Religion.* Moscow: Foreign Languages Publishing House, 1957.

———— "1844 Manuscripts." In *Karl Marx: Early Writings,* ed. T. B. Bottomore. London: Watts, 1963.

———— "Critical Marginal Notes on the Article 'The King of Prussia and Social Reform; By a Prussian'" (1844). In *Writings of the Young Marx on Philosophy and Society,* ed. Loyd D. Easton and Kurt H. Guddat. Garden City, N.Y.: Doubleday, 1967.

———— *Theses on Feuerbach* (1845). In *Marx and Engels: Collected Works,* vol. 5. London: Lawrence and Wishart, 1976.

———— *The Poverty of Philosophy* (1847). Moscow: Foreign Languages Publishing House, n.d.

———— "Moralising Criticism and Critical Morality" (1847). In *Marx and Engels: Collected Works,* vol. 6. London: Lawrence and Wishart, 1976.

———— *Grundrisse* (1857). Trans. Martin Nicolaus. Harmondsworth: Penguin, 1973.

———— *A Contribution to the Critique of Political Economy* (1859). Chicago: Charles H. Kerr, 1918.

———— "Inaugural Address of the Working Men's International Association" (1864). In *Marx and Engels: Selected Works in Two Volumes,* vol. 1. Moscow: Foreign Languages Publishing House, 1958.

———— "Wages, Price, and Profit" (1865). In *Marx and Engels: Selected Works in Two Volumes,* vol. 1. Moscow: Foreign Languages Publishing House, 1958.

———— *Capital* (1867), vol. 1. Trans. Ben Fowkes. Harmondsworth: Penguin, 1976.

———— "Report to the Brussels Congress" (1868). In *The First International and After,* ed. David Fernbach. Harmondsworth: Penguin, 1974.

———— *The Civil War in France* (1871). In *Karl Marx: Selected Writings,* ed. David McLellan. Oxford: Oxford University Press, 1977.

———— "Critique of the Gotha Programme" (1875). In *Marx and Engels: Selected Works in Two Volumes,* vol. 2. Moscow: Foreign Languages Publishing House, 1958.

———— Letter to Friedrich Sorge, 19 October 1877. In *Letters to Americans, 1848–1895, by Karl Marx and Frederick Engels,* ed. Alexander Trachtenberg. New York: International Publishers, 1963.

———— and Friedrich Engels. *The German Ideology* (1845–1846). London: Lawrence and Wishart, 1965.

———— and Friedrich Engels. *Die deutsche Ideologie* (1845–1846). In *Marx/ Engels Werke,* vol. 3. Berlin: Dietz, 1973.

———— and Friedrich Engels. "The Communist Manifesto" (1848). In *Marx and Engels: Collected Works,* vol. 6. London: Lawrence and Wishart, 1976.

McLellan, David. *Marx before Marxism.* London: Macmillan, 1970.

———— *The Thought of Karl Marx: An Introduction.* London: Macmillan, 1971.

Menger, Anton. *The Right to the Whole Produce of Labour.* London: Macmillan, 1899.

Meyerson, Harold, and Ernie Harburg. *Who Put the Rainbow in "The Wizard of Oz"?* Ann Arbor: University of Michigan Press, 1993.

Miller, David. "Equality and Justice." *Ratio,* 10 (1997): 222–237.

Mishel, Lawrence, and David M. Frankel. *The State of Working America.* Armonk, N.Y.: M. E. Sharpe, 1991.

Murphy, Liam. "The Demands of Beneficence." *Philosophy and Public Affairs,* 22 (1993): 267–292.

———— "Institutions and the Demands of Justice." *Philosophy and Public Affairs,* 27 (1998): 251–291.

Nagel, Thomas. "Libertarianism without Foundations." In Jeffrey Paul, ed., *Reading Nozick.* Totowa, N.J.: Rowman and Littlefield, 1981.

Narveson, Jan. *The Libertarian Idea.* Philadelphia: Temple University Press, 1988.

Nozick, Robert. *Anarchy, State, and Utopia.* New York: Basic Books, 1974.

———— *Philosophical Explanations.* Cambridge, Mass.: Harvard University Press, 1981.

———— *The Nature of Rationality.* Princeton: Princeton University Press, 1993.

Okin, Susan Moller. *Justice, Gender, and the Family.* New York: Basic Books, 1989.

———— "Political Liberalism, Justice, and Gender." *Ethics,* 105 (1994): 23–43.

Parfit, Derek. *Reasons and Persons.* Oxford: Clarendon, 1984.

———— *Equality or Priority?* Lindley Lecture. Lawrence: University of Kansas Press, 1995.

Plato. *The Republic.* Trans. Benjamin Jowett. New York: Quality Paperback Bookclub, 1992.

Pogge, Thomas W. *Realizing Rawls.* Ithaca, N.Y.: Cornell University Press, 1989.

Quine, W. V. O. "Two Dogmas of Empiricism." In Quine, *From a Logical Point of View.* Cambridge, Mass.: Harvard University Press, 1961.

Rawls, John. "Justice as Fairness." In Peter Laslett and W. G. Runciman, eds., *Philosophy, Politics, and Society,* 2nd series. Oxford: Blackwell, 1962. Reprinted from *The Journal of Philosophy,* 54 (1957): 653–662.

———— *A Theory of Justice.* Cambridge, Mass.: Harvard University Press, 1971.

———— "Kantian Constructivism in Moral Theory." *Journal of Philosophy,* 88 (1980): 515–572.

———— "Justice as Fairness: A Briefer Restatement." Typescript, Harvard University, 1989.

———— *Political Liberalism.* New York: Columbia University Press, 1996.

———— "The Idea of Public Reason Revisited." *University of Chicago Law Review,* 64 (1997): 765–807.

Roemer, John. *A Future for Socialism.* Cambridge, Mass.: Harvard University Press, 1994.

Rubel, Maximilien, and Margaret Manale. *Marx without Myth.* Oxford: Blackwell, 1975.

Sartre, Jean-Paul. *Anti-Semite and Jew.* New York: Schocken, 1948.

Silber, Irwin, ed. *Lift Every Voice! The Second People's Song Book.* New York: People's Artists, 1953.

Smilansky, Saul. "On Practicing What We Preach." *American Philosophical Quarterly,* 31 (1994): 73–79.

Smith, John Maynard. "An Eye on Life." *The Guardian,* "On Line" section (1 October 1998): 3.

Turner, Denys. "Religion: Illusions and Liberation." In Terrell Carver, ed., *The Cambridge Companion to Marx.* Cambridge: Cambridge University Press, 1991.

Wilde, Oscar. *The Soul of Man under Socialism.* London: Journeyman, 1988.

Williams, Andrew, "Incentives, Inequality, and Publicity." *Philosophy and Public Affairs,* 27 (1998): 226–248.

Williams, Bernard. *Shame and Necessity.* Cambridge: Cambridge University Press, 1993.

Wood, Allen. *Hegel's Ethical Thought.* Cambridge: Cambridge University Press, 1990.

CREDITS

I thank the following publishers for permission to draw on the indicated
material:

Cambridge University Press for material from the Introduction and chapter 6
of G. A. Cohen, *Self-Ownership, Freedom and Equality* (Cambridge, 1995),
that appears in Lecture 6.

Princeton University Press for material from G. A. Cohen, "Where the Action
Is," *Philosophy and Public Affairs,* 26, no. 1 (Winter 1997), that appears in
Lectures 8 and 9.

Curtis Brown Group Ltd. for material from David Lodge, *Small World*
(Harmondsworth, 1984), pp. 17–19, that appears in Lecture 10.

Kluwer Academic Publishers for material from G. A. Cohen, "If You're an
Egalitarian, How Come You're So Rich?" *Journal of Ethics,* 3 (2000), that
appears in Lecture 10.

INDEX

Miller, A. V., 191n2
Miller, Arthur, 181
Miller, David, 215n16
Mishel, Lawrence, 212n30
modes of production, 55–57, 68, 70
Molotov-Ribbentrop Pact, 187n10
Montefiore, Alan, 155
Montreal, 11, 21–31, 34–38, 154, 187n9
Morgenbesser, Sidney, 197n6
Morris Winchewsky School, 22–24, 27, 29, 31, 32, 39
Murphy, Liam, 211n25, 218n44

Nagel, Thomas, 168–175, 217nn33,34, 218nn37,41,44, 219n45, 220n51
Narveson, Jan, 218n37
National Federation of Labour Youth, 25, 26, 187n10
natural resources. *See* ecological crisis
Nazism, 23
Nebuchadnezzar, 23
New Economic Policy, 21
Nozick, Robert, 117, 168–170, 184n7, 185n12, 197n9, 217n33, 220n52
nurture (of belief), 7–13

obstetric motif. *See* Marxism, obstetric motif in
Okin, Susan, 123, 206n19
Oshanin, L., 42
Otsuka, Michael, 184n4
Owen, Robert, 102
Oxford, 17–18, 37

Padlock Law, 24, 187n7
Parfit, Derek, 132, 208n42, 217n27
Pasolini, Pier Paolo, 6
philosophy: Hegel on, 58–59, 61, 84; Feuerbach on, 94; Marx on, 95–100
Pinzauti, Piero, 198n26
Plato, 62, 97–98, 100
Plotinus, 83
Pogge, Thomas, 183n2
political economy, 45, 48–49, 50, 72
Pollitt, Harry, 187n8
Principle, the (about reasons for belief), 11–13, 184nn46, 185n9
prioritarianism, 162–163
problem of evil, 82, 116

production relations, 69
productive forces, 49, 69, 104
proletariat, 48, 51–52, 54, 63, 70, 75, 77–78, 99–100, 104–112, 117, 193n29, 195n44, 200n6, 201n10, 202nn12,14, 203n20
Putnam, Hilary, 18
Pythagoras, 59–62

Quine, W. V. O., 17

racism, 188n13, 211n19. *See also* anti-Semitism
rationality (and belief), 8–16, 18–19, 184nn7,8, 185n12, 186n15, 216n21
Rawls, John, 1, 2, 4–6, 117, 120–142, 144–147, 148–149, 162, 183n2, 205nn8,14, 206nn19,21,23, 207nn28,31, 208nn35,36,38, 209nn1,7,8,11,13, 210nn14,17, 211nn18,19,23,25, 212n32, 213n36, 217n33
reform, social, 66, 71–72
religion, 4–5, 32, 77, 79–81, 96–97, 100, 192n16, 199n36. *See also* Christianity; God; Hinduism; Judaism
revolution, 68; moral, 2, 120; Bolshevik, 20–21; socialist, 42–43, 64, 69, 72, 100, 104, 107, 111, 196n47, 202n12, 203n20
Ricardo, David, 48, 190n6
Rice, Les, 202n15
Roemer, John, 103, 105, 196n49
Rorty, Amélie, 190n9
Rose, Fred, 23
Rosen, Michael, 197n10
Rosenfeld, Morris, 20
Rubel, Maximilien, 190n10
Ruge, Arnold, 66, 68, 80
Russell, Bertrand, 58

Sacks, Jonathan, 38
Saint-Simon, Henri, comte de, 110
Sartre, Jean-Paul, 34, 37
scarcity, 49, 115. *See also* abundance
Scheffler, Samuel, 213n36
Schopenhauer, Arthur, 59–62, 192n13
Scott, Stephen, 186n13, 187n7
self-ownership principle, 106–108, 200n9, 201n11
Shelley, Percy Bysshe, 201n9
slavery, 212n28

Harvard University Press is a member of Green Press Initiative
(greenpressinitiative.org), a nonprofit organization working to
help publishers and printers increase their use of recycled paper
and decrease their use of fiber derived from endangered forests.
This book was printed on recycled paper containing 30%
post-consumer waste and processed chlorine free.